THE NEW FOLGER LIBRARY SHAKESPEARE

Designed to make Shakespeare's great plays available to all readers, the New Folger Library edition of Shakespeare's plays provides accurate texts in modern spelling and punctuation, as well as scene-by-scene action summaries, full explanatory notes, many pictures clarifying Shakespeare's language, and notes recording all significant departures from the early printed versions. Each play is prefaced by a brief introduction, by a guide to reading Shakespeare's language, and by accounts of his life and theater. Each play is followed by an annotated list of further readings and by a "Modern Perspective" written by an expert on that particular play.

Barbara A. Mowat is Director of Research at the Folger Shakespeare Library, Executive Editor of *Shakespeare Quarterly*, Chair of the Folger Institute, and author of *The Dramaturgy of Shakespeare's Romances* and of essays on Shakespeare's plays and on the editing of the plays.

Paul Werstine is Professor of English at the Graduate School and at King's University College at the University of Western Ontario. He is general editor of the New Variorum Shakespeare and author of many papers and articles on the printing and editing of Shakespeare's plays.

The Folger Shakespeare Library

The Folger Shakespeare Library in Washington, D.C., a privately funded research library dedicated to Shakespeare and the civilization of early modern Europe, was founded in 1932 by Henry Clay and Emily Jordan Folger. In addition to its role as the world's preeminent Shakespeare collection and its emergence as a leading center for Renaissance studies, the Folger Library offers a wide array of cultural and educational programs and services for the general public.

EDITORS

BARBARA A. MOWAT
Director of Research
Folger Shakespeare Library

PAUL WERSTINE
Professor of English
King's University College at the University of
Western Ontario, Canada

FOLGER SHAKESPEARE LIBRARY

Henry VIII

By

WILLIAM SHAKESPEARE

EDITED BY BARBARA A. MOWAT
AND PAUL WERSTINE

WASHINGTON SQUARE PRESS
NEW YORK LONDON TORONTO SYDNEY

A WASHINGTON SQUARE PRESS *Original* Publication

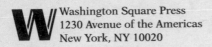 Washington Square Press
1230 Avenue of the Americas
New York, NY 10020

ISBN-13: 978-0-7432-7330-5
ISBN-10:   0-7432-7330-3

Washington Square Press New Folger Edition February 2007

10 9 8 7 6 5 4 3 2 1

WASHINGTON SQUARE PRESS and colophon are
registered trademarks of Simon & Schuster, Inc.

Manufactured in the United States of America

For information regarding special discounts for bulk purchases,
please contact Simon & Schuster Special Sales at 1-800-456-6798
or business@simonandschuster.com.

From the Director of the Library

Shakespeare has never been more alive as author and playwright than he is today, with productions being staged all over the world, new film versions appearing on screen every year, and millions of students in classrooms at all levels absorbed in the human drama and verbal richness of his works.

The New Folger Library Shakespeare editions welcome the interested reader with newly edited texts, commentary in a friendly facing-page format, and illustrations, drawn from the Folger archives, that wonderfully illuminate references and images in the plays. A synopsis of every scene makes the action clear.

In these editions, students, teachers, actors, and thousands of other readers will find the best of modern textual scholarship, along with up-to-date critical essays, written especially for these volumes, that offer original and often surprising interpretations of Shakespeare's characters, action, and language.

I thank editors Barbara Mowat and Paul Werstine for undertaking this ambitious project, which is nothing less than an entirely new look at the texts from the earliest printed versions. Lovers of Shakespeare everywhere must be grateful for the breadth of their learning, the liveliness of their imaginations, and the scholarly rigor that they bring to the challenge of re-editing the plays.

Gail Kern Paster, Director
The Folger Shakespeare Library

Contents

Editors' Preface

In recent years, ways of dealing with Shakespeare's texts and with the interpretation of his plays have been undergoing significant change. This edition, while retaining many of the features that have always made the Folger Shakespeare so attractive to the general reader, at the same time reflects these current ways of thinking about Shakespeare. For example, modern readers, actors, and teachers have become interested in the differences between, on the one hand, the early forms in which Shakespeare's plays were first published and, on the other hand, the forms in which editors through the centuries have presented them. In response to this interest, we have based our edition on what we consider the best early printed version of a particular play (explaining our rationale in a section called "An Introduction to This Text") and have marked our changes in the text—unobtrusively, we hope, but in such a way that the curious reader can be aware that a change has been made and can consult the "Textual Notes" to discover what appeared in the early printed version.

Current ways of looking at the plays are reflected in our brief prefaces, in many of the commentary notes, in the annotated lists of "Further Reading," and especially in each play's "Modern Perspective," an essay written by an outstanding scholar who brings to the reader his or her fresh assessment of the play in the light of today's interests and concerns.

As in the Folger Library General Reader's Shakespeare, which this edition replaces, we include explanatory notes designed to help make Shakespeare's language clearer to a modern reader, and we place the notes on the page facing the text that they explain. We also follow the earlier edition in including illustrations—of objects, of clothing, of mythological figures—from books and manuscripts in the Folger Library collection. We provide fresh accounts of the life of Shakespeare, of the publishing of his plays, and of the theaters in which his plays were performed, as well as an introduction to the text itself. We also include a section called "Reading Shakespeare's Language," in which we try to help readers learn to "break the code" of Elizabethan poetic language.

For each section of each volume, we are indebted to a host of generous experts and fellow scholars. The "Reading Shakespeare's Language" sections, for example, could not have been written had not Arthur King, of Brigham Young University, and Randall Robinson, author of *Unlocking Shakespeare's Language*, led the way in untangling Shakespearean language puzzles and shared their insights and methodologies generously with us. "Shakespeare's Life" profited by the careful reading given it by the late S. Schoenbaum; "Shakespeare's Theater" was read and strengthened by Andrew Gurr, John Astington, and William Ingram; and "The Publication of Shakespeare's Plays" is indebted to the comments of Peter W. M. Blayney. We, as editors, take sole responsibility for any errors in our editions.

We are grateful to the authors of the "Modern Perspectives"; to the Huntington and Newberry Libraries for fellowship support; to King's University College for the grants it has provided to Paul Werstine; to the Social Sciences and Humanities Research Council of Canada, which provided him with a Research Time

Stipend for 1990–91; to R. J. Shroyer of the University of Western Ontario for essential computer support; to the Folger Institute's Center for Shakespeare Studies for its sponsorship of a workshop on "Shakespeare's Texts for Students and Teachers" (funded by the National Endowment for the Humanities and led by Richard Knowles of the University of Wisconsin), a workshop from which we learned an enormous amount about what is wanted by college and high-school teachers of Shakespeare today; to Alice Falk for her expert copyediting; and especially to Stephen Llano, our production editor at Washington Square Press. Among the texts we consulted, we found Gordon McMullan's Arden *King Henry VIII* (2000) particularly helpful.

Our biggest debt is to the Folger Shakespeare Library—to Gail Kern Paster, Director of the Library, whose interest and support are unfailing, and to Werner Gundersheimer, the Library's Director from 1984 to 2002, who made possible our edition; to Deborah Curren-Aquino, who provides extensive editorial and production support; to Jean Miller, the Library's former Art Curator, who combs the Library holdings for illustrations, and to Julie Ainsworth, Head of the Photography Department, who carefully photographs them; to Peggy O'Brien, former Director of Education at the Folger and now Director of Education Programs at the Corporation for Public Broadcasting, who gave us expert advice about the needs being expressed by Shakespeare teachers and students (and to Martha Christian and other "master teachers" who used our texts in manuscript in their classrooms); to Allan Shnerson and Mary Bloodworth for their expert computer support; to the staff of the Academic Programs Division, especially Solvei Robertson (whose help is crucial), Liz Pohland, Mimi Godfrey, Kathleen Lynch, Carol Brobeck, Owen Williams, Virginia Millington, and Karen Rogers; and, finally, to the generously supportive staff of the Library's Reading Room.

Barbara A. Mowat and Paul Werstine

Shakespeare's *Henry VIII*

In *Henry VIII*, the last of his plays about English history, Shakespeare presents monarchy in a state of crisis.*
Noblemen are embattled with the enormously powerful Lord Chancellor Cardinal Wolsey, as both parties level charges of treason against each other almost indiscriminately. Wolsey, without the king's knowledge, has taxed the people to the point of rebellion. Yet the politics of the play are so subtle that the true cause of this crisis is not clear. In the case of the duke of Buckingham, for example, witnesses brought before Henry by Cardinal Wolsey claim that the duke, deceived by the prophecies of an evil monk, is conspiring to usurp Henry's throne. Nonetheless, as Buckingham goes to his death for treason, he seems the innocent victim of suborned testimony. Perhaps, then, the root of the crisis is Henry's failure to recognize Wolsey's exploitation of the king's favor, which, we learn later, has enabled him to amass a huge fortune through extortion and to feed his own pride and spite. Or perhaps the crisis arises from the ambition of noblemen who would strip Henry and his heirs of the throne.

The monarchy also faces a succession crisis, for Henry is without a male heir. Though Henry's queen, Katherine, has been pregnant many times, all but one of the pregnancies have resulted in miscarriages or in infants who died soon after birth. Worse, the single survivor is the girl Mary. After meeting the young and

*For our use of the name "Shakespeare" in this edition, see our Appendix on Authorship, page 251.

beautiful Anne Bullen, one of Katherine's ladies-in-waiting, Henry says that he is tormented by the suspicion that God has denied him a male heir because his marriage to Katherine—the widow of his brother—is invalid. The royal marriage begins to come apart. Again the precise nature of the crisis is put in question. Is Henry indeed experiencing a crisis of conscience about the sanctity of his marriage, or is he experiencing a crisis of desire provoked by the opportunity to take the young and beautiful Anne as a new wife and queen?

Whatever the ethics of Shakespeare's Henry, Katherine's integrity glows so splendidly in the play's action and dialogue that her role has long been coveted by actors. She first takes the stage as the advocate for all the English people crushed by Wolsey's oppressive taxes, and then she is properly suspicious, as Henry is not, of the motives of the witnesses who send Buckingham to his death. Her fierce opposition to Wolsey is repeatedly justified by the play's depiction of the cardinal's vices. When she is summoned to the church court that is deliberating on the propriety of her marriage, her defense of her conduct as Henry's wife is resounding in its eloquence. She has been admired for centuries by readers and playgoers alike.

After you have read the play, we invite you to turn to the essay printed after it, "*Henry VIII:* A Modern Perspective," by Barbara A. Mowat of the Folger Shakespeare Library.

Reading Shakespeare's Language: *Henry VIII*

For many people today, reading Shakespeare's language can be a problem—but it is a problem that can be solved. (For our use of the name "Shakespeare" in this play, see our Appendix on Authorship, p. 251.) Those who have studied Latin (or even French or German or Spanish), and those who are used to reading poetry, will have little difficulty understanding the language of poetic drama. Others, though, need to develop the skills of untangling unusual sentence structures and of recognizing and understanding poetic compressions, omissions, and wordplay. And even those skilled in reading unusual sentence structures may have occasional trouble with Shakespeare's words. Four hundred years of "static" intervene between his speaking and our hearing. Most of his vocabulary is still in use, but a few of his words are no longer used and many of his words now have meanings quite different from those they had in the seventeenth century. In the theater, most of these difficulties are solved for us by actors who study the language and articulate it for us so that the essential meaning is heard—or, when combined with stage action, is at least *felt*. When we are reading on our own, we must do what each actor does: go over the lines (often with a dictionary close at hand) until the puzzles are solved and the lines yield up their poetry and the characters speak in words and phrases that are, suddenly, rewarding and wonderfully memorable.

Shakespeare's Words

As you begin to read the opening scenes of a Shakespeare play, you may notice occasional unfamiliar words. Some are unfamiliar simply because we no longer use them. In the early scenes of *Henry VIII*, for example, one finds the words *keech* (i.e., a lump of congealed fat), *otherwhere* (i.e., elsewhere), *outworths* (i.e., is more valuable than), and *unpartial* (i.e., impartial). Words of this kind are explained in notes to the text and will become familiar the more Shakespeare plays you read.

In *Henry VIII*, as in all of Shakespeare's writing, more problematic are the words that are still in use but that now have different meanings. In the opening scenes of *Henry VIII*, for example, the word *guarded* is used where we would say "trimmed," *sad* where we would say "serious," *morrow* where we would say "morning," and *deceived* where we would say "disappointed." Such words will be explained in the notes to the text, but they, too, will become familiar as you continue to read Shakespeare's language.

Some words are strange not because of the "static" introduced by changes in language over the past centuries but because these are words that Shakespeare is using to build a dramatic world that has its own space, time, and history. In the opening scene of *Henry VIII*, for example, the dramatist quickly constructs the court of this early-sixteenth-century English monarch in which courtiers of different backgrounds compete for places on the king's "honorable board of council." There are courtiers "propped" by ancestors, those who have done "high feats" for the crown, and those "allied to eminent assistants." In their struggle for "honor," they accuse their rivals of "fierce vanities," "malice," "insolence," "device," and "practice." Such language quickly constructs Henry VIII's court; the words and the world they create will become increasingly familiar as you get further into the play.

Shakespeare's Sentences

In an English sentence, meaning is quite dependent on the place given each word. "The dog bit the boy" and "The boy bit the dog" mean very different things, even though the individual words are the same. Because English places such importance on the positions of words in sentences, on the way words are arranged, unusual arrangements can puzzle a reader. Shakespeare frequently shifts his sentences away from "normal" English arrangements—often to create the rhythm he seeks, sometimes to use a line's poetic rhythm to emphasize a particular word, sometimes to give a character his or her own speech patterns or to allow the character to speak in a special way. When we attend a good performance of the play, the actors will have worked out the sentence structures and will articulate the sentences so that the meaning is clear. When reading the play, we need to do as the actor does: that is, when puzzled by a character's speech, check to see if words are being presented in an unusual sequence.

Often Shakespeare rearranges subjects and verbs (i.e., instead of "He goes" we find "Goes he"). In *Henry VIII*, Buckingham uses such a construction in explaining why Charles the Holy Roman Emperor fears the English-French treaty—"from this league / *Peeped harms* that menaced him" (1.1.213–14). So does Lovell when he later says "so *run the conditions*" (1.3.31). The "normal" order would be "harms peeped" and "the conditions run." Shakespeare also frequently places the object before the subject and verb (i.e., instead of "I hit him," we might find "Him I hit"). Buckingham provides an example of this inversion when he says "all *this business / Our* reverend *cardinal carried*" (1.1.119–20), and the king another example when he says of Buckingham's surveyor that "*the treasons* of his master / *He shall* again *relate*" (1.2.7–8). The "normal" order would be "our cardinal carried this business" and "he shall relate the treasons."

Inversions are not the only unusual sentence structures in Shakespeare's language. Often in his sentences words that would normally appear together are separated from each other. Again, this is commonly done to create a particular rhythm or to stress a particular word, or else to draw attention to a needed piece of information. Take, for example, Norfolk's "Today the French, / All clinquant, all in gold, like heathen gods, / Shone down the English" (1.1.24–26). Here the subject ("the French") is separated from its verb ("shone") by the subject's three modifiers: "All clinquant [glittering]," "all in gold," and "like heathen gods." As Norfolk's purpose is to describe to Buckingham the splendor of the ceremonies at the Field of the Cloth of Gold, these modifiers have an importance that allows them briefly to shoulder aside the verb. Or take Buckingham's accusation against Wolsey for prompting Henry unwisely to sign a treaty:

> This holy fox,
> Or wolf, or both—for he is equal rav'nous
> As he is subtle, and as prone to mischief
> As able to perform 't, his mind and place
> Infecting one another, yea reciprocally—
> Only to show his pomp as well in France
> As here at home, suggests the King our master
> To this last costly treaty[.]
>
> (1.1.188–95)

Here the subject and verb ("This holy fox . . . suggests") are separated by a coordinate conjunction and a noun ("or wolf"), another conjunction and an appositive ("or both"), then a balanced subordinate clause ("for he is equal rav'nous / As he is subtle, and as prone to mischief / As able to perform 't"), then an absolute construction ("his mind and place / Infecting one another, yea reciprocally"), and finally an infinitive ("Only to show his pomp as well in France / As here at home"). This pileup of interruptions emphasizes Buckingham's almost overmastering contempt for Wolsey's pride and fear of his cunning malice. In order to create sentences that seem more like the English of everyday speech, one can rearrange the words, putting together the word clusters ("This holy fox suggests the king to this treaty, for he is equal ravenous . . ."). The result will usually be an increase in clarity but a loss of rhythm or a shift in emphasis.

Often in *Henry VIII,* rather than separating basic sentence elements, Shakespeare simply holds them back, delaying them until other material to which he wants to give greater emphasis has been presented. He puts this kind of construction in the mouth of Buckingham to stress how the character missed all that took place at the Field of the Cloth of Gold: "All the whole time / I was my chamber's prisoner" (1.1.17–18). The basic sentence elements ("I was") are here withheld for a moment as Buckingham indicates the length of the sickness that kept him from appearing in public; this indication provides the motivation for Norfolk's account of all that Buckingham missed, an account that takes up much of the play's first scene. When, as he feared, Buckingham is arrested at the end of this scene, again Shakespeare delays the crucial sentence elements of subject, verb, and object ("I arrest thee") until a list of Buckingham's titles has been presented and

our awareness thereby directed to the great height
from which he is now falling.

> My lord the Duke of Buckingham and Earl
> Of Hertford, Stafford, and Northampton, I
> Arrest thee[.]
>
>   (1.1.233–35)

Finally, in Shakespeare's plays, sentences are sometimes complicated not because of unusual structures or
interruptions but because the dramatist omits words
and parts of words that English sentences normally
require. (In conversation, we, too, often omit words. We
say, "Heard from him yet?" and our hearer supplies the
missing "Have you.") Shakespeare captures the same
conversational tone in the play's initial exchange
between Buckingham and Norfolk. When Buckingham
asks Norfolk "How have you done / Since last we saw in
France?" the dramatist omits "each other" after "saw"
leaving his audience or readers to supply the words.
From Norfolk's response "I thank your Grace, / Healthful" Shakespeare leaves out the words "I have been"
before "healthful" (1.1.1–4). In 1.2, when Henry VIII
hears that such high taxes are being exacted in his name
that some subjects are about to rebel, the urgency of his
demands for detail is dramatically rendered through his
radical ellipses, his questions stripped of most of the
usual sentence elements: "Taxation? / Wherein? And
what taxation?" (1.2.43–44) and "Still exaction! / The
nature of it?" (61–62). Though Shakespeare follows each
of these sets of stripped-down questions with a more
fully formed question, even those questions are cryptic:
"My Lord Cardinal, / You that are blamed for it alike
with us, / Know you of this taxation?" and "In what
kind, let's know, / Is this exaction?" (44–46, 62–63). The
effect obtained is of volatile, barely contained emotion.

Shakespeare's Wordplay

Shakespeare plays with language so often and so variously that entire books are written on the topic. Here we will mention only two kinds of wordplay, metaphors and puns. A metaphor is a play on words in which one object or idea is expressed as if it were something else, something with which the metaphor suggests it shares common features. For instance, when Buckingham, as he is arrested, declares "The net has fall'n upon me" (1.1.238), he uses a metaphor that presents his arrest as the trapping of an animal in a successfully laid snare. "Those suns of glory" (1.1.8) is another metaphor, this one glorifying Henry VIII of England and Francis I of France by describing them as the brightest of lights. This metaphor is repeated later in the scene, first by Norfolk, who refers to the kings as "these suns— / For so they phrase 'em" (39–40). Buckingham himself uses it again in the context of other metaphors in an attack on Wolsey:

> I wonder
> That such a keech can with his very bulk
> Take up the rays o' th' beneficial sun
> And keep it from the earth.

> (1.1.63–66)

In this passage, Wolsey is metaphorically said to be a "keech," or lump of fat, grown so vast in bulk that he shadows the earth, depriving it of the sun's rays. In the context of earlier references to the king as sun, it seems reasonable to interpret the lines as accusing Wolsey of absorbing so much of the king's favor that no one else can experience it. A further extension of the metaphor may be found at the scene's conclusion when Buckingham laments how he has fallen out of the king's favor:

> I am the shadow of poor Buckingham,
> Whose figure even this instant cloud puts on
> By dark'ning my clear sun.
>
> (266–68)

This challenging metaphor may be interpreted to mean, among other things, that Buckingham views his disgrace as a passage out of the light of the sun-king and into the shade of a cloud.

A pun is a play on words that sound the same but that have different meanings (or on a single word that has more than one meaning). A number of puns in this play are bawdy. When Lord Sands is talking with his friends the Lord Chamberlain and Sir Thomas Lovell about wooing women, the Lord Chamberlain asks Sands "Your colt's tooth [i.e., youthful desire] is not cast yet?" Sands answers "not while I have a stump" (1.3.58, 60), punning on "stump," which can mean not only part of a broken tooth left in the gum but also a penis. Other puns are not bawdy but savagely ironic. Queen Katherine uses such a pun in addressing the Cardinals Wolsey and Campeius:

> Holy men I thought you,
> Upon my soul, two reverend cardinal virtues;
> But cardinal sins and hollow hearts I fear you.
>
> (3.1.116–18)

The word *cardinal*, as used in line 117, means "chief," but puns on the ecclesiastical rank of *cardinal* and on the term *cardinal virtues*, which refers to justice, temperance, prudence, and fortitude. In line 118, once again "cardinal" alludes to the men's ecclesiastic rank and puns on the term *cardinal sins*—that is, the Seven

Deadly Sins, usually identified as pride, greed, envy, wrath, sloth, gluttony, and lechery.

Implied Stage Action

Finally, in reading Shakespeare's plays we should always remember that what we are reading is a performance script. The dialogue is written to be spoken by actors who, at the same time, are moving, gesturing, picking up objects, weeping, shaking their fists. Some stage action is described in what are called "stage directions"; some is signaled within the dialogue itself. We must learn to be alert to such signals as we stage the play in our imaginations.

Often the dialogue offers an immediate indication of the action that is to accompany it. For example, when Wolsey, in conversation with Cromwell, says "Let's dry our eyes" (3.2.511), it is clear that both are shedding tears over Wolsey's fall from greatness. Therefore we feel fairly confident about adding to their preceding speech prefixes the stage direction *"weeping,"* putting it in half-square brackets to signal that it is our interpolation rather than an instruction appearing in the earliest printed text. Again, when Henry VIII says of Cardinal Campeius "once more in mine arms I bid him welcome" (2.2.118), it is fairly clear that the king embraces the cardinal, and so we add the stage direction *"He embraces Campeius,"* in brackets, at the end of the king's speech. However, the line *"once more* in mine arms I bid him welcome" might be interpreted to mean that Henry has already bid the cardinal welcome by embracing him. In Henry's earlier speeches to the cardinal there is no allusion to an earlier embrace, and therefore we have added no stage direction to indicate one. While it is possible that they have embraced before, it is also possible that the king means only "once more . . . I bid him welcome." We have left to the reader to decide whether king or cardinal embrace once or twice.

Occasionally, in *Henry VIII*, signals to the reader are not in the least clear. In 1.4, for example, Wolsey is sitting in a raised chair watching the masquers dance when he offers to give up his seat of honor for one among the masquers that he knows to be of a higher rank than himself. The response comes that Wolsey must determine which of the masquers holds that noble rank. Wolsey then says: "Let me see, then. By all your good leaves, gentlemen. Here I'll make my royal choice." To which the king responds "You have found him, cardinal" (112–16). The stage action accompanying this dialogue could range all the way from Wolsey's staying in his seat and pointing to the masked king to Wolsey's prostrating himself before this figure. After considering royal protocol and dramatic effectiveness, we decided to add stage directions, in brackets, that have Wolsey leave "his state" and then bow "before the king," at which point the king unmasks. Actors and directors, and you as a reader, are free to decide on other actions and gestures.

Again, in 3.2, directions for stage action are most ambiguous. Wolsey meets Cromwell, who tells him he has delivered Wolsey's packet to the king; Wolsey speaks in soliloquy of his determination that Henry not marry Anne Bullen; the king enters, unobserved by Wolsey, and is told that Wolsey has been acting very strange.

> He bites his lip, and starts,
> Stops on a sudden, looks upon the ground,
> Then lays his finger on his temple, straight
> Springs out into fast gait, then stops again,
> Strikes his breast hard, and anon he casts
> His eye against the moon. In most strange postures
> We have seen him set himself.
>
> (148–54)

It is quite possible that Norfolk, the speaker here, is describing exactly what Wolsey has been doing as he speaks in soliloquy. On the other hand, Wolsey might have stood perfectly still while speaking, with Norfolk simply using this opportunity to describe Wolsey as behaving in a highly suspicious manner. In this case, we added no directions for Wolsey's actions, leaving the decision about them to the actor, director, or imaginative reader.

Practice in reading the language of stage action repays one many times over when one reaches scenes heavily dependent on stage business. Think, for example, of the scene (5.2) that begins with Cranmer refused admittance to the Privy Council, observed first by Doctor Butts, then by the king and Doctor Butts from a window above, followed by the setting up of the Privy Council meeting, the summoning of Cranmer before the Council, his impassioned defense of himself, his presentation of the king's ring, the entrance of the king, and the final general embracing of Cranmer by the members of the Council. For a reader, such a scene requires a vivid stage-related imagination. With such an imagination, such an ability to read the language of stage action, scenes like this one—along with, for example, the coronation scene (4.1) and the baptism scene (5.4)—come to life in the mind much as they do on the stage.

It is immensely rewarding to work carefully with Shakespeare's language—with the words, the sentences, the wordplay, and the implied stage action—as readers for the past four centuries have discovered. It may be more pleasurable to attend a good performance of a play—though not everyone has thought so. But the joy of being able to stage a Shakespeare play in one's imagination, to return to passages that continue to yield further meanings (or further questions) the more one reads them—these are pleasures that, for many, rival (or at least augment) those of the performed text, and certainly make it worth considerable effort to "break the code" of Jacobean poetic drama and let free the remarkable language that makes up a Shakespeare text.

Shakespeare's Life

Surviving documents that give us glimpses into the life of William Shakespeare show us a playwright, poet, and actor who grew up in the market town of Stratford-upon-Avon, spent his professional life in London, and returned to Stratford a wealthy landowner. He was born in April 1564, died in April 1616, and is buried inside the chancel of Holy Trinity Church in Stratford.

We wish we could know more about the life of the world's greatest dramatist. His plays and poems are testaments to his wide reading—especially to his knowledge of Virgil, Ovid, Plutarch, Holinshed's *Chronicles*, and the Bible—and to his mastery of the English language, but we can only speculate about his education. We know that the King's New School in Stratford-upon-Avon was considered excellent. The school was one of the English "grammar schools" established to educate young men, primarily in Latin grammar and literature. As in other schools of the time, students began their studies at the age of four or five in the attached "petty school," and there learned to read and write in English, studying primarily the catechism from the Book of Common Prayer. After two years in the petty school, students entered the lower form (grade) of the grammar school, where they began the serious study of Latin grammar and Latin texts that would occupy most of the remainder of their school days. (Several Latin texts that Shakespeare used repeatedly in writing his plays and poems were texts that schoolboys memorized and recited.) Latin comedies were introduced early in the lower form; in the upper form, which the boys entered at age ten or eleven, students wrote their own Latin orations and declamations, studied Latin historians and rhetoricians, and began the study of Greek using the Greek New Testament.

Since the records of the Stratford "grammar school" do not survive, we cannot prove that William Shakespeare attended the school; however, every indication (his father's position as an alderman and bailiff of Stratford, the playwright's own knowledge of the Latin classics, scenes in the plays that recall grammar-school experiences—for example, *The Merry Wives of Windsor*, 4.1) suggests that he did. We also lack generally accepted documentation about Shakespeare's life after his schooling ended and his professional life in London began. His marriage in 1582 (at age eighteen) to Anne Hathaway and the subsequent births of his daughter Susanna (1583) and the twins Judith and Hamnet (1585) are recorded, but how he supported himself and where he lived are not known. Nor do we know when and why he left Stratford for the London theatrical world, nor how he rose to be the important figure in that world that he had become by the early 1590s.

We do know that by 1592 he had achieved some prominence in London as both an actor and a playwright. In that year was published a book by the playwright Robert Greene attacking an actor who had the audacity to write blank-verse drama and who was "in his own conceit [i.e., opinion] the only Shake-scene in a country." Since Greene's attack includes a parody of a line from one of Shakespeare's early plays, there is little doubt that it is Shakespeare to whom he refers, a "Shake-scene" who had aroused Greene's fury by successfully competing with university-educated dramatists like Greene himself. It was in 1593 that Shakespeare became a published poet. In that year he published his long narrative poem *Venus and Adonis;* in 1594, he followed it with *The Rape of Lucrece.* Both poems were dedicated to the young earl of Southampton (Henry Wriothesley), who may have become Shakespeare's patron.

It seems no coincidence that Shakespeare wrote these narrative poems at a time when the theaters were closed because of the plague, a contagious epidemic disease that devastated the population of London. When the theaters reopened in 1594, Shakespeare apparently resumed his double career of actor and playwright and began his long (and seemingly profitable) service as an acting-company shareholder. Records for December of 1594 show him to be a leading member of the Lord Chamberlain's Men. It was this company of actors, later named the King's Men, for whom he would be a principal actor, dramatist, and shareholder for the rest of his career.

So far as we can tell, that career spanned about twenty years. In the 1590s, he wrote his plays on English history as well as several comedies and at least two tragedies (*Titus Andronicus* and *Romeo and Juliet*). These histories, comedies, and tragedies are the plays credited to him in 1598 in a work, *Palladis Tamia,* that in one chapter compares English writers with "Greek, Latin, and Italian Poets." There the author, Francis Meres, claims that Shakespeare is comparable to the Latin dramatists Seneca for tragedy and Plautus for comedy, and calls him "the most excellent in both kinds for the stage." He also names him "Mellifluous and honey-tongued Shakespeare": "I say," writes Meres, "that the Muses would speak with Shakespeare's fine filed phrase, if they would speak English." Since Meres also mentions Shakespeare's "sugared sonnets among his private friends," it is assumed that many of Shakespeare's sonnets (not published until 1609) were also written in the 1590s.

In 1599, Shakespeare's company built a theater for themselves across the river from London, naming it the Globe. The plays that are considered by many to be Shakespeare's major tragedies (*Hamlet, Othello, King Lear,* and *Macbeth*) were written while the company was resident in this theater, as were such comedies as *Twelfth Night* and *Measure for Measure.* Many of Shakespeare's plays were performed at court (both for Queen Elizabeth I and, after her death in 1603, for King James I), some were presented at the Inns of Court (the residences of London's legal societies), and some were doubtless performed in other towns, at the universities, and at great houses when the King's Men went on tour; otherwise, his plays from 1599 to 1608 were, so far as we know, performed only at the Globe. Between 1608 and 1612, Shakespeare wrote several plays—among them *The Winter's Tale* and *The*

Tempest—presumably for the company's new indoor Blackfriars theater, though the plays seem to have been performed also at the Globe and at court. Surviving documents describe a performance of *The Winter's Tale* in 1611 at the Globe, for example, and performances of *The Tempest* in 1611 and 1613 at the royal palace of Whitehall.

Shakespeare wrote very little after 1612, the year in which he probably wrote *Henry VIII*. (It was at a performance of *Henry VIII* in 1613 that the Globe caught fire and burned to the ground.) Sometime between 1610 and 1613 he seems to have returned to live in Stratford-upon-Avon, where he owned a large house and considerable property, and where his wife and his two daughters and their husbands lived. (His son Hamnet had died in 1596.) During his professional years in London, Shakespeare had presumably derived income from the acting company's profits as well as from his own career as an actor, from the sale of his play manuscripts to the acting company, and, after 1599, from his shares as an owner of the Globe. It was presumably that income, carefully invested in land and other property, which made him the wealthy man that surviving documents show him to have become. It is also assumed that William Shakespeare's growing wealth and reputation played some part in inclining the crown, in 1596, to grant John Shakespeare, William's father, the coat of arms that he had so long sought. William Shakespeare died in Stratford on April 23, 1616 (according to the epitaph carved under his bust in Holy Trinity Church) and was buried on April 25. Seven years after his death, his collected plays were published as *Mr. William Shakespeares Comedies, Histories, & Tragedies* (the work now known as the First Folio).

The Globe

A stylized representation of the Globe theater.
From Claes Jansz Visscher, *Londinum florentissima
Britanniae urbs . . .* [c. 1625].

The years in which Shakespeare wrote were among the most exciting in English history. Intellectually, the discovery, translation, and printing of Greek and Roman classics were making available a set of works and worldviews that interacted complexly with Christian texts and beliefs. The result was a questioning, a vital intellectual ferment, that provided energy for the period's amazing dramatic and literary output and that fed directly into Shakespeare's plays. The Ghost in *Hamlet,* for example, is wonderfully complicated in part because he is a figure from Roman tragedy—the spirit of the dead returning to seek revenge—who at the same time inhabits a Christian hell (or purgatory); Hamlet's description of humankind reflects at one moment the Neoplatonic wonderment at mankind ("What a piece of work is a man!") and, at the next, the Christian disparagement of human sinners ("And yet, to me, what is this quintessence of dust?").

As intellectual horizons expanded, so also did geographical and cosmological horizons. New worlds—both North and South America—were explored, and in them were found human beings who lived and worshiped in ways radically different from those of Renaissance Europeans and Englishmen. The universe during these years also seemed to shift and expand. Copernicus had earlier theorized that the earth was not the center of the cosmos but revolved as a planet around the sun. Galileo's telescope, created in 1609, allowed scientists to see that Copernicus had been correct; the universe was not organized with the earth at the center, nor was it so nicely circumscribed as people had, until that time, thought. In terms of expanding horizons, the impact of these discoveries on people's beliefs—religious, scientific, and philosophical—cannot be overstated.

London, too, rapidly expanded and changed during the years (from the early 1590s to around 1610) that Shakespeare lived there. London—the center of England's government, its economy, its royal court, its overseas trade—was, during these years, becoming an exciting metropolis, drawing to it thousands of new citizens every year. Troubled by overcrowding, by poverty, by recurring epidemics of the plague, London was also a mecca for the wealthy and the aristocratic, and for those who sought advancement at court, or power in government or finance or trade. One hears in Shakespeare's plays the voices of London—the struggles for power, the fear of venereal disease, the language of buying and selling. One hears as well the voices of Stratford-upon-Avon—references to the nearby Forest of Arden, to sheepherding, to small-town gossip, to village fairs and markets. Part of the richness of Shakespeare's work is the influence felt there of the various worlds in which he lived: the world of metropolitan London, the world of small-town and rural England, the world of the theater, and the worlds of craftsmen and shepherds.

That Shakespeare inhabited such worlds we know from surviving London and Stratford documents, as well as from the evidence of the plays and poems themselves. From such records we can sketch the dramatist's life. We know from his works that he was a voracious reader. We know from legal and business documents that he was a multifaceted theater man who became a wealthy landowner. We know a bit about his family life and a fair amount about his legal and financial dealings. Most scholars today depend upon such evidence as they draw their picture of the world's greatest playwright. Such, however, has not always been the case. Until the late eighteenth century, the William Shakespeare who lived in most biographies was the creation of legend and tradition. This was the Shakespeare who was supposedly caught poaching deer at Charlecote, the estate of Sir Thomas Lucy close by Stratford; this was the Shakespeare who fled from Sir Thomas's vengeance and made his way in London by taking care of horses outside a playhouse; this was the Shakespeare who reportedly could barely read but whose natural gifts were extraordinary, whose father was a butcher who allowed his gifted son sometimes to help in the butcher shop, where William supposedly killed calves "in a high style," making a speech for the occasion. It was this legendary William Shakespeare whose Falstaff (in *1* and *2 Henry IV*) so pleased Queen Elizabeth that she demanded a play about Falstaff in love, and demanded that it be written in fourteen days (hence the existence of *The Merry Wives of Windsor*). It was this legendary Shakespeare who reached the top of his acting career in the roles of the Ghost in *Hamlet* and old Adam in *As You Like It*—and who died of a fever contracted by drinking too hard at "a merry meeting" with the poets Michael Drayton and Ben Jonson. This legendary Shakespeare is a rambunctious, undisciplined man, as attractively "wild" as his plays were seen by earlier generations to be. Unfortunately, there is no trace of evidence to support these wonderful stories.

Perhaps in response to the disreputable Shakespeare of legend—or perhaps in response to the fragmentary and, for some, all-too-ordinary Shakespeare documented by surviving records—some people since the mid–nineteenth century have argued that William Shakespeare could not have written the plays that bear his name. These persons have put forward some dozen names as more likely authors, among them Queen Elizabeth, Sir Francis Bacon, Edward de Vere (earl of Oxford), and Christopher Marlowe. Such attempts to find what for these people is a more believable author of the plays is a tribute to the regard in which the plays are held. Unfortunately for their claims, the documents that exist that provide evidence for the facts of Shakespeare's life tie him inextricably to the body of plays and poems that bear his name. Unlikely as it seems to those who want the works to have been written by an aristocrat, a university graduate, or an "important" person, the plays and poems seem clearly to have been produced by a man from Stratford-upon-Avon with a very good "grammar school" education and a life of experience in London and in the world of the London theater. How this particular man produced the works that dominate the cultures of much of the world almost four hundred years after his death is one of life's mysteries—and one that will continue to tease our imaginations as we continue to delight in his plays and poems.

Shakespeare's Theater

The actors of Shakespeare's time performed plays in a great variety of locations. They played at court (that is, in the great halls of such royal residences as Whitehall, Hampton Court, and Greenwich); they played in halls at the universities of Oxford and Cambridge, and at the Inns of Court (the residences in London of the legal societies); and they also played in the private houses of great lords and civic officials. Sometimes acting companies went on tour from London into the provinces, often (but not only) when outbreaks of bubonic plague in the capital forced the closing of theaters to reduce the possibility of contagion in crowded audiences. In the provinces the actors usually staged their plays in churches (until around 1600) or in guildhalls. Though surviving records show only a handful of occasions when actors played at inns while on tour, London inns were important playing places up until the 1590s.

The building of theaters in London had begun only shortly before Shakespeare wrote his first plays in the 1590s. These theaters were of two kinds: outdoor or public playhouses that could accommodate large numbers of playgoers, and indoor or private theaters for much smaller audiences. What is usually regarded as the first London outdoor public playhouse was called simply the Theatre. James Burbage—the father of Richard Burbage, who was perhaps the most famous actor in Shakespeare's company—built it in 1576 in an area north of the city of London called Shoreditch. Among the more famous of the other public playhouses that capitalized on the new fashion were the Curtain and the Fortune (both also built north of the city), the Rose, the Swan, the Globe, and the Hope (all located on the Bankside, a region just across the Thames south of the city of London). All these playhouses had to be built outside the jurisdiction of the city of London because many civic officials were hostile to the performance of drama and repeatedly petitioned the royal council to abolish it.

The theaters erected on the Bankside (a region under the authority of the Church of England, whose head was the monarch) shared the neighborhood with houses of prostitution and with the Paris Garden, where the blood sports of bearbaiting and bullbaiting were carried on. There may have been no clear distinction between playhouses and buildings for such sports, for the Hope was used for both plays and baiting, and Philip Henslowe, owner of the Rose and, later, partner in the ownership of the Fortune, was also a partner in a monopoly on baiting. All these forms of entertainment were easily accessible to Londoners by boat across the Thames or over London Bridge.

Evidently Shakespeare's company prospered on the Bankside. They moved there in 1599. Threatened by difficulties in renewing the lease on the land where their first playhouse (the Theatre) had been built, Shakespeare's company took advantage of the Christmas holiday in 1598 to dismantle the Theatre and transport its timbers across the Thames to the Bankside, where, in 1599, these timbers were used in the building of the Globe. The weather in late December 1598 is recorded as having been especially harsh. It was so cold that the Thames was "nigh [nearly] frozen," and there was heavy snow. Perhaps the weather aided Shakespeare's company in eluding their landlord, the snow hiding their activity and the freezing of the Thames allowing them to slide the timbers across to the Bankside without paying tolls for repeated trips over London Bridge. Attractive as this narrative is, it remains just as likely that the heavy snow hampered transport of the timbers in wagons through the London streets to the river. It also must be remembered that the Thames was, according to report, only "nigh frozen" and therefore as impassable as it ever was. Whatever the precise circumstances of this fascinating event in English theater history, Shakespeare's company was able to begin playing at their new Globe theater on the Bankside in 1599. After the first Globe burned down in 1613 during the staging of Shakespeare's *Henry VIII* (its thatch roof was set alight by cannon fire called for by the performance), Shakespeare's company immediately rebuilt on the same location. The second Globe seems to have been a grander structure than its predecessor. It remained in use until the beginning of the English Civil War in 1642, when Parliament officially closed the theaters. Soon thereafter it was pulled down.

The public theaters of Shakespeare's time were very different buildings from our theaters today. First of all, they were open-air playhouses. As recent excavations of the Rose and the Globe confirm, some were polygonal or roughly circular in shape; the Fortune, however, was square. The most recent estimates of their size put the diameter of these buildings at 72 feet (the Rose) to 100 feet (the Globe), but they were said to hold vast audiences of two or three thousand, who must have been squeezed together quite tightly. Some of these spectators paid extra to sit or stand in the two or three levels of roofed galleries that extended, on the upper levels, all the way around the theater and surrounded an open space. In this space were the stage and, perhaps, the tiring house (what we would call dressing rooms), as well as the so-called yard. In the yard stood the spectators who chose to pay less, the ones whom Hamlet contemptuously called "groundlings." For a roof they had only the sky, and so they were exposed to all kinds of weather. They stood on a floor that was sometimes made of mortar and sometimes of ash mixed with the shells of hazelnuts, which, it has recently been discovered, were standard flooring material in the period.

Unlike the yard, the stage itself was covered by a roof. Its ceiling, called "the heavens," is thought to have been elaborately painted to depict the sun, moon, stars, and planets. Just how big the stage was remains hard to determine. We have a single sketch of part of the interior of the Swan. A Dutchman named Johannes de Witt visited this theater around 1596 and sent a sketch of it back to his friend, Arend van Buchel. Because van Buchel found de Witt's letter and sketch of interest, he copied both into a book. It is van Buchel's copy, adapted, it seems, to the shape and size of the page in his book, that survives. In this sketch, the stage appears to be a large rectangular platform that thrusts far out into the yard, perhaps even as far as the center of the circle formed by the surrounding galleries. This drawing, combined with the specifications for the size of the stage in the building contract for the Fortune, has led scholars to conjecture that the stage on which Shakespeare's plays were performed must have measured approximately 43 feet in width and 27 feet in depth, a vast acting area. But the digging up of a large part of the Rose by archaeologists has provided evidence of a quite different stage design. The Rose stage was a platform tapered at the corners and much shallower than what seems to be depicted in the van Buchel sketch. Indeed, its measurements seem to be about 37.5 feet across at its widest point and only 15.5 feet deep. Because the surviving indications of stage size and design differ from each other so much, it is possible that the stages in other playhouses, like the Theatre, the Curtain, and the Globe (the outdoor playhouses where Shakespeare's plays were performed), were different from those at both the Swan and the Rose.

After about 1608 Shakespeare's plays were staged not only at the Globe but also at an indoor or private playhouse in Blackfriars. This theater had been constructed in 1596 by James Burbage in an upper hall of a former Dominican priory or monastic house. Although Henry VIII had dissolved all English monasteries in the 1530s (shortly after he had founded the Church of England), the area remained under church, rather than hostile civic, control. The hall that Burbage had purchased and renovated was a large one in which Parliament had once met. In the private theater that he constructed, the stage, lit by candles, was built across the narrow end of the hall, with boxes flanking it. The rest of the hall offered seating room only. Because there was no provision for standing room, the largest audience it could hold was less than a thousand, or about a quarter of what the Globe could accommodate. Admission to Blackfriars was correspondingly more expensive. Instead of a penny to stand in the yard at the Globe, it cost a minimum of sixpence to get into Blackfriars. The best seats at the Globe (in the Lords' Room in the gallery above and behind the stage) cost sixpence; but the boxes flanking the stage at Blackfriars were half a crown, or five times sixpence. Some spectators who were particularly interested in displaying themselves paid even more to sit on stools on the Blackfriars stage.

Whether in the outdoor or indoor playhouses, the stages of Shakespeare's time were different from ours. They were not separated from the audience by the dropping of a curtain between acts and scenes. Therefore the playwrights of the time had to find other ways of signaling to the audience that one scene (to be imagined as occurring in one location at a given time) had ended and the next (to be imagined at perhaps a different location at a later time) had begun. The customary way used by Shakespeare and many of his contemporaries was to have everyone onstage exit at the end of one scene and have one or more different characters enter to begin the next. In a few cases, where characters remain onstage from one scene to another, the dialogue or stage action makes the change of location clear, and the characters are generally to be imagined as having moved from one place to another. For example, in *Romeo and Juliet*, Romeo and his friends remain onstage in Act 1 from scene 4 to scene 5, but they are represented as having moved between scenes from the street that leads to Capulet's house into Capulet's house itself. The new location is signaled in part by the appearance onstage of Capulet's servingmen carrying napkins, something they would not take into the streets. Playwrights had to be quite resourceful in the use of hand properties, like the napkin, or in the use of dialogue to specify where the action was taking place in their plays because, in contrast to most of today's theaters, the playhouses of Shakespeare's time did not use movable scenery to dress the stage and make the setting precise. As another consequence of this difference, however, the playwrights of Shakespeare's time did not have to specify exactly where the action of their plays was set when they did not choose to do so, and much of the action of their plays is tied to no specific place.

Usually Shakespeare's stage is referred to as a "bare stage," to distinguish it from the stages of the past two or three centuries with their elaborate sets. But the stage in Shakespeare's time was not completely bare. Philip Henslowe, owner of the Rose, lists in his inventory of stage properties a rock, three tombs, and two mossy banks. Stage directions in plays of the time also call for such things as thrones (or "states"), banquets (presumably tables with plaster replicas of food on them), and beds and tombs to be pushed onto the stage. Thus the stage often held more than the actors.

The actors did not limit their performing to the stage alone. Occasionally they went beneath the stage, as the Ghost appears to do in the first act of *Hamlet*. From there they could emerge onto the stage through a trapdoor. They could retire behind the hangings across the back of the stage (or the front of the tiring house), as, for example, the actor playing Polonius does when he hides behind the arras. Sometimes the hangings could be drawn back during a performance to "discover" one or more actors behind them. When performance required that an actor appear "above," as when Juliet is imagined to stand at the window of her chamber in the famous and misnamed "balcony scene," then the actor probably climbed the stairs to the gallery over the back of the stage and temporarily shared it with some of the spectators. The stage was also provided with ropes and winches so that actors could descend from, and re-ascend to, the "heavens."

Perhaps the greatest difference between dramatic performances in Shakespeare's time and ours was that in Shakespeare's England the roles of women were played by boys. (Some of these boys grew up to take male roles in their maturity.) There were no women in the acting companies, only in the audience. It had not always been so in the history of the English stage. There are records of women on English stages in the thirteenth and fourteenth centuries, two hundred years before Shakespeare's plays were performed. After the accession of James I in 1603, the queen of England and her ladies took part in entertainments at court called masques, and with the reopening of the theaters in 1660 at the restoration of Charles II, women again took their place on the public stage.

The chief competitors for the companies of adult actors such as the one to which Shakespeare belonged and for which he wrote were companies of exclusively boy actors. The competition was most intense in the early 1600s. There were then two principal children's companies: the Children of Paul's (the choirboys from St. Paul's Cathedral, whose private playhouse was near the cathedral); and the Children of the Chapel Royal (the choirboys from the monarch's private chapel, who performed at the Blackfriars theater built by Burbage in 1596, which Shakespeare's company had been stopped from using by local residents who objected to crowds). In *Hamlet* Shakespeare writes of "an aerie [nest] of children, little eyases [hawks], that cry out on the top of question and are most tyrannically clapped for 't. These are now the fashion and . . . berattle the common stages [attack the public theaters]." In the long run, the adult actors prevailed. The Children of Paul's dissolved around 1606. By about 1608 the Children of the Chapel Royal had been forced to stop playing at the Blackfriars theater, which was then taken over by the King's company of players, Shakespeare's own troupe.

Acting companies and theaters of Shakespeare's time were organized in different ways. For example, Philip Henslowe owned the Rose and leased it to companies of actors, who paid him from their takings. Henslowe would act as manager of these companies, initially paying playwrights for their plays and buying properties, recovering his outlay from the actors. With the building of the Globe, however, Shakespeare's company managed itself, with the principal actors, Shakespeare among them, having the status of "sharers" and the right to a share in the takings, as well as the responsibility for a part of the expenses. Five of the sharers, including Shakespeare, owned the Globe. As actor, as sharer in an acting company and in ownership of theaters, and as playwright, Shakespeare was about as involved in the theatrical industry as one could imagine. Although Shakespeare and his fellows prospered, their status under the law was conditional upon the protection of powerful patrons. "Common players"—those who did not have patrons or masters—were classed in the language of the law with "vagabonds and sturdy beggars." So the actors had to secure for themselves the official rank of servants of patrons. Among the patrons under whose protection Shakespeare's company worked were the lord chamberlain and, after the accession of King James in 1603, the king himself.

In the early 1990s we seemed on the verge of learning a great deal more about the theaters in which Shakespeare and his contemporaries performed—or, at least, opening up new questions about them. At that time about 70 percent of the Rose had been excavated, as had about 10 percent of the second Globe, the one built in 1614. It was then hoped that more would become available for study. However, excavation was halted at that point, and it is not known if or when it will resume.

The Publication of Shakespeare's Plays

Eighteen of Shakespeare's plays found their way into print during the playwright's lifetime, but there is nothing to suggest that he took any interest in their publication. These eighteen appeared separately in editions called quartos. Their pages were not much larger than the one you are now reading, and these little books were sold unbound for a few pence. The earliest of the quartos that still survive were printed in 1594, the year that both *Titus Andronicus* and a version of the play now called *2 King Henry VI* became available. While almost every one of these early quartos displays on its title page the name of the acting company that performed the play, only about half provide the name of the playwright, Shakespeare. The first quarto edition to bear the name Shakespeare on its title page is *Love's Labor's Lost* of 1598. A few of these quartos were popular with the book-buying public of Shakespeare's lifetime; for example, quarto *Richard II* went through five editions between 1597 and 1615. But most of the quartos were far from best sellers; *Love's Labor's Lost* (1598), for instance, was not reprinted in quarto until 1631. After Shakespeare's death, two more of his plays appeared in quarto format: *Othello* in 1622 and *The Two Noble Kinsmen*, coauthored with John Fletcher, in 1634.

In 1623, seven years after Shakespeare's death, *Mr. William Shakespeares Comedies, Histories, & Tragedies* was published. This printing offered readers in a single book thirty-six of the thirty-eight plays now thought to have been written by Shakespeare, including eighteen that had never been printed before. And it offered them in a style that was then reserved for serious literature and scholarship. The plays were arranged in double columns on pages nearly a foot high. This large page size is called "folio," as opposed to the smaller "quarto," and the 1623 volume is usually called the Shakespeare First Folio. It is reputed to have sold for the lordly price of a pound. (One copy at the Folger Library is marked fifteen shillings—that is, three-quarters of a pound.)

In a preface to the First Folio entitled "To the great Variety of Readers," two of Shakespeare's former fellow actors in the King's Men, John Heminge and Henry Condell, wrote that they themselves had collected their dead companion's plays. They suggested that they had seen his own papers: "we have scarce received from him a blot in his papers." The title page of the Folio declared that the plays within it had been printed "according to the True Original Copies." Comparing the Folio to the quartos, Heminge and Condell disparaged the quartos, advising their readers that "before you were abused with divers stolen and surreptitious copies, maimed, and deformed by the frauds and stealths of injurious impostors." Many Shakespeareans of the eighteenth and nineteenth centuries believed Heminge and Condell and regarded the Folio plays as superior to anything in the quartos.

Once we begin to examine the Folio plays in detail, it becomes less easy to take at face value the word of Heminge and Condell about the superiority of the Folio texts. For example, of the first nine plays in the

Folio (one-quarter of the entire collection), four were
essentially reprinted from earlier quarto printings that
Heminge and Condell had disparaged; and four have
now been identified as printed from copies written in
the hand of a professional scribe of the 1620s named
Ralph Crane; the ninth, *The Comedy of Errors*, was
apparently also printed from a manuscript, but one
whose origin cannot be readily identified. Evidently,
then, eight of the first nine plays in the First Folio
were not printed, in spite of what the Folio title page
announces, "according to the True Original Copies," or
Shakespeare's own papers, and the source of the ninth
is unknown. Since today's editors have been forced to
treat Heminge and Condell's pronouncements with
skepticism, they must choose whether to base their
own editions upon quartos or the Folio on grounds
other than Heminge and Condell's story of where the
quarto and Folio versions originated.

Editors have often fashioned their own narratives
to explain what lies behind the quartos and Folio.
They have said that Heminge and Condell meant
to criticize only a few of the early quartos, the ones
that offer much shorter and sometimes quite different, often garbled, versions of plays. Among the
examples of these are the 1600 quarto of *Henry V* (the
Folio offers a much fuller version) or the 1603 *Hamlet* quarto (in 1604 a different, much longer form of
the play got into print as a quarto). Early-twentieth-
century editors speculated that these questionable
texts were produced when someone in the audience
took notes from the plays' dialogue during performances and then employed "hack poets" to fill out
the notes. The poor results were then sold to a publisher and presented in print as Shakespeare's plays.
More recently this story has given way to another in
which the shorter versions are said to be re-creations

from memory of Shakespeare's plays by actors who wanted to stage them in the provinces but lacked manuscript copies. Most of the quartos offer much better texts than these so-called bad quartos. Indeed, in most of the quartos we find texts that are at least equal to or better than what is printed in the Folio. Many Shakespeare enthusiasts persuaded themselves that most of the quartos were set into type directly from Shakespeare's own papers, although there is nothing on which to base this conclusion except the desire for it to be true. Thus speculation continues about how the Shakespeare plays got to be printed. All that we have are the printed texts.

The book collector who was most successful in bringing together copies of the quartos and the First Folio was Henry Clay Folger, founder of the Folger Shakespeare Library in Washington, D.C. While it is estimated that there survive around the world only about 230 copies of the First Folio, Mr. Folger was able to acquire more than seventy-five copies, as well as a large number of fragments, for the library that bears his name. He also amassed a substantial number of quartos. For example, only fourteen copies of the First Quarto of *Love's Labor's Lost* are known to exist, and three are at the Folger Shakespeare Library. As a consequence of Mr. Folger's labors, scholars visiting the Folger Library have been able to learn a great deal about sixteenth- and seventeenth-century printing and, particularly, about the printing of Shakespeare's plays. And Mr. Folger did not stop at the First Folio, but collected many copies of later editions of Shakespeare, beginning with the Second Folio (1632), the Third (1663–64), and the Fourth (1685). Each of these later folios was based on its immediate predecessor and was edited anonymously. The first editor of Shakespeare whose name we know was Nicholas Rowe, whose first edition came out in 1709. Mr. Folger collected this edition and many, many more by Rowe's successors.

An Introduction to This Text

Henry VIII was first printed in the 1623 collection of Shakespeare's plays now known as the First Folio. The present edition is based directly upon that printing.* For the convenience of the reader, we have modernized the punctuation and the spelling of the Folio. Sometimes, in this play as in all our editions, we go so far as to modernize certain old forms of words; for example, when *a* means *he*, we usually change it to *he; we change *mo* to *more*, and *ye* to *you*. (We are aware that scholars engaged in dividing up authorship of *Henry VIII* between Shakespeare and John Fletcher have taken the presence of the form *ye* as evidence of Fletcher's hand. In modernizing *ye* to *you*, we seek not to conceal evidence of collaboration but only to render the play in this respect as readable for a contemporary audience as the rest of the plays in this series. For our decision to set aside questions of authorship in this edition, see the Appendix on Authorship, page 251.) It is not our practice in editing any of the plays to modernize words that sound distinctly different from modern forms. For example, when the early printed texts read *sith* or *apricocks* or *porpentine*, we have not modernized to *since, apricots, porcupine*. When the forms

---

*We have also consulted the computerized text of the First Folio provided by the Text Archive of the Oxford University Computing Centre, to which we are grateful.

an, and, or *and if* appear instead of the modern form *if,* we have reduced *and* to *an* but have not changed any of these forms to their modern equivalent, *if.* We also modernize and, where necessary, correct passages in foreign languages, unless an error in the early printed text can be reasonably explained as a joke.

Whenever we change the wording of the First Folio or add anything to its stage directions, we mark the change by enclosing it in superior half-brackets (⌐ ¬). We want our readers to be immediately aware when we have intervened. (Only when we correct an obvious typographical error in the First Folio does the change not get marked.) Whenever we change either the First Folio's wording or its punctuation so that meaning changes, we list the change in the textual notes at the back of the book, even if all we have done is fix an obvious error.

We regularize spellings of a number of the proper names in the dialogue and stage directions, as is the usual practice in editions of the play. For example, the First Folio occasionally uses the forms "Sandys" and "Campian," but our edition uses only the more usual Folio spellings "Sands" and "Campeius."

However, in another respect our treatment of certain names in this play differs from that in many other editions. A number of historical figures are named but do not appear as characters on stage and are given different names or titles in different places in the Folio text. For example, the monk who is alleged to have prophesied to the duke of Buckingham is named three different ways in the Folio: *"Michaell Hopkins"* (1.1.262), *"Nicholas Henton"* (1.2.169), and *"Hopkins"* (2.1.28). Many editors have interpreted some or all of these differences to have arisen through scribal or printing error. These editors point out that in the principal source for the play, Ralph Holinshed's *Chronicles,* this figure's name is Nicholas Hopkins. These editors also observe how closely many of the play's speeches follow Holinshed's language and thus conclude that the dramatist would have intended to reproduce the name from Holinshed. Such editors also reasonably observe that Nicholas may have been misnamed *"Michaell"* because his name had been abbreviated to "Nic.," the abbreviation then misread by a scribe or printer as "Mic." and wrongly expanded to *"Michaell."* When Hopkins is called *"Henton,"* all editors properly note that *Henton* was the name of the monk's monastery, and some also presume a scribe's or printer's confusion of place-name for person's name. Thus these editors impose the consistent designation "Nicholas Hopkins" on the play's text. A slightly different example involves Buckingham's chancellor or secretary. This figure is called both *"Gilbert Pecke,* his Councellour" (1.1.258) and "Sir *Gilbert Pecke* his Chancellour" (2.1.26). Noticing how graphically similar "Councellour" is to "Chancellour," many editors, again suspecting a scribe's or printer's error, have changed "Councellour" to "Chancellour," not taking into consideration that a chancellor—that is, an official secretary—and particularly one with the rank of knight, might well be expected to advise his master and thus also be a counselor.

Our conception of the play's relation to its sources and of its treatment of proper names and titles of offices is somewhat different. While we are aware of how closely in particular places the language of the play follows that of its sources, we are also aware of how widely the play often departs from its sources and from history. For example, the first act presents Henry's meeting with Francis I of France at the Field of the Cloth of Gold as happening just before the arrest of Buckingham, which itself takes place just before Henry meets Anne Bullen at Wolsey's supper. In Holinshed and in history, the meeting at the Field of the Cloth of Gold took place in May–June 1520, Buckingham's arrest almost a year later in April 1521, and Henry's meeting Anne at Wolsey's in 1527—six years before Buckingham's execution, an event that comes *after* it in the play. Therefore we felt we could not presume that the dramatist, in creating the play as fiction, would be careful to follow sources on every possible occasion. We have also considered the variation evident in the play's naming of the character Sands—a speaking role in the play and thus of much greater prominence than Hopkins and Peck, who are merely mentioned. When Sands appears in the first act in connection with the supper at Wolsey's, he is called "Lord *Sands*" (1.3.57, 1.4.51). However, when he reappears in the following scene, he is *"Sir Walter Sands"* (2.1.70 SD). The inconsistency is easily explained, and it does, we freely admit, derive from the play's historical sources. In 1521, the year of Buckingham's execution, which is the subject of 2.1, Sands was only a knight (Sir *William* Sands, according to Holinshed). Before 1527, the year of the supper at Wolsey's, Sands was ennobled, becoming Lord Sands, as he is called in the scenes associated with that occasion (1.3, 1.4). However, the inconsistency in the presentation of Sands's rank, which cannot be either a scribe's or a printer's error, indicates a remarkable indifference on the part of the dramatist to consistency of naming. Therefore we fear that if we were to make consistent the names of such minor figures as Hopkins and Henton, we might not necessarily be recovering the play's text from the errors of scribes and printers; instead we might be imposing much later standards of consistency and historical accuracy on a work of fiction created in a period during which such standards were foreign to dramatists' practice.

This edition differs from many earlier ones in its efforts to aid the reader in imagining the play as a performance. Thus stage directions and speech prefixes are written and arranged with reference to the stage. For example, when one goes to a modern production of *Henry VIII*, early in the fourth act one simultaneously watches the procession returning from Anne Bullen's coronation and listens to the commentary on it provided by the two gentlemen onstage. Like the audience in the theater, these gentlemen watch it, but they also identify by name those who walk in it, and admire it to each other. However, in the First Folio and in the subsequent editorial tradition, the elaborate stage direction describing the procession appears en masse before the gentlemen's commentary on it. By dividing up this stage direction and associating the particular figures who are named in it with the dialogue's commentary specifically related to them, we hope to help our readers stage this sequence in the play in their own imaginations in a way that more closely approximates an experience in the theater.

Whenever it is reasonably certain, in our view, that a speech is accompanied by a particular action, we provide a stage direction describing the action, setting the added direction in brackets to signal that it is not found in the Folio. (Occasional exceptions to this rule occur when the action is so obvious that to add a stage direction would insult the reader). Stage directions for the entrance of a character in mid-scene are, with rare exceptions, placed so that they immediately precede the character's participation in the scene, even though these entrances may appear somewhat earlier in the early printed texts. Whenever we move a stage direction, we record this change in the textual notes. Latin stage directions (e.g., *Exeunt*) are translated into English (e.g., *They exit*).

We expand the often severely abbreviated forms of names used as speech headings in early printed texts into the full names of the characters. We also regularize the speakers' names in speech headings, using only a single designation for each character, even though the early printed texts sometimes use a variety of designations. An exception occurs with Katherine, who is a queen for the play's first three acts but no longer one when she appears in the fourth act. Thus we call her "QUEEN KATHERINE" in speech prefixes until Act 4, when she becomes simply "KATHERINE." Variations in the speech headings of the early printed texts are recorded in the textual notes.

In the present edition, as well, we mark with a dash any change of address within a speech, unless a stage direction intervenes. When the -ed ending of a word is to be pronounced, we mark it with an accent. Like editors for the past two centuries, we print metrically linked lines in the following way:

WOLSEY
 Is he in person ready?
SECRETARY   Ay, please your Grace.
                                        (1.1.139–40)

However, when there are a number of short verse-lines that can be linked in more than one way, we do not, with rare exceptions, indent any of them.

The Explanatory Notes

The notes that appear on the pages facing the text are designed to provide readers with the help that they may need to enjoy the play. Whenever the meaning of a word in the text is not readily accessible in a good contemporary dictionary, we offer the meaning in a note. Sometimes we provide a note even when the relevant meaning is to be found in the dictionary but when the word has acquired since Shakespeare's time other potentially confusing meanings. In our notes, we try to offer modern synonyms for Shakespeare's words. We also try to indicate to the reader the connection between the word in the play and the modern synonym. For example, Shakespeare sometimes uses the word *head* to mean *source*, but, for modern readers, there may be no connection evident between these two words. We provide the connection by explaining Shakespeare's usage as follows: "**head:** fountainhead, source." On some occasions, a whole phrase or clause needs explanation. Then we rephrase in our own words the difficult passage, and add at the end synonyms for individual words in the passage. When scholars have been unable to determine the meaning of a word or phrase, we acknowledge the uncertainty. Biblical quotations are from the Geneva Bible (1560), modernized.

HENRY VIII

Henry VIII, king of England.
From John Taylor, *All the workes of . . .* (1630).

Characters in the Play

KING Henry the Eighth

Duke of NORFOLK
Duke of SUFFOLK

Cardinal WOLSEY, Archbishop of Canterbury
SECRETARIES to Wolsey
CROMWELL, servant to Wolsey, later secretary to the Privy
  Council
Cardinal CAMPEIUS, Papal Legate
GARDINER, secretary to the king, later Bishop of Winchester
PAGE to Gardiner

QUEEN KATHERINE, Henry's first wife, later Princess Dowager
GRIFFITH, attendant on Katherine
PATIENCE, woman to Katherine
Queen's GENTLEMAN USHER
CAPUCHIUS, ambassador from the Emperor Charles

Duke of BUCKINGHAM
Lord ABERGAVENNY, Buckingham's son-in-law
Earl of SURREY, Buckingham's son-in-law
Sir Nicholas VAUX
Knevet, former SURVEYOR to Buckingham
BRANDON
SERGEANT at Arms
FIRST GENTLEMAN
SECOND GENTLEMAN

ANNE Bullen, Katherine's lady-in-waiting, later Henry's
  second wife and queen
OLD LADY, with Anne Bullen
Lord CHAMBERLAIN

3

Lord SANDS (also Sir Walter SANDS)
Sir Thomas LOVELL
Sir Henry GUILFORD

Bishop of LINCOLN
CRANMER, later Archbishop of Canterbury
Lord CHANCELLOR
GARTER King of Arms
THIRD GENTLEMAN
Sir Anthony DENNY
Doctor BUTTS
KEEPER
PORTER and his MAN
SCRIBES
CRIER
PROLOGUE
EPILOGUE

Spirits, Princess Elizabeth as an infant, Duchess of
Norfolk, Marquess and Marchioness of Dorset, Lords,
Nobles, Countesses, Bishops, Judges, Priests, Ladies,
Gentlemen, Gentlemen Ushers, Lord Mayor, Four
Representatives of the Cinque Ports, Aldermen, Women,
Musicians, Choristers, Guards, Tipstaves, Halberds,
Vergers, Attendants, Servants, Messenger, Pages, Footboys,
Grooms

HENRY VIII

ACT 1

2. **brow:** countenance, facial expression

3. **Sad:** solemn, serious; **high:** elevated, lofty; **working:** moving; **state:** stateliness, dignity; magnificence

9. **truth:** a possible allusion (as also in lines 18 and 21) to the play's alternate title, *All Is True*

10. **a show:** a spectacle, such as a procession or masque

11. **pass:** be approved

12. **undertake:** venture to assert; **shilling:** twelve pence (For the cost of attending a play, see "Shakespeare's Theater," page xl.)

14–16. **merry...yellow:** a possible allusion to the play *When You See Me, You Know Me*, a comedy that featured Henry VIII fighting, in disguise, and also featured Henry's professional fool or jester **targets:** shields **motley coat:** fool's garment (**Motley** means variegated, multicolored. See picture, page 82.). **guarded:** trimmed

17. **deceived:** disappointed

18. **rank:** classify

20. **Our own brains:** perhaps, the labor of **our own brains;** or, perhaps, **our** (reputation for) intelligence; **opinion:** expectation

21. **To...intend:** perhaps, of purposing to present only the truth

22. **understanding:** intelligent (with possible wordplay referring to those standing below in the yard around the raised stage)

24. **first:** foremost; **happiest:** most fortunate

25. **sad:** serious

27. **As:** i.e., **as** if

29. **thousand:** i.e., a **thousand**

PROLOGUE

I come no more to make you laugh. Things now
That bear a weighty and a serious brow,
Sad, high, and working, full of state and woe,
Such noble scenes as draw the eye to flow,
We now present. Those that can pity here   5
May, if they think it well, let fall a tear;
The subject will deserve it. Such as give
Their money out of hope they may believe
May here find truth too. Those that come to see
Only a show or two, and so agree   10
The play may pass, if they be still and willing,
I'll undertake may see away their shilling
Richly in two short hours. Only they
That come to hear a merry, bawdy play,
A noise of targets, or to see a fellow   15
In a long motley coat guarded with yellow,
Will be deceived. For, gentle hearers, know
To rank our chosen truth with such a show
As fool and fight is, besides forfeiting
Our own brains and the opinion that we bring   20
To make that only true we now intend,
Will leave us never an understanding friend.
Therefore, for goodness' sake, and as you are known
The first and happiest hearers of the town,
Be sad, as we would make you. Think you see   25
The very persons of our noble story
As they were living. Think you see them great,
And followed with the general throng and sweat
Of thousand friends. Then, in a moment, see
How soon this mightiness meets misery.   30
And if you can be merry then, I'll say
A man may weep upon his wedding day.

⌜*He exits.*⌝

1.1 The Duke of Buckingham, learning the details of the costly and ultimately fruitless meeting of French and English at the Field of the Cloth of Gold, threatens to expose the powerful Cardinal Wolsey, whose manipulation of the event and of the failed treaty makes him a traitor in Buckingham's eyes. Before Buckingham can act, Wolsey has him arrested.

------

1. **morrow:** morning; **well met:** an expression of welcome

2. **saw:** i.e., **saw** each other

4. **Healthful:** healthy; **fresh:** eager, ready

7. **Stayed me:** held me back

8. **suns of glory:** i.e., the two kings, Henry VIII of England and Francis I of France (See pictures, pages 2 and 34.)

9. **vale of Andren:** site of the Field of the Cloth of Gold, so called in part because of the splendor of the events (described in lines 19–50 below) and, perhaps, in part because the tent in which the kings met in the **vale** was made of cloth of gold (**Andren** or Andres is the village north of the valley.)

10. **Guynes:** the town in which Henry and his army were based; **Arde:** the French village where Francis I was based (The **vale of Andren** lay between the two towns.)

13. **as:** i.e., **as** if

15. **weighed:** been equivalent (in value, power) to

ACT 1

Scene 1

*Enter the Duke of Norfolk at one door; at the other, the
Duke of Buckingham and the Lord Abergavenny.*

BUCKINGHAM
Good morrow, and well met. How have you done
Since last we saw in France?

NORFOLK   I thank your Grace,
Healthful, and ever since a fresh admirer
Of what I saw there.   5

BUCKINGHAM   An untimely ague
Stayed me a prisoner in my chamber when
Those suns of glory, those two lights of men,
Met in the vale of Andren.

NORFOLK   'Twixt Guynes and Arde.   10
I was then present, saw them salute on horseback,
Beheld them when they lighted, how they clung
In their embracement, as they grew together—
Which had they, what four throned ones could have
        weighed   15
Such a compounded one?

BUCKINGHAM   All the whole time
I was my chamber's prisoner.

NORFOLK   Then you lost
The view of earthly glory. Men might say   20
Till this time pomp was single, but now married
To one above itself. Each following day

9

23. **master:** schoolmaster, teacher

24. **its:** i.e., its own

25. **clinquant:** glittering; **heathen gods:** See Psalm 115.4: "Their idols are silver and gold. . . ."

26. **they:** i.e., **the English**

27. **India:** i.e., as if possessed of the gold mines of the Indies

29. **cherubins:** cherubs, winged infant angels (See picture, page 56.) **madams:** ladies of high rank

31. **pride:** splendid adornment

32. **painting:** cosmetic (Flushed with exertion, the ladies seemed heavily rouged.) **masque:** masquerade, masked ball; or, perhaps, a dramatic spectacle performed in part by courtiers and court ladies in the seventeenth century)

33. **cried:** i.e., extolled (as)

34–38. **The two . . . one:** i.e., whichever king was in view seemed the superior, although both were **equal;** when both were visible at once, they were said to be identical **Still:** always

38. **discerner:** observer; one who makes distinctions

39. **Durst:** dared; **censure:** disagreement with this judgment; or, choosing one above the other

40. **phrase:** call

41. **noble spirits:** courtiers; **arms:** i.e., a tournament; **they:** perhaps, the **noble spirits;** or, perhaps, the two kings (who, according to Holinshed, "surmounted all the rest in prowess and valiantness")

42. **compass:** range, scope; **former:** i.e., what was formerly taken to be

43. **credit:** i.e., such right to be trusted

(continued)

Became the next day's master, till the last
Made former wonders its. Today the French,
All clinquant, all in gold, like heathen gods,   25
Shone down the English, and tomorrow they
Made Britain India: every man that stood
Showed like a mine. Their dwarfish pages were
As cherubins, all gilt. The madams too,
Not used to toil, did almost sweat to bear   30
The pride upon them, that their very labor
Was to them as a painting. Now this masque
Was cried incomparable; and th' ensuing night
Made it a fool and beggar. The two kings,
Equal in luster, were now best, now worst,   35
As presence did present them: him in eye
Still him in praise; and being present both,
'Twas said they saw but one, and no discerner
Durst wag his tongue in censure. When these suns—
For so they phrase 'em—by their heralds challenged   40
The noble spirits to arms, they did perform
Beyond thought's compass, that former fabulous story,
Being now seen possible enough, got credit
That *Bevis* was believed.

BUCKINGHAM   O, you go far.   45

NORFOLK
As I belong to worship, and affect
In honor honesty, the tract of everything
Would by a good discourser lose some life
Which action's self was tongue to. All was royal;
To the disposing of it naught rebelled.   50
Order gave each thing view. The office did
Distinctly his full function.

BUCKINGHAM   Who did guide,
I mean who set the body and the limbs
Of this great sport together, as you guess?   55

NORFOLK
One, certes, that promises no element
In such a business.

44. **Bevis:** *Bevis of Hampton,* a popular fourteenth-century verse romance filled with improbable adventures (See picture, page 154.)

46. **worship:** high rank; **affect:** aspire to

47. **In honor:** in obedience to the principles governing the nobility; **tract:** discussion

48. **discourser:** narrator, speaker; **life:** liveliness

49. **action's . . . to:** i.e., the **action** itself expressed

50. **disposing:** management

51. **view:** visibility

51–52. **The office . . . function:** i.e., each official did his individual part to the full

54. **set:** put

55. **sport:** i.e., tournament

56. **certes:** certainly; **promises:** i.e., leads one to expect (he will have); **element:** constituent part

59. **ordered:** managed; **discretion:** power

61. **speed:** destroy

63. **vanities:** inanities; wastes of time

64. **keech:** i.e., son of a butcher (literally, a lump of congealed fat)

68. **stuff:** capability; inward character; **puts:** incites, urges

69. **grace:** good fortune, favorable position

70. **Chalks:** marks out as a course to be followed; **called upon:** invited, encouraged

71. **neither:** nor

72. **assistants:** supporters, promoters

73. **self-drawing web:** i.e., **web** drawn out of himself; **gives us note:** lets us know

76. **next . . . King:** second only to the king's

(continued)

BUCKINGHAM   I pray you who, my lord?
NORFOLK
  All this was ordered by the good discretion
  Of the right reverend Cardinal of York.   60
BUCKINGHAM
  The devil speed him! No man's pie is freed
  From his ambitious finger. What had he
  To do in these fierce vanities? I wonder
  That such a keech can with his very bulk
  Take up the rays o' th' beneficial sun   65
  And keep it from the earth.
NORFOLK   Surely, sir,
  There's in him stuff that puts him to these ends;
  For, being not propped by ancestry, whose grace
  Chalks successors their way, nor called upon   70
  For high feats done to th' crown, neither allied
  To eminent assistants, but spiderlike,
  Out of his self-drawing web, ⌈he⌉ gives us note
  The force of his own merit makes his way—
  A gift that heaven gives for him which buys   75
  A place next to the King.
ABERGAVENNY   I cannot tell
  What heaven hath given him—let some graver eye
  Pierce into that—but I can see his pride
  Peep through each part of him. Whence has he that?   80
  If not from hell, the devil is a niggard,
  Or has given all before, and he begins
  A new hell in himself.
BUCKINGHAM   Why the devil,
  Upon this French going-out, took he upon him,   85
  Without the privity o' th' King, t' appoint
  Who should attend on him? He makes up the file
  Of all the gentry, for the most part such
  To whom as great a charge as little honor
  He meant to lay upon; and his own letter,   90
  The honorable board of council out,
  Must fetch him in he papers.

82. **he:** i.e., Wolsey

85. **going-out:** expedition

86. **privity:** knowledge, implying consent

87. **attend on him:** i.e., accompany the king; **file:** list

88–90. **such . . . lay upon:** i.e., **such** as he intended to burden with **great** expense for **little honor**

91. **The honorable . . . out:** i.e., without reference to the Privy Council, the king's selected advisers including great aristocrats and churchmen

92. **fetch him in:** i.e., take in everyone; **he papers:** i.e., whose name he sets down on paper

95. **sickened:** made sick, hurt; **estates:** fortunes

96. **abound:** be wealthy

97–98. **many . . . on 'em:** i.e., many have destroyed themselves financially by selling off property in order to buy suitable clothes (Proverbial: "to break one's back"; "to wear a whole lordship on one's back")

99. **vanity:** worthless action

100–101. **minister . . . issue:** afford occasion for conversation to little purpose (with possible wordplay on **poor issue** as "impoverished offspring")

107. **not consulting:** i.e., without **consulting** each other

108. **general:** universal

109. **Dashing:** destroying; spattering; **aboded:** presaged

110. **on 't:** i.e., of it

111. **is budded out:** i.e., has developed (as expected)

(continued)

ABERGAVENNY   I do know
　Kinsmen of mine, three at the least, that have
　By this so sickened their estates that never   95
　They shall abound as formerly.
BUCKINGHAM   O, many
　Have broke their backs with laying manors on 'em
　For this great journey. What did this vanity
　But minister communication of   100
　A most poor issue?
NORFOLK   Grievingly I think
　The peace between the French and us not values
　The cost that did conclude it.
BUCKINGHAM   Every man,   105
　After the hideous storm that followed, was
　A thing inspired and, not consulting, broke
　Into a general prophecy: that this tempest,
　Dashing the garment of this peace, aboded
　The sudden breach on 't.   110
NORFOLK   Which is budded out,
　For France hath flawed the league and hath attached
　Our merchants' goods at Bordeaux.
ABERGAVENNY   Is it therefore
　Th' ambassador is silenced?   115
NORFOLK   Marry, is 't.
ABERGAVENNY
　A proper title of a peace, and purchased
　At a superfluous rate!
BUCKINGHAM   Why, all this business
　Our reverend cardinal carried.   120
NORFOLK   Like it your Grace,
　The state takes notice of the private difference
　Betwixt you and the Cardinal. I advise you—
　And take it from a heart that wishes towards you
　Honor and plenteous safety—that you read   125
　The Cardinal's malice and his potency
　Together; to consider further that

112. **flawed:** marred; **league:** peace treaty; **attached:** seized

114. **therefore:** on that account

115. **silenced:** i.e., required to keep to his house

116. **Marry:** indeed (a mild oath)

117. **proper title of:** i.e., good name for (ironic, and with wordplay on **title** as "legal right to possession of a property," which can be **purchased**)

118. **superfluous:** inordinate; **rate:** price

120. **carried:** conducted, managed

121. **Like it:** if it please (formulaic politeness)

122. **state:** government (perhaps the king, perhaps the Privy Council); **difference:** quarrel

125. **read:** consider

128. **would:** wishes to; **wants:** lacks

129. **A minister:** i.e., the means (namely, **his power**)

133. **Bosom up:** take to heart; hide in your **bosom**

134. **Lo:** see

135 SD. **purse:** bag containing the Great Seal of England, which was used to authorize all documents issued by the sovereign, and which was the insignia of the Lord Chancellor's office; **passage:** passing

136. **The Duke of Buckingham's surveyor:** overseer of **the Duke of Buckingham's** estates

137. **examination:** deposition

138, 140. **so please you, please your Grace:** formulaic politeness

142. **big:** haughty

143. **butcher's cur:** a proverbially vicious kind of dog (with a reference to Wolsey's supposed parentage)

144–45. **best . . . slumber:** Proverbial: "It is evil waking of a sleeping dog."

(continued)

What his high hatred would effect wants not
A minister in his power. You know his nature,
That he's revengeful, and I know his sword   130
Hath a sharp edge; it's long, and 't may be said
It reaches far, and where 'twill not extend,
Thither he darts it. Bosom up my counsel;
You'll find it wholesome. Lo where comes that rock
That I advise your shunning.   135

*Enter Cardinal Wolsey, the purse borne before him,
certain of the Guard, and two Secretaries with papers.
The Cardinal in his passage fixeth his eye on Buckingham,
and Buckingham on him, both full of disdain.*

WOLSEY, ⌐*aside to a Secretary*¬
  The Duke of Buckingham's surveyor, ha?
  Where's his examination?
SECRETARY   Here, so please you.
          ⌐*He hands Wolsey a paper.*¬

WOLSEY
  Is he in person ready?
SECRETARY   Ay, please your Grace.   140
WOLSEY
  Well, we shall then know more, and Buckingham
  Shall lessen this big look.
          Cardinal ⌐*Wolsey*¬ *and his train exit.*

BUCKINGHAM
  This butcher's cur is venomed-mouthed, and I
  Have not the power to muzzle him; therefore best
  Not wake him in his slumber. A beggar's book   145
  Outworths a noble's blood.
NORFOLK   What, are you chafed?
  Ask God for temp'rance. That's th' appliance only
  Which your disease requires.
BUCKINGHAM   I read in 's looks   150
  Matter against me, and his eye reviled
  Me as his abject object. At this instant

145. **book:** learning
146. **Outworths:** is more valuable than
147. **chafed:** vexed, angry
148. **appliance:** medication
151. **Matter:** allegations
152. **abject:** despicable; despised
153. **bores:** cheats, mocks
156. **choler:** anger
157. **go about:** take in hand, undertake
159. **full:** very; **his:** i.e., its (Proverbial: "**A** free horse will soon tire.")
160. **Self-mettle:** i.e., its natural vigor or spirit; **him:** i.e., it
161. **like you:** i.e., as **you can**
164. **cry down:** put down by more vehement crying
165. **Ipswich:** a provincial town, Wolsey's birthplace (For Wolsey, see picture, page 52.)
166. **difference in:** i.e., distinction (in rank) among
167. **advised:** cautious
170. **run at:** attack
171. **overrunning:** outrunning
172. **mounts the liquor:** causes the liquid to rise (by boiling it)
175. **More stronger:** i.e., **stronger**
176. **sap:** liquid, fluid
180. **prescription:** explicit direction; **top-proud:** proud to the highest degree
181. **from the flow . . . not:** i.e., **I** do **not** accuse out of rancor
182. **motions:** motives, reasons; emotions; **intelligence:** communication of spies

(continued)

He bores me with some trick. He's gone to th' King.
I'll follow and outstare him.

NORFOLK   Stay, my lord,   155
And let your reason with your choler question
What 'tis you go about. To climb steep hills
Requires slow pace at first. Anger is like
A full hot horse who, being allowed his way,
Self-mettle tires him. Not a man in England   160
Can advise me like you; be to yourself
As you would to your friend.

BUCKINGHAM   I'll to the King,
And from a mouth of honor quite cry down
This Ipswich fellow's insolence, or proclaim   165
There's difference in no persons.

NORFOLK   Be advised.
Heat not a furnace for your foe so hot
That it do singe yourself. We may outrun
By violent swiftness that which we run at   170
And lose by overrunning. Know you not
The fire that mounts the liquor till 't run o'er
In seeming to augment it wastes it? Be advised.
I say again there is no English soul
More stronger to direct you than yourself,   175
If with the sap of reason you would quench
Or but allay the fire of passion.

BUCKINGHAM   Sir,
I am thankful to you, and I'll go along
By your prescription. But this top-proud fellow—   180
Whom from the flow of gall I name not, but
From sincere motions—by intelligence,
And proofs as clear as founts in July when
We see each grain of gravel, I do know
To be corrupt and treasonous.   185

NORFOLK   Say not "treasonous."

BUCKINGHAM
To th' King I'll say 't, and make my vouch as strong

183. **founts:** springs

187. **vouch:** allegation

188. **Attend:** listen; **fox:** Proverbial: "As **subtle** (line 190) as a **fox**."

189. **wolf:** Proverbial: "As **ravenous** as a **wolf**." **equal:** i.e., equally

190. **subtle:** i.e., cunning; **mischief:** wickedness

191. **place:** office in the service of the king

194. **suggests:** prompts, tempts

195. **interview:** ceremonial meeting of princes

197. **rinsing:** The Folio's spelling of this word, *wrenching,* carries a second meaning, "violent twisting."

199. **Pray . . . favor:** a polite request to be allowed to continue

200. **combination:** alliance; **drew:** i.e., **drew** up

202. **end:** purpose

207. **Charles the Emperor:** Charles V, emperor of the Germanic Holy Roman Empire, and king of Spain (See picture, page 182.)

209. **color:** pretext, excuse

210. **whisper:** i.e., **whisper** to

212. **England and France:** i.e., the kings of **England and France**

213. **Breed:** cause; **prejudice:** damage, loss

214. **privily:** secretly

215. **trow:** believe

217. **ere:** before

219. **desired:** requested; or, perhaps, demanded

220. **he:** i.e., Wolsey

As shore of rock. Attend. This holy fox,
Or wolf, or both—for he is equal rav'nous
As he is subtle, and as prone to mischief   190
As able to perform 't, his mind and place
Infecting one another, yea reciprocally—
Only to show his pomp as well in France
As here at home, suggests the King our master
To this last costly treaty, th' interview   195
That swallowed so much treasure and like a glass
Did break i' th' rinsing.

NORFOLK   Faith, and so it did.

BUCKINGHAM
Pray give me favor, sir. This cunning cardinal
The articles o' th' combination drew   200
As himself pleased; and they were ratified
As he cried "Thus let be," to as much end
As give a crutch to th' dead. But our Count Cardinal
Has done this, and 'tis well, for worthy Wolsey,
Who cannot err, he did it. Now this follows—   205
Which, as I take it, is a kind of puppy
To th' old dam treason: Charles the Emperor,
Under pretense to see the Queen his aunt—
For 'twas indeed his color, but he came
To whisper Wolsey—here makes visitation;   210
His fears were that the interview betwixt
England and France might through their amity
Breed him some prejudice, for from this league
Peeped harms that menaced him; privily
Deals with our cardinal and, as I trow—   215
Which I do well, for I am sure the Emperor
Paid ere he promised, whereby his suit was granted
Ere it was asked. But when the way was made
And paved with gold, the Emperor thus desired
That he would please to alter the King's course   220
And break the foresaid peace. Let the King know—
As soon he shall by me—that thus the Cardinal

227. Something: somewhat, a little; **mistaken:** misunderstood, misjudged; **in 't:** i.e., in connection with it

229. pronounce: report; **in that very shape:** i.e., exactly as

230. in proof: i.e., under examination; when put to the test

231. office: duty

237. Lo: look

239. device: plot; scheme; **practice:** machination, trickery

241. look on: i.e., **look** at, see

242. business present: i.e., **present business**

243. Tower: i.e., **Tower** of London, a royal fortress, part of which served as a prison (See picture, page 214.)

244. nothing: not at all

Does buy and sell his honor as he pleases
And for his own advantage.

NORFOLK   I am sorry   225
To hear this of him, and could wish he were
Something mistaken in 't.

BUCKINGHAM   No, not a syllable.
I do pronounce him in that very shape
He shall appear in proof.   230

Enter Brandon, a Sergeant-at-Arms before him, and two
or three of the Guard.

BRANDON
Your office, Sergeant: execute it.

SERGEANT, ⌜*to Buckingham*⌝   Sir,
My lord the Duke of Buckingham and Earl
Of Hertford, Stafford, and Northampton, I
Arrest thee of high treason, in the name   235
Of our most sovereign king.

BUCKINGHAM, ⌜*to Norfolk*⌝   Lo you, my lord,
The net has fall'n upon me. I shall perish
Under device and practice.

BRANDON   I am sorry   240
To see you ta'en from liberty, to look on
The business present. 'Tis his Highness' pleasure
You shall to th' Tower.

BUCKINGHAM   It will help me nothing
To plead mine innocence, for that dye is on me   245
Which makes my whit'st part black. The will of heaven
Be done in this and all things. I obey.
O my Lord Abergavenny, fare you well.

BRANDON
Nay, he must bear you company.—The King
Is pleased you shall to th' Tower, till you know   250
How he determines further.

ABERGAVENNY   As the Duke said,
The will of heaven be done, and the King's pleasure
By me obeyed.

256. **attach:** seize, arrest; **bodies:** persons (legal terminology)

258. **counselor:** At 2.1.26, Peck is designated as Buckingham's **chancellor** or official secretary. Since a **counselor** could simply be someone who gives advice, it seems unnecessary to change the word here to **chancellor,** as is often done by editors.

260. **limbs o':** parts that make up

261. **Chartreux:** Carthusian order

262. **Michael Hopkins:** For problems with this monk's name, see longer note, page 239.

264. **false:** (1) lying; (2) treacherous; **o'ergreat:** i.e., overly great; too great

265. **spanned:** measured out, reaching its limit (Psalm 39.6–7: "Behold, thou hast made my days as it were a span long.")

266. **shadow:** ghost; image (with wordplay on the usual sense of **shadow,** spelled out in lines 267–68, where the rays of the **sun** [the king] are darkened and Buckingham's **figure** clouded)

267. **figure:** shape; **even this instant cloud:** perhaps, "right now a **cloud**"; perhaps, "**even this** imminent affliction"; **puts on:** assumes, dons

268. **clear:** bright

1.2 Queen Katherine reveals that Wolsey is heavily taxing the English in the king's name, and Henry pronounces a pardon to all who have resisted the tax. Wolsey then accuses Buckingham of treason, and his accusation is supported by Buckingham's former surveyor and confidant. Henry orders that Buckingham be tried as a traitor.

(continued)

BRANDON   Here is a warrant from   255
　　The King t' attach Lord Mountacute, and the bodies
　　Of the Duke's confessor, John de la Car,
　　One Gilbert Peck, his counselor—
BUCKINGHAM   So, so;
　　These are the limbs o' th' plot. No more, I hope.   260
BRANDON
　　A monk o' th' Chartreux.
BUCKINGHAM   O, Michael Hopkins?
BRANDON   He.
BUCKINGHAM
　　My surveyor is false. The o'ergreat cardinal
　　Hath showed him gold. My life is spanned already.   265
　　I am the shadow of poor Buckingham,
　　Whose figure even this instant cloud puts on
　　By dark'ning my clear sun. ⌜*To Norfolk.*⌝ My ⌜lord,⌝
　　farewell.

                                             They exit.

Scene 2

*Cornets. Enter King Henry, leaning on the Cardinal's
shoulder, ⌜with⌝ the Nobles, Sir Thomas Lovell, and
⌜Attendants, including a Secretary of the Cardinal.⌝
The Cardinal places himself under the King's feet on
　　　　　　　his right side.*

KING, ⌜*to Wolsey*⌝
　　My life itself, and the best heart of it,
　　Thanks you for this great care. I stood i' th' level
　　Of a full-charged confederacy, and give thanks
　　To you that choked it.—Let be called before us
　　That gentleman of Buckingham's; in person   5
　　I'll hear him his confessions justify,
　　And point by point the treasons of his master
　　He shall again relate.

0 SD. **places himself under the King's feet:** i.e., sits below the king, who has ascended a throne perhaps raised on a dais

1. **best heart:** i.e., most vital essence

2. **level:** line of fire

3. **full-charged:** fully loaded

4. **choked:** suppressed

5. **gentleman of Buckingham's:** i.e., **Buckingham's** overseer or surveyor

6. **justify:** support by evidence, prove

8 SD. **within:** offstage; **state:** throne (See pictures, pages 50 and 236.)

9. **we:** the royal "we" (See also **us** in line 10.)

10. **take place:** sit

13. **moiety:** half

14. **Repeat:** state, recount; **will:** wish, desire

15. **Thank:** i.e., I **thank**

22. **true:** loyal; **condition:** character, nature

23. **grievance:** distress, hardship; **commissions:** orders, commands (in this case for the levying of taxes)

24. **flawed:** damaged

27. **putter-on:** instigator

28. **exactions:** arbitrary and excessive taxes

29. **soil:** blemish

36. **clothiers:** i.e., makers of woollen clothes (See *Act 25 Henry VIII, c. 18*, "Clothears, or makers of woollen clothes.")

A noise within crying "Room for the Queen!" Enter the
Queen ⌈Katherine,⌉ ushered by the Duke of Norfolk, and
⌈the Duke of⌉ Suffolk. She kneels. ⌈The⌉ King riseth from
his state.

QUEEN KATHERINE
Nay, we must longer kneel; I am a suitor.

KING
Arise, and take place by us.   10
              ⌈He⌉ takes her up, kisses and placeth her by him.
                                      Half your suit
Never name to us; you have half our power.
The other moiety ere you ask is given;
Repeat your will, and take it.

QUEEN KATHERINE   Thank your Majesty.   15
That you would love yourself, and in that love
Not unconsidered leave your honor nor
The dignity of your office, is the point
Of my petition.

KING   Lady mine, proceed.   20

QUEEN KATHERINE
I am solicited, not by a few,
And those of true condition, that your subjects
Are in great grievance. There have been commissions
Sent down among 'em which hath flawed the heart
Of all their loyalties, wherein, although   25
My good Lord Cardinal, they vent reproaches
Most bitterly on you as putter-on
Of these exactions, yet the King our master,
Whose honor heaven shield from soil, even he
    escapes not   30
Language unmannerly—yea, such which breaks
The sides of loyalty and almost appears
In loud rebellion.

NORFOLK   Not "almost appears"—
It doth appear. For, upon these taxations,   35
The clothiers all, not able to maintain

37. **to them longing:** dependent on them; **put off:** dismissed, laid off

38. **spinsters:** women (rarely, men) who spin thread; **carders:** those who prepare wool for spinning by combing it with wire-tooth brushes called cards; **fullers:** those who tread on or beat cloth to clean and thicken it (See picture, page 102.)

39. **other life:** i.e., other ways of earning a living

41. **Daring . . . teeth:** challenging the outcome with defiance; **uproar:** insurrection, popular uprising

42. **danger:** harm, damage, mischief; **serves among them:** is at their disposal

48. **know . . . part:** i.e., have the knowledge of only **a single** individual; **aught:** i.e., anything that

49. **front:** march in the first rank; **file:** line of soldiers

50. **tell steps:** i.e., march (literally, count off **steps**)

52. **frame:** bring to pass, produce

53. **alike:** equally (i.e., by the **others** who **tell steps with** you)

54. **which would not:** who **would** prefer **not** to

55. **their acquaintance:** i.e., known by them

56. **would:** wishes to; **note:** information

60. **hard:** harsh; **exclamation:** derogatory outcry

62–63. **The nature . . . exaction:** i.e., what kind of tax is it?

64. **venturous:** bold, daring

65. **boldened:** emboldened, made bold

66. **grief:** grievance

69. **substance:** wealth, possessions; **levied:** raised, imposed

(continued)

The many to them longing, have put off
The spinsters, carders, fullers, weavers, who,
Unfit for other life, compelled by hunger
And lack of other means, in desperate manner   40
Daring th' event to th' teeth, are all in uproar,
And danger serves among them.

KING   Taxation?
Wherein? And what taxation? My Lord Cardinal,
You that are blamed for it alike with us,   45
Know you of this taxation?

WOLSEY   Please you, sir,
I know but of a single part in aught
Pertains to th' state, and front but in that file
Where others tell steps with me.   50

QUEEN KATHERINE   No, my lord?
You know no more than others? But you frame
Things that are known alike, which are not wholesome
To those which would not know them, and yet must
Perforce be their acquaintance. These exactions   55
Whereof my sovereign would have note, they are
Most pestilent to th' hearing, and to bear 'em
The back is sacrifice to th' load. They say
They are devised by you, or else you suffer
Too hard an exclamation.   60

KING   Still exaction!
The nature of it? In what kind, let's know,
Is this exaction?

QUEEN KATHERINE   I am much too venturous
In tempting of your patience, but am boldened   65
Under your promised pardon. The subjects' grief
Comes through commissions which compels from
    each
The sixth part of his substance, to be levied
Without delay, and the pretense for this   70
Is named your wars in France. This makes bold
    mouths.

70. **pretense:** ground or reason; purpose (with probable wordplay on the meaning "pretext")

77. **would:** wish

79. **primer:** greater; **baseness:** i.e., mischief (literally, moral turpitude, contemptible meanness) Editors sometimes emend to "business."

81. **pleasure:** wish, will, desire

82. **for:** as for

84. **single voice:** individual vote (in the Privy Council)

85. **approbation:** sanction

86. **neither know:** i.e., **know neither**

87. **faculties:** personal qualities; **will be:** insist on being

89. **place:** service to the crown or state; **brake:** briers, thicket

90. **stint:** discontinue

92. **To cope:** of meeting with

94. **is new trimmed:** i.e., has been newly fitted out for the sea

96. **sick:** envious; **once:** in short

97. **what worst:** i.e., what we do **worst**

98. **Hitting:** being agreeable to; **a grosser quality:** i.e., ignorant or coarse people

98–99. **cried up / For:** extolled as

100. **motion:** activity; proposal

102. **state-statues only:** mere images of statesmen (a nonce word)

105. **example:** precedent; **issue:** outcome

Tongues spit their duties out, and cold hearts freeze
Allegiance in them. Their curses now
Live where their prayers did; and it's come to pass   75
This tractable obedience is a slave
To each incensèd will. I would your Highness
Would give it quick consideration, for
There is no primer baseness.
KING   By my life,   80
This is against our pleasure.
WOLSEY   And for me,
I have no further gone in this than by
A single voice, and that not passed me but
By learnèd approbation of the judges. If I am   85
Traduced by ignorant tongues, which neither know
My faculties nor person, yet will be
The chronicles of my doing, let me say
'Tis but the fate of place, and the rough brake
That virtue must go through. We must not stint   90
Our necessary actions in the fear
To cope malicious censurers, which ever,
As ravenous fishes, do a vessel follow
That is new trimmed, but benefit no further
Than vainly longing. What we oft do best,   95
By sick interpreters, once weak ones, is
Not ours or not allowed; what worst, as oft,
Hitting a grosser quality, is cried up
For our best act. If we shall stand still
In fear our motion will be mocked or carped at,   100
We should take root here where we sit,
Or sit state-statues only.
KING   Things done well,
And with a care, exempt themselves from fear;
Things done without example, in their issue   105
Are to be feared. Have you a precedent
Of this commission? I believe, not any.
We must not rend our subjects from our laws

109. **stick:** fix, fasten (**Stick them in** is set in opposition to **rend** [them] **from** [line 108].)

110. **trembling contribution:** tax to be trembled at with fear

111. **lop:** smaller branches and twigs

114. **this is questioned:** i.e., the tax is disputed

120. **grievèd:** aggrieved, vexed, troubled

121. **Hardly:** harshly; **conceive:** think; **noised:** spread about; rumored

122. **our:** i.e., my (Wolsey presumes to use the royal plural in addressing his secretary, but not the king.) **revokement:** revocation, repeal

123. **anon:** soon

126. **Is run in:** incurs

128. **rare:** distinguished

129. **bound:** indebted, obligated (for natural endowments)

131. **out of:** beyond

132. **benefits:** natural gifts or advantages

135. **fair:** attractive, beautiful; **complete:** accomplished

137. **ravished:** enraptured, entranced

139. **habits:** guises; behaviors

And stick them in our will. Sixth part of each?
A trembling contribution! Why, we take   110
From every tree lop, bark, and part o' th' timber,
And though we leave it with a root, thus hacked,
The air will drink the sap. To every county
Where this is questioned send our letters with
Free pardon to each man that has denied   115
The force of this commission. Pray look to 't;
I put it to your care.
WOLSEY, ⌜*aside to his Secretary*⌝ A word with you.
Let there be letters writ to every shire
Of the King's grace and pardon. The grievèd commons   120
Hardly conceive of me. Let it be noised
That through our intercession this revokement
And pardon comes. I shall anon advise you
Further in the proceeding.   *Secretary exits.*

Enter ⌜Buckingham's⌝ Surveyor.

QUEEN KATHERINE, ⌜*to the King*⌝
I am sorry that the Duke of Buckingham   125
Is run in your displeasure.
KING   It grieves many.
The gentleman is learnèd and a most rare speaker;
To nature none more bound; his training such
That he may furnish and instruct great teachers   130
And never seek for aid out of himself. Yet see,
When these so noble benefits shall prove
Not well disposed, the mind growing once corrupt,
They turn to vicious forms ten times more ugly
Than ever they were fair. This man so complete,   135
Who was enrolled 'mongst wonders, and when we
Almost with ravished list'ning could not find
His hour of speech a minute—he, my lady,
Hath into monstrous habits put the graces
That once were his, and is become as black   140
As if besmeared in hell. Sit by us. You shall hear—

142. **gentleman in trust:** i.e., trusted official

144. **fore-recited:** earlier disclosed; **practices:** treacheries, schemes

147. **careful:** heedful, concerned; **collected:** gathered

148. **Out of:** from

152. **carry it so:** conduct matters so as

158. **conception:** plan; **point:** instance

159. **Not . . . person:** i.e., not assisted by the success of **his wish** (i.e., that you be childless)

163. **Deliver:** tell; **charity:** Christian love of one's fellow man; forbearance, tolerance

166. **fail:** death; **To this point:** i.e., on this matter

167. **speak aught:** say anything

168. **this:** i.e., the expectation of being king

169. **Nicholas Henton:** Perhaps the same man who at 1.1.262 was called Michael Hopkins. (See longer note to 1.1.262, page 239.)

171. **Chartreux:** Carthusian

Francis I, king of France. (1.1.8)
From Jean de Serres,
A generall historie of France . . . (1611).

This was his gentleman in trust—of him
Things to strike honor sad.—Bid him recount
The fore-recited practices, whereof
We cannot feel too little, hear too much.   145

WOLSEY
Stand forth, and with bold spirit relate what you
Most like a careful subject have collected
Out of the Duke of Buckingham.

KING   Speak freely.

SURVEYOR
First, it was usual with him—every day   150
It would infect his speech—that if the King
Should without issue die, he'll carry it so
To make the scepter his. These very words
I've heard him utter to his son-in-law,
Lord Abergavenny, to whom by oath he menaced   155
Revenge upon the Cardinal.

WOLSEY   Please your Highness, note
This dangerous conception in this point:
Not friended by his wish to your high person,
His will is most malignant, and it stretches   160
Beyond you to your friends.

QUEEN KATHERINE   My learnèd Lord Cardinal,
Deliver all with charity.

KING, ⌜*to Surveyor*⌝   Speak on.
How grounded he his title to the crown   165
Upon our fail? To this point hast thou heard him
At any time speak aught?

SURVEYOR   He was brought to this
By a vain prophecy of Nicholas Henton.

KING
What was that Henton?   170

SURVEYOR   Sir, a Chartreux friar,
His confessor, who fed him every minute
With words of sovereignty.

176. **the Rose:** Buckingham's London manor house

177. **demand:** ask

178. **speech:** talk

181. **Presently:** immediately

182. **doubted:** feared; suspected

186. **choice:** appropriate; **hour:** time

187. **moment:** weight, importance

188–91. **Whom ... utter:** i.e., who, after the **monk** (of line 184) made the **chaplain** swear under **the seal** of confession to tell the monk's words only to Buckingham **Whom:** who (referring to the monk)

191. **demure:** solemn; **confidence:** assurance, certitude

192. **pausingly:** with pausing; **ensued:** followed; **nor 's:** i.e., nor his

199. **spleen:** resentment

200. **spoil:** destroy

201. **heartily:** earnestly, sincerely

202. **on:** i.e., go on

205. **illusions:** deceptions

208. **forged him:** i.e., led him to contrive; **design:** plan, project; **being:** i.e., the monk's prophecy **being**

KING   How know'st thou this?

SURVEYOR

  Not long before your Highness sped to France,   175
  The Duke being at the Rose, within the parish
  Saint Laurence Poultney, did of me demand
  What was the speech among the Londoners
  Concerning the French journey. I replied
  Men fear the French would prove perfidious,   180
  To the King's danger. Presently the Duke
  Said 'twas the fear indeed, and that he doubted
  'Twould prove the verity of certain words
  Spoke by a holy monk "that oft," says he,
  "Hath sent to me, wishing me to permit   185
  John de la Car, my chaplain, a choice hour
  To hear from him a matter of some moment;
  Whom after under the ⌜confession's⌝ seal
  He solemnly had sworn that what he spoke
  My chaplain to no creature living but   190
  To me should utter, with demure confidence
  This pausingly ensued: 'Neither the King, nor 's heirs—
  Tell you the Duke—shall prosper. Bid him strive
  To ⌜gain⌝ the love o' th' commonalty; the Duke
  Shall govern England.' "   195

QUEEN KATHERINE   If I know you well,
  You were the Duke's surveyor, and lost your office
  On the complaint o' th' tenants. Take good heed
  You charge not in your spleen a noble person
  And spoil your nobler soul. I say, take heed—   200
  Yes, heartily beseech you.

KING   Let him on.—
  Go forward.

SURVEYOR   On my soul, I'll speak but truth.
  I told my lord the Duke, by th' devil's illusions   205
  The monk might be deceived, and that 'twas dangerous
  For ⌜him⌝ to ruminate on this so far until
  It forged him some design, which, being believed,

209. **much like:** very likely; **Tush:** exclamation of impatient contempt or disparagement

211. **failed:** died

213. **gone off:** i.e., been taken **off**

214. **rank:** violent; rebellious

215. **mischief:** evil

221. **being my:** i.e., **Blumer being my** (Blumer is the Folio spelling; in Holinshed, the name is Bulmer.)

222. **retained him his:** engaged **him** as **his** own servant

223. **committed:** sent to prison

225. **act:** perform

226. **Th' usurper Richard:** King Richard III, who ruled from 1483 to 1485, after having taken the throne from his nephew, the boy King Edward V (See Shakespeare's play *Richard III*, esp. 5.1, for the particular incident alluded to here. See also picture, page 166.) **Salisbury:** where Richard gathered his forces for the Battle of Bosworth Field

227. **Made suit:** petitioned; **in 's:** i.e., in Richard's

228. **made semblance of his duty:** pretended to kneel before the king

231. **freedom:** liberty of action

233. **God mend all:** a conventional pious wish

234. **would out of thee:** i.e., that you want to utter

236. **him:** i.e., himself (upright)

237. **on 's:** i.e., on his; **mounting:** raising

238. **discharge:** let fly; give vent to; **tenor:** import

It was much like to do. He answered "Tush,
It can do me no damage," adding further   210
That had the King in his last sickness failed,
The Cardinal's and Sir Thomas Lovell's heads
Should have gone off.

KING   Ha! What, so rank? Ah ha!
There's mischief in this man! Canst thou say further? 215

SURVEYOR
I can, my liege.

KING   Proceed.

SURVEYOR   Being at Greenwich,
After your Highness had reproved the Duke
About Sir William Blumer—   220

KING
I remember of such a time, being my sworn servant,
The Duke retained him his. But on. What hence?

SURVEYOR
"If," quoth he, "I for this had been committed,"
As to the Tower, I thought, "I would have played
The part my father meant to act upon   225
Th' usurper Richard, who, being at Salisbury,
Made suit to come in 's presence; which if granted,
As he made semblance of his duty, would
Have put his knife into him."

KING   A giant traitor!   230

WOLSEY
Now, madam, may his Highness live in freedom
And this man out of prison?

QUEEN KATHERINE   God mend all.

KING, ⌈*to Surveyor*⌉
There's something more would out of thee. What sayst?

SURVEYOR
After "the Duke his father" with "the knife,"   235
He stretched him, and with one hand on his dagger,
Another spread on 's breast, mounting his eyes,
He did discharge a horrible oath whose tenor

239. **evil used:** treated poorly; **outgo:** surpass
240. **performance:** i.e., **performance** of an act
242. **period:** conclusion, appointed end, goal
243. **us:** me; **attached:** arrested
244. **present:** immediate
247. **to th' height:** in the highest degree

1.3 Three courtiers discuss the royal proclamation against young fops who have adopted French manners and dress after returning from France. The courtiers then look forward together to the festive supper to be hosted by Wolsey that evening.

———————

1. **spells:** enthralling charms (with wordplay on incantations, occult powers); **juggle:** change; beguile (with wordplay on "conjure")
2. **strange mysteries:** surprising or foreign practices (with wordplay on "obscure secret things")
5. **let 'em be:** i.e., even if they are
7. **late:** recent
8. **fit . . . face:** one or two strange facial expressions or grimaces; **shrewd:** cunning, artful
9. **hold 'em:** i.e., maintain the expressions; **directly:** (1) at once; (2) absolutely
11. **Pepin or Clotharius:** ancient French or Frankish kings; **keep state:** maintain their dignity
12. **legs:** i.e., ways of walking and bowing (*To make a leg* was to bow.)
14. **see:** i.e., saw; **pace:** walk
14–15. **spavin / Or springhalt:** diseases of horses' legs
16. **Death:** i.e., by God's **death** (a strong oath)

(continued)

Was, were he evil used, he would outgo
His father by as much as a performance   240
Does an irresolute purpose.

KING   There's his period,
To sheathe his knife in us! He is attached.
Call him to present trial. If he may
Find mercy in the law, 'tis his; if none,   245
Let him not seek 't of us. By day and night,
He's traitor to th' height!

                                        They exit.

Scene 3

Enter Lord Chamberlain and Lord Sands.

CHAMBERLAIN
Is 't possible the spells of France should juggle
Men into such strange mysteries?

SANDS   New customs,
Though they be never so ridiculous—
Nay, let 'em be unmanly—yet are followed.   5

CHAMBERLAIN
As far as I see, all the good our English
Have got by the late voyage is but merely
A fit or two o' th' face; but they are shrewd ones,
For when they hold 'em, you would swear directly
Their very noses had been counselors   10
To Pepin or Clotharius, they keep state so.

SANDS
They have all new legs and lame ones; one would
    take it,
That never see 'em pace before, the spavin
⌜Or⌝ springhalt reigned among 'em.   15

CHAMBERLAIN   Death! My lord,
Their clothes are after such a pagan cut to 't,
That, sure, they've worn out Christendom.

17. **Their . . . to 't:** a combination of two constructions: (1) **their clothes are** fashioned **after such a pagan cut;** (2) **their clothes** have **a pagan cut to** them

18. **worn out Christendom:** i.e., exhausted all the fashions of the Christian world

19. **How now:** i.e., **how** is it **now**

21. **Faith:** a mild oath, equivalent to "indeed"

23. **clapped upon:** put up on

26. **quarrels:** i.e., duels

27. **monsieurs:** i.e., *messieurs* (Mispronunciation may be designed to be mocking and comic.)

29. **the Louvre:** palace of the French kings

31. **conditions:** provisions (of **the proclamation** [line 22])

32. **fool and feather:** Proverbial: "A **fool and** his **feather**."

33. **their . . . ignorance:** i.e., the items they wrongly think are matters of honor (with wordplay on **points** as laces that fasten articles of clothing together)

34. **as:** i.e., such **as; fireworks:** i.e., whoring (**Fireworks** is a possible metaphor for venereal disease, which the English associated with the French.)

36. **renouncing clean:** i.e., (and they must) completely renounce

37. **tennis:** *Real tennis*, from which the modern game is derived, was invented in France. **tall stockings:** The wearing of long **stockings** and **short breeches** (line 38) was a French style for men in Shakespeare's time. (See picture, page 208.)

38. **blistered breeches:** i.e., **breeches** ornamented with puffs; **types:** distinguishing marks

(continued)

42

Enter Sir Thomas Lovell.

                       How now?
What news, Sir Thomas Lovell?   20
LOVELL   Faith, my lord,
I hear of none but the new proclamation
That's clapped upon the court gate.
CHAMBERLAIN   What is 't for?
LOVELL
The reformation of our traveled gallants   25
That fill the court with quarrels, talk, and tailors.
CHAMBERLAIN
I'm glad 'tis there; now I would pray our monsieurs
To think an English courtier may be wise
And never see the Louvre.
LOVELL   They must either—   30
For so run the conditions—leave those remnants
Of fool and feather that they got in France,
With all their honorable points of ignorance
Pertaining thereunto, as fights and fireworks,
Abusing better men than they can be   35
Out of a foreign wisdom, renouncing clean
The faith they have in tennis and tall stockings,
Short blistered breeches, and those types of travel,
And understand again like honest men,
Or pack to their old playfellows. There, I take it,   40
They may *cum privilegio* ⌈*"oui"*⌉ away
The lag end of their lewdness and be laughed at.
SANDS
'Tis time to give 'em physic, their diseases
Are grown so catching.
CHAMBERLAIN   What a loss our ladies 45
Will have of these trim vanities!
LOVELL   Ay, marry,
There will be woe indeed, lords. The sly whoresons

39. understand: i.e., (they must) have comprehension (with wordplay on "stand under" meaning "be subject," or be proper English subjects, **honest men**)

40. pack: be off, depart

41. cum privilegio: i.e., with privilege, with impunity (See longer note, page 239.) **oui:** yes (French)

42. lag end: last part, after the best has been used; **lewdness:** (1) foolishness; (2) wickedness; (3) lasciviousness

43. physic: medicine

46. trim vanities: i.e., well-dressed conceited courtiers

48. whoresons: bastards (a term of abuse)

49. speeding: rapid, effective

50. has no fellow: cannot be equaled

51. fiddle 'em: i.e., cheat or swindle them

52. converting of: i.e., changing

53–54. beaten . . . play: i.e., long forced out of the game (of seduction)

54. plainsong: simple melody (as opposed to **a French song** [line 50])

55. by 'r Lady: i.e., by Our **Lady** (the Virgin Mary)

56. Held: will be regarded as; **current music:** music that is in vogue, presently fashionable

58. colt's tooth: i.e., youthful lascivious desires

60. stump: part of a broken tooth left in the gum (with wordplay on penis)

66. makes: provides, gives

71. dews: See Psalm 133.3: "the dew of Hermon . . . falleth upon the mountains of Zion: for there the Lord appointed the blessing and life

(continued)

Have got a speeding trick to lay down ladies.
A French song and a fiddle has no fellow.   50
SANDS
The devil fiddle 'em! I am glad they are going,
For sure there's no converting of 'em. Now
An honest country lord, as I am, beaten
A long time out of play, may bring his plainsong,
And have an hour of hearing, and, by 'r Lady,   55
Held current music too.
CHAMBERLAIN   Well said, Lord Sands.
Your colt's tooth is not cast yet?
SANDS   No, my lord,
Nor shall not while I have a stump.   60
CHAMBERLAIN   Sir Thomas,
Whither were you a-going?
LOVELL   To the Cardinal's.
Your Lordship is a guest too.
CHAMBERLAIN   O, 'tis true.   65
This night he makes a supper, and a great one,
To many lords and ladies. There will be
The beauty of this kingdom, I'll assure you.
LOVELL
That churchman bears a bounteous mind indeed,
A hand as fruitful as the land that feeds us.   70
His dews fall everywhere.
CHAMBERLAIN   No doubt he's noble;
He had a black mouth that said other of him.
SANDS
He may, my lord. 'Has wherewithal. In him,
Sparing would show a worse sin than ill doctrine.   75
Men of his way should be most liberal;
They are set here for examples.
CHAMBERLAIN   True, they are so,
But few now give so great ones. My barge stays.
Your Lordship shall along.—Come, good Sir Thomas,   80
We shall be late else, which I would not be,

forever" (with wordplay on *dues* as legal charges, tolls, tribute, fees)

73. **black:** slanderous (A **black mouth** was also a sign of imminent death.) **other of:** anything else about

74. **He may:** perhaps, Wolsey has the ability; **'Has:** i.e., he has; **wherewithal:** i.e., money

75. **than ill:** i.e., **than** (preaching or believing) evil or erroneous

76. **way:** course of life, vocation

79. **barge:** usual means of travel within London by way of the Thames; **stays:** awaits

80. **shall along:** i.e., **shall** come **along**

81. **else:** otherwise

82. **spoke to:** asked, appealed to

83. **comptrollers:** stewards, or masters of ceremonies

84. **I . . . Lordship's:** i.e., I will follow your direction

1.4 At the supper, Wolsey and his guests are visited by Henry and his courtiers, all disguised as shepherds. Henry dances with Anne Bullen and exclaims over her beauty.

---

0 SD. **Hautboys:** powerful double-reed woodwind instruments (See picture, page 162.) **state:** canopy, such as usually hangs above a throne (See picture, page 50.)

1. **his Grace:** i.e., Wolsey

3. **fair content:** delightful or desirable pleasure

(continued)

For I was spoke to, with Sir Henry Guilford
This night to be comptrollers.

SANDS   I am your Lordship's.

They exit.

Scene 4

Hautboys. A small table under a state for the Cardinal, a
longer table for the guests. Then enter Anne Bullen and
divers other ladies and gentlemen as guests at one door;
at another door enter Sir Henry Guilford.

GUILFORD
Ladies, a general welcome from his Grace
Salutes you all. This night he dedicates
To fair content and you. None here, he hopes,
In all this noble bevy has brought with her
One care abroad. He would have all as merry   5
As, first, good company, good wine, good welcome
Can make good people.

Enter Lord Chamberlain, Lord Sands, and
⌐Sir Thomas¬ Lovell.

              O, my lord, you're tardy!
The very thought of this fair company
Clapped wings to me.   10

CHAMBERLAIN   You are young, Sir Harry Guilford.

SANDS
Sir Thomas Lovell, had the Cardinal
But half my lay thoughts in him, some of these
Should find a running banquet, ere they rested,
I think would better please 'em. By my life,   15
They are a sweet society of fair ones.

LOVELL
O, that your Lordship were but now confessor
To one or two of these!

9. **fair:** beautiful

10. **Clapped:** promptly put

13. **lay thoughts:** i.e., sexual **thoughts** of a layman, as opposed to a supposedly celibate clergyman

14. **running banquet:** light refreshment taken hurriedly between meals (with the suggestion of casual sexual encounters)

16. **society:** company, small party

22. **down:** feather; **afford:** bestow, grant, yield

24. **Place you:** arrange; i.e., seat

34. **O . . . too:** Proverbial: "**Love** is a madness."

36. **kiss you:** i.e., kiss (**you** is the ethic dative); **twenty:** perhaps, **twenty** women; perhaps, **twenty** times; **with a breath:** in the time it takes to draw **a breath**

37. **Well said:** i.e., **well** done

41. **Pass away:** leave

42. **cure:** sphere of spiritual ministration (continuing the metaphor begun with **penance,** line 40) A **cure** is also (1) the spiritual charge given a curate; (2) medical treatment.

43. **Let me alone:** i.e., trust me

43 SD. **takes his state:** seats himself in a raised chair under the canopy (See note to 1.4.0 SD.)

SANDS   I would I were.
They should find easy penance.   20

LOVELL   Faith, how easy?

SANDS
As easy as a down bed would afford it.

CHAMBERLAIN
Sweet ladies, will it please you sit?—Sir Harry,
Place you that side; I'll take the charge of this.
⌐*The guests are seated.*⌐
His Grace is ent'ring. Nay, you must not freeze; 25
Two women placed together makes cold weather.
My Lord Sands, you are one will keep 'em waking.
Pray sit between these ladies.

SANDS   By my faith,
And thank your Lordship.—By your leave, sweet ladies. 30
⌐*He sits between Anne Bullen and another lady.*⌐
If I chance to talk a little wild, forgive me;
I had it from my father.

ANNE   Was he mad, sir?

SANDS
O, very mad, exceeding mad, in love too;
But he would bite none. Just as I do now, 35
He would kiss you twenty with a breath.
⌐*He kisses Anne.*⌐

CHAMBERLAIN   Well said,
my lord.
So, now you're fairly seated, gentlemen,
The penance lies on you if these fair ladies 40
Pass away frowning.

SANDS   For my little cure,
Let me alone.

Hautboys. Enter Cardinal Wolsey, ⌐*with Attendants and
Servants,*⌐ *and takes his state.*

WOLSEY
You're welcome, my fair guests. That noble lady

49. **bowl:** i.e., **bowl** that

52. **beholding:** beholden, obliged; **Cheer:** entertain; enliven, animate

58. **gamester:** mirthful or playful person (Sands responds as if, by **gamester,** Anne meant "gambler," another meaning of the word.)

61. **pledge it:** drink in response (He goes on, in line 62, to turn the generalized **it** into **a thing** to which they are drinking.)

64. **anon:** soon

64 SD. **Chambers:** small cannon

68. **end:** purpose

69. **laws of war:** One of such **laws** is the prohibition against violence to noncombatants.

71. **strangers:** foreigners

73. **make:** come; **as:** i.e., **as** if they are

Henry VIII in his chair of state. (1.2.8 SD)
From Alfred Benjamin Wyon,
The great seals of England . . . (1887).

Or gentleman that is not freely merry   45
Is not my friend. This to confirm my welcome,
And to you all good health.   ⌐*He drinks to them.*⌐
SANDS   Your Grace is noble.
Let me have such a bowl may hold my thanks
And save me so much talking.   50
WOLSEY   My Lord Sands,
I am beholding to you. Cheer your neighbors.—
Ladies, you are not merry.—Gentlemen,
Whose fault is this?
SANDS   The red wine first must rise   55
In their fair cheeks, my lord. Then we shall have 'em
Talk us to silence.
ANNE   You are a merry gamester,
My Lord Sands.
SANDS   Yes, if I make my play.   60
Here's to your Ladyship, and pledge it, madam,
                                ⌐*He drinks to her.*⌐
For 'tis to such a thing—
ANNE   You cannot show me.
SANDS
I told your Grace they would talk anon.
                    Drum and Trumpet. Chambers discharged.
WOLSEY   What's that?   65
CHAMBERLAIN
Look out there, some of you.   ⌐*Servants exit.*⌐
WOLSEY   What warlike voice,
And to what end, is this?—Nay, ladies, fear not.
By all the laws of war you're privileged.

                        Enter a Servant.

CHAMBERLAIN
How now, what is 't?   70
SERVANT   A noble troop of strangers,
For so they seem. They've left their barge and landed,
And hither make, as great ambassadors
From foreign princes.

76–77. the French tongue: The French language seems here regarded as the proper language of diplomacy.

78. receive: welcome

80. attend: wait on; accompany

81. broken: interrupted; **banquet:** feast; **mend it:** put it right

83 SD. masquers: participants in an impromptu masquerade; **habited:** costumed

86. fame: rumor

90. conduct: direction

91. leave: permission

92. revels: lively entertainment, including dancing and games

THOMAS WOLSAVS CARD·

Cardinal Wolsey.
From Henry Holland, *Herøologia* . . . [1620].

WOLSEY   Good Lord Chamberlain,   75
  Go, give 'em welcome—you can speak the French
    tongue—
  And pray receive 'em nobly, and conduct 'em
  Into our presence, where this heaven of beauty
  Shall shine at full upon them. Some attend him.   80
        ⌐*Lord Chamberlain exits, with Attendants.*⌐
                  All rise, and tables removed.
  You have now a broken banquet, but we'll mend it.
  A good digestion to you all; and once more
  I shower a welcome on you. Welcome all!

Hautboys. Enter King and others as masquers, habited
  like shepherds, ushered by the Lord Chamberlain.
  They pass directly before the Cardinal and gracefully
                  salute him.

  A noble company! What are their pleasures?
CHAMBERLAIN
  Because they speak no English, thus they prayed   85
  To tell your Grace: that, having heard by fame
  Of this so noble and so fair assembly
  This night to meet here, they could do no less,
  Out of the great respect they bear to beauty,
  But leave their flocks and, under your fair conduct,   90
  Crave leave to view these ladies and entreat
  An hour of revels with 'em.
WOLSEY   Say, Lord Chamberlain,
  They have done my poor house grace, for which I
    pay 'em   95
  A thousand thanks and pray 'em take their pleasures.
        ⌐*The masquers*⌐ *choose Ladies.* ⌐*The*⌐
                King ⌐*chooses*⌐ *Anne Bullen.*
KING
  The fairest hand I ever touched! O beauty,
  Till now I never knew thee.
                              Music, Dance.
WOLSEY My lord!

104. **this place:** the raised and canopied chair of state

111. **it:** i.e., Wolsey's chair

113. **By all your good leaves:** a plural version of "**by your** leave," a conventional request for permission

119. **unhappily:** unfavorably

121. **pleasant:** jocular, humorous

125. **one of her Highness' women:** i.e., (she is) **one of** the Queen's ladies-in-waiting

126. **dainty:** delicately beautiful

127. **were:** would be; **take you out:** i.e., to dance with you

128. **kiss:** For the possible relation between dancing and kissing, see longer note, page 240.

130. **Let it go round:** let everyone drink

ANNA BVLLEN REGINA ANGLIÆ.
Henrici VIII Vxor 2ª Elizabethæ Reginæ
Mater fuit decollata Londini, 19 Maij Æ 1536.

Anne Bullen.
By Wenceslaus Hollar (1649), after Holbein (1536).
From the Folger Library Collection.

CHAMBERLAIN   Your Grace?   100
WOLSEY   Pray tell 'em thus much
  from me:
  There should be one amongst 'em by his person
  More worthy this place than myself, to whom,
  If I but knew him, with my love and duty   105
  I would surrender it.
CHAMBERLAIN   I will, my lord.
                ⌜*Whisper with the masquers.*⌝
WOLSEY
  What say they?
CHAMBERLAIN   Such a one they all confess
  There is indeed, which they would have your Grace   110
  Find out, and he will take it.
WOLSEY   Let me see, then.
              ⌜*He leaves his state.*⌝
  By all your good leaves, gentlemen.
              ⌜*He bows before the King.*⌝
              Here I'll make
  My royal choice.   115
KING, ⌜*unmasking*⌝ You have found him, cardinal.
  You hold a fair assembly; you do well, lord.
  You are a churchman, or I'll tell you, cardinal,
  I should judge now unhappily.
WOLSEY   I am glad   120
  Your Grace is grown so pleasant.
KING   My Lord Chamberlain,
  Prithee come hither. What fair lady's that?
CHAMBERLAIN
  An't please your Grace, Sir Thomas Bullen's daughter,
  The Viscount Rochford, one of her Highness' women.   125
KING
  By heaven, she is a dainty one.—Sweetheart,
  I were unmannerly to take you out
  And not to kiss you. ⌜*He kisses Anne.*⌝ A health,
    gentlemen!
  Let it go round.   ⌜*He drinks a toast.*⌝ 130

131. **banquet:** course of candies, fruit, and wine, served either as a separate entertainment or as a continuation of the principal meal, but in the latter case usually in a different room; a dessert

132. **privy chamber:** innermost and most private room in a house

142. **measure:** stately dance

144. **best in favor:** (1) most beautiful; (2) most favored by the king; (3) most favored by the ladies; **knock it:** strike up

144 SD. **Trumpets:** i.e., musicians playing a trumpet fanfare

"Cherubins." (1.1.29)
From Martin Luther,
Der Zwey vnd zwentzigste Psalm Dauids . . . (1525).

WOLSEY
  Sir Thomas Lovell, is the banquet ready
  I' th' privy chamber?
LOVELL   Yes, my lord.
WOLSEY   Your Grace,
  I fear, with dancing is a little heated.   135
KING
  I fear, too much.
WOLSEY   There's fresher air, my lord,
  In the next chamber.
KING
  Lead in your ladies ev'ry one.—Sweet partner,
  I must not yet forsake you.—Let's be merry,   140
  Good my Lord Cardinal. I have half a dozen healths
  To drink to these fair ladies, and a measure
  To lead 'em once again, and then let's dream
  Who's best in favor. Let the music knock it.
                              They exit, with Trumpets.

HENRY VIII

ACT 2

2.1 Buckingham, convicted of treason, is led to execution. He declares his innocence, forgives his enemies, and vows his loyalty to Henry. Two gentlemen then discuss the rumor that Henry is separating from Katherine.

---

0 SD. **several:** separate

3. **Hall:** Westminster **Hall**

13. **condemned:** sentenced; **upon 't:** i.e., on being found guilty

16. **passed it:** did it proceed

17. **in a little:** briefly

18. **his accusations:** the charges against him

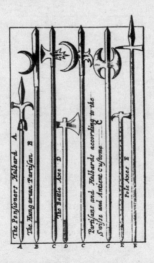

Halberds and other weapons. (2.1.70 SD)
From Louis de Gaya, *A treatise of the arms* . . . (1678).

ACT 2

Scene 1

Enter two Gentlemen at several doors.

FIRST GENTLEMAN
  Whither away so fast?
SECOND GENTLEMAN   O, God save you.
  E'en to the Hall to hear what shall become
  Of the great Duke of Buckingham.
FIRST GENTLEMAN   I'll save you   5
  That labor, sir. All's now done but the ceremony
  Of bringing back the prisoner.
SECOND GENTLEMAN   Were you there?
FIRST GENTLEMAN
  Yes, indeed was I.
SECOND GENTLEMAN Pray speak what has happened.   10
FIRST GENTLEMAN
  You may guess quickly what.
SECOND GENTLEMAN   Is he found guilty?
FIRST GENTLEMAN
  Yes, truly, is he, and condemned upon 't.
SECOND GENTLEMAN
  I am sorry for 't.
FIRST GENTLEMAN So are a number more.   15
SECOND GENTLEMAN But pray, how passed it?
FIRST GENTLEMAN
  I'll tell you in a little. The great duke
  Came to the bar, where to his accusations

61

19. **still:** always

20. **sharp:** acute, sagacious; **reasons:** arguments

21. **contrary:** opposed side

22. **Urged on:** presented; **examinations:** statements, depositions; **proofs:** written statements of what witnesses are prepared to swear to

24. **viva voce:** i.e., to testify orally

26. **Sir:** courtesy title for a priest; **chancellor:** official secretary

28. **Hopkins:** See longer note to 1.1.262, page 239; **mischief:** harm

32. **which:** perhaps, whom; **fain:** gladly

34. **his peers:** other nobles

37. **Was either pitied in him or forgotten:** i.e., either aroused only pity for him or was disregarded or taken no note of

40. **judgment:** sentence

41. **agony:** anguish of mind

42. **ill:** offensive

43. **fell to himself:** regained self-control

46. **Sure:** i.e., surely

47. **He . . . womanish:** Proverbial: "To fear is womanish."

48. **grieve at:** be resentful about

50. **end:** root cause

He pleaded still not guilty and alleged
Many sharp reasons to defeat the law.   20
The King's attorney on the contrary
Urged on the examinations, proofs, confessions
Of divers witnesses, which the Duke desired
To him brought *viva voce* to his face;
At which appeared against him his surveyor,   25
Sir Gilbert Peck his chancellor, and John Car,
Confessor to him, with that devil monk,
Hopkins, that made this mischief.
SECOND GENTLEMAN   That was he
That fed him with his prophecies?   30
FIRST GENTLEMAN   The same.
All these accused him strongly, which he fain
Would have flung from him, but indeed he could not.
And so his peers upon this evidence
Have found him guilty of high treason. Much   35
He spoke, and learnèdly, for life, but all
Was either pitied in him or forgotten.
SECOND GENTLEMAN
After all this, how did he bear himself?
FIRST GENTLEMAN
When he was brought again to th' bar to hear
His knell rung out, his judgment, he was stirred   40
With such an agony he sweat extremely
And something spoke in choler, ill and hasty.
But he fell to himself again, and sweetly
In all the rest showed a most noble patience.
SECOND GENTLEMAN
I do not think he fears death.   45
FIRST GENTLEMAN   Sure he does not;
He never was so womanish. The cause
He may a little grieve at.
SECOND GENTLEMAN   Certainly
The Cardinal is the end of this.   50
FIRST GENTLEMAN   'Tis likely,

52–53. **Kildare's . . . removed:** i.e., after the earl of Kildare, Lord Deputy of Ireland, was summoned to England in disgrace **attainder:** stain of dishonor

54. **Earl Surrey:** i.e., the **earl** of **Surrey**

55. **father:** i.e., father-in-law

57. **deep envious:** profoundly malicious

58. **his:** i.e., the earl of Surrey's

60. **generally:** by everyone

60–61. **whoever . . . employment:** i.e., **the cardinal will find** a post for whomever **the King favors**

64. **him:** i.e., Wolsey; **perniciously:** to the death

68. **mirror:** model, paragon

69. **Stay:** i.e., break off your speech

70 SD. **Tipstaves:** court officers carrying staves tipped with metal as the badge of their office; **Halberds:** soldiers carrying **halberds** (See picture, page 60.) **accompanied with:** i.e., **accompanied** by; **Sir Walter Sands:** See longer note, page 240.

71. **close:** hidden

73. **thus far:** i.e., this **far**

74. **lose:** forget

77. **sink:** destroy

79. **The law I bear no malice:** i.e., **I bear no malice** to **the law**

80. **upon the premises:** i.e., based on what has just been said (by the witnesses); **but:** only

By all conjectures; first, Kildare's attainder,
Then Deputy of Ireland, who, removed,
Earl Surrey was sent thither, and in haste too,
Lest he should help his father.   55

SECOND GENTLEMAN   That trick of state
Was a deep envious one.

FIRST GENTLEMAN   At his return
No doubt he will requite it. This is noted,
And generally: whoever the King favors,   60
The Card'nal instantly will find employment,
And far enough from court too.

SECOND GENTLEMAN   All the commons
Hate him perniciously and, o' my conscience,
Wish him ten fathom deep. This duke as much   65
They love and dote on, call him bounteous
    Buckingham,
The mirror of all courtesy.

FIRST GENTLEMAN   Stay there, sir,
And see the noble ruined man you speak of.   70

*Enter Buckingham from his arraignment, Tipstaves before
him, the ax with the edge towards him, Halberds on each
side, accompanied with Sir Thomas Lovell, Sir Nicholas
    Vaux, Sir Walter Sands, and Common People, etc.*

SECOND GENTLEMAN
Let's stand close and behold him.

BUCKINGHAM   All good people,
You that thus far have come to pity me,
Hear what I say, and then go home and lose me.
I have this day received a traitor's judgment,   75
And by that name must die. Yet heaven bear witness,
And if I have a conscience, let it sink me
Even as the ax falls, if I be not faithful!
The law I bear no malice for my death;
'T has done, upon the premises, but justice.   80
But those that sought it I could wish more ⌈Christian.⌉

82. **Be what they will:** i.e., whatever or whoever they be; **heartily:** sincerely

83. **look:** be sure; take care; **mischief:** harm, evil

87. **sue:** petition, appeal (i.e., for mercy)

88. **make faults:** do wrongs

91. **only bitter:** i.e., the **only** cause of bitterness; **only dying:** perhaps, the **only** death

93. **divorce of steel:** His execution would be through divorcing head from body with an axe. (See picture, page 70.)

95. **a' God's:** i.e., in **God's**

96. **for charity:** i.e., out of **charity,** as an act of loving-kindness

98. **frankly:** unconditionally; freely

99–100. **I as . . . forgiven:** an echo of the biblical prayer "**forgive** us . . . **as** we **forgive** those who trespass against us" **free:** unreservedly

102. **take:** i.e., make

103. **envy:** malice

104. **make:** perhaps, **make** up, form (often emended to "mark")

104. **Commend . . . Grace:** remember me kindly to the king

107. **Yet are:** i.e., are still; **forsake:** leave entirely

108. **cry:** call in supplication

109. **tell:** count

112. **monument:** tomb

114. **charge:** responsibility, custody

115. **undertakes you:** takes you in charge

Be what they will, I heartily forgive 'em.
Yet let 'em look they glory not in mischief,
Nor build their evils on the graves of great men,
For then my guiltless blood must cry against 'em.   85
For further life in this world I ne'er hope,
Nor will I sue, although the King have mercies
More than I dare make faults. You few that loved me
And dare be bold to weep for Buckingham,
His noble friends and fellows, whom to leave   90
Is only bitter to him, only dying,
Go with me like good angels to my end,
And as the long divorce of steel falls on me,
Make of your prayers one sweet sacrifice,
And lift my soul to heaven.—Lead on, a' God's name.   95

LOVELL
I do beseech your Grace, for charity,
If ever any malice in your heart
Were hid against me, now to forgive me frankly.

BUCKINGHAM
Sir Thomas Lovell, I as free forgive you
As I would be forgiven. I forgive all.   100
There cannot be those numberless offenses
'Gainst me that I cannot take peace with. No black
   envy
Shall make my grave. Commend me to his Grace.
And if he speak of Buckingham, pray tell him   105
You met him half in heaven. My vows and prayers
Yet are the King's and, till my soul forsake,
Shall cry for blessings on him. May he live
Longer than I have time to tell his years.
Ever beloved and loving may his rule be;   110
And when old Time shall lead him to his end,
Goodness and he fill up one monument!

LOVELL
To th' waterside I must conduct your Grace,
Then give my charge up to Sir Nicholas Vaux,
Who undertakes you to your end.   115

118. **fit:** supply; **furniture:** accessories, ornaments

121. **state:** high rank; pomp and ceremony

125. **truth:** steadfast allegiance; **seal it:** i.e., ratify (as by a seal) my superior allegiance

128. **raised head:** mounted an insurrection; **Richard:** See note to 1.2.226 and picture, page 166.

129. **succor:** aid

132. **succeeding:** i.e., **succeeding** to the throne after the defeat and death of Richard III at Bosworth Field

133. **prince:** sovereign ruler, king

140. **happier:** more fortunate

142. **Fell:** i.e., were brought down

147. **loose:** careless, unguarded

149. **rub:** obstacle (a technical term from the game of bowls, where a **rub** is any obstruction that hinders or deflects the course of the bowl) See picture below.

A game of bowls. (2.1.149)
From *Le centre de l'amour . . .* [1650?].

VAUX, ⌜*calling as to Officers offstage*⌝   Prepare there!
  The Duke is coming. See the barge be ready,
  And fit it with such furniture as suits
  The greatness of his person.
BUCKINGHAM   Nay, Sir Nicholas,   120
  Let it alone. My state now will but mock me.
  When I came hither, I was Lord High Constable
  And Duke of Buckingham; now, poor Edward Bohun.
  Yet I am richer than my base accusers,
  That never knew what truth meant. I now seal it,   125
  And with that blood will make 'em one day groan for 't.
  My noble father, Henry of Buckingham,
  Who first raised head against usurping Richard,
  Flying for succor to his servant Banister,
  Being distressed, was by that wretch betrayed,   130
  And, without trial, fell. God's peace be with him.
  Henry the Seventh, succeeding, truly pitying
  My father's loss, like a most royal prince
  Restored me to my honors and out of ruins
  Made my name once more noble. Now his son,   135
  Henry the Eighth, life, honor, name, and all
  That made me happy at one stroke has taken
  Forever from the world. I had my trial,
  And must needs say a noble one, which makes me
  A little happier than my wretched father.   140
  Yet thus far we are one in fortunes: both
  Fell by our servants, by those men we loved most—
  A most unnatural and faithless service.
  Heaven has an end in all; yet, you that hear me,
  This from a dying man receive as certain: 145
  Where you are liberal of your loves and counsels
  Be sure you be not loose; for those you make friends
  And give your hearts to, when they once perceive
  The least rub in your fortunes, fall away
  Like water from you, never found again   150

151. **sink:** ruin

152. **forsake you:** leave you entirely

159. **authors:** i.e., agents of Buckingham's downfall and death

162. **fall:** happen

164. **keep it from us:** i.e., protect and shield us from it

165. **faith:** faithfulness, fidelity

170. **confident:** trustful, trusting

171. **of late:** i.e., in recent

172. **buzzing:** rumor

174. **held not:** did not last, or remain valid

176. **straight:** straightaway, immediately

177. **allay:** subdue, quell

178. **durst:** dared; **disperse it:** spread it around

180. **found:** i.e., discovered to be

181. **held for certain:** believed as a certainty

182. **venture at:** make an attempt at; **the Cardinal:** i.e., Wolsey

183. **about him near:** i.e., close to the king

An executioner. (2.1.93)
From [Richard Verstegen,] *Theatre des cruautez des hereticques de nostre temps* . . . (1607).

But where they mean to sink you. All good people,
Pray for me. I must now forsake you. The last hour
Of my long weary life is come upon me.
Farewell. And when you would say something that
   is sad,   155
Speak how I fell. I have done; and God forgive me.
                              Duke and train exit.

FIRST GENTLEMAN
O, this is full of pity, sir! It calls,
I fear, too many curses on their heads
That were the authors.

SECOND GENTLEMAN   If the Duke be guiltless,   160
'Tis full of woe. Yet I can give you inkling
Of an ensuing evil, if it fall,
Greater than this.

FIRST GENTLEMAN   Good angels keep it from us!
What may it be? You do not doubt my faith, sir?   165

SECOND GENTLEMAN
This secret is so weighty 'twill require
A strong faith to conceal it.

FIRST GENTLEMAN   Let me have it.
I do not talk much.

SECOND GENTLEMAN   I am confident;   170
You shall, sir. Did you not of late days hear
A buzzing of a separation
Between the King and Katherine?

FIRST GENTLEMAN   Yes, but it held not;
For when the King once heard it, out of anger   175
He sent command to the Lord Mayor straight
To stop the rumor and allay those tongues
That durst disperse it.

SECOND GENTLEMAN   But that slander, sir,
Is found a truth now, for it grows again
Fresher than e'er it was, and held for certain   180
The King will venture at it. Either the Cardinal,
Or some about him near, have, out of malice

184. **possessed him:** caused **him** to be **possessed; scruple:** thought that troubles the conscience

185. **undo:** destroy; **To confirm this too:** i.e., as further confirmation of the imminent **separation** (line 172)

186. **Cardinal Campeius:** Lorenzo **Cardinal** Campeggio (Latinized as **Campeius**), papal legate; **is arrived, and lately:** i.e., has recently **arrived**

188. **'Tis the Cardinal:** i.e., it is Wolsey who is responsible

189. **revenge him:** avenge himself; **the Emperor:** Charles V, great-nephew to Queen Katherine (See note to 1.1.207.)

191. **Toledo:** a city in Spain; **this:** i.e., the **separation; purposed:** proposed; designed

192. **have . . . mark:** i.e., are accurate (literally, [your arrow] has **hit the** target) See picture, page 80.

193. **smart:** pain

196. **too open:** i.e., too much in the public view

197. **think:** consider

2.2 Norfolk, Suffolk, and the Lord Chamberlain join in denouncing Wolsey. They hold him responsible for dividing Henry from Katherine, and see the threatened divorce as serving Wolsey's desire that Henry marry the French king's sister. When Norfolk and Suffolk break in on the king's privacy, he rebukes them and sends them away while welcoming Wolsey and Cardinal Campeius, the papal legate. Henry is delighted that the divorce proceedings can go forward.

(continued)

To the good queen, possessed him with a scruple
That will undo her. To confirm this too,   185
Cardinal Campeius is arrived, and lately,
As all think, for this business.

FIRST GENTLEMAN   'Tis the Cardinal;
And merely to revenge him on the Emperor
For not bestowing on him at his asking   190
The archbishopric of Toledo this is purposed.

SECOND GENTLEMAN
I think you have hit the mark. But is 't not cruel
That she should feel the smart of this? The Cardinal
Will have his will, and she must fall.

FIRST GENTLEMAN   'Tis woeful.   195
We are too open here to argue this.
Let's think in private more.

                                        They exit.

Scene 2

Enter Lord Chamberlain, reading this letter.

⌜CHAMBERLAIN⌝ *My lord, the horses your Lordship sent
for, with all the care I had I saw well chosen, ridden,
and furnished. They were young and handsome and
of the best breed in the north. When they were ready
to set out for London, a man of my Lord Cardinal's,   5
by commission and main power, took 'em from me
with this reason: his master would be served before
a subject, if not before the King, which stopped our
mouths, sir.*
I fear he will indeed; well, let him have them.   10
He will have all, I think.

        *Enter to the Lord Chamberlain, the Dukes
            of Norfolk and Suffolk.*

NORFOLK   Well met, my Lord Chamberlain.
CHAMBERLAIN   Good day to both your Graces.

2. **ridden:** broken in

3. **furnished:** equipped

5. **my Lord Cardinal's:** i.e., Wolsey's

6. **commission:** order, warrant; **main power:** sheer force

7. **reason:** rationale

12. **Well met:** an expression of welcome

15. **private:** alone

16. **sad:** serious

18. **his brother's wife:** Queen Katherine was married in 1501 to Henry's elder brother Arthur, who died in 1502. A papal dispensation allowed Henry to marry Katherine in 1509 when he became king.

24–25. **That blind . . . list:** Norfolk here associates Wolsey with the goddess **Fortune,** who **turns** her wheel to control the rise and fall of human beings, and who is often pictured as blind. (See pictures, pages 94, 158, and 184.) **eldest son:** i.e., **son** and heir **list:** chooses, wishes

25. **know him:** i.e., perceive him clearly

26. **know himself:** understand **himself** (Proverbial: "Nosce te ipsum [know thyself].") **else:** otherwise

27. **he works:** i.e., Wolsey **works**

29. **league:** alliance

37. **jewel:** costly ornament

42. **course:** i.e., **course** of action

44. **news:** tidings, reports bringing new information about recent events

SUFFOLK
How is the King employed?

CHAMBERLAIN   I left him private,   15
Full of sad thoughts and troubles.

NORFOLK   What's the cause?

CHAMBERLAIN
It seems the marriage with his brother's wife
Has crept too near his conscience.

SUFFOLK   No, his conscience   20
Has crept too near another lady.

NORFOLK   'Tis so;
This is the Cardinal's doing. The king-cardinal,
That blind priest, like the eldest son of Fortune,
Turns what he list. The King will know him one day.   25

SUFFOLK
Pray God he do! He'll never know himself else.

NORFOLK
How holily he works in all his business,
And with what zeal! For, now he has cracked the
    league
Between us and the Emperor, the Queen's great-   30
    nephew,
He dives into the King's soul and there scatters
Dangers, doubts, wringing of the conscience,
Fears and despairs—and all these for his marriage.
And out of all these to restore the King,   35
He counsels a divorce, a loss of her
That like a jewel has hung twenty years
About his neck, yet never lost her luster;
Of her that loves him with that excellence
That angels love good men with; even of her   40
That, when the greatest stroke of fortune falls,
Will bless the King. And is not this course pious?

CHAMBERLAIN
Heaven keep me from such counsel! 'Tis most true:
These news are everywhere, every tongue speaks 'em,

45. **true:** loyal

46. **main:** chief, principal; **end:** goal

47. **The French king's sister:** i.e., the duchess d'Alençon (reputed to be Wolsey's choice for Henry's second wife)

48. **slept upon:** i.e., been blind to

54. **honors:** titles, ranks

55. **lump:** i.e., of clay (Wolsey is figured as a potter.)

56. **pitch:** stature; status, degree

59. **made:** assured of success; **stand:** remain

60. **His:** i.e., Wolsey's

61. **alike:** in the same way; indifferently; **breath I not believe in:** i.e., nothing but air

63. **the Pope:** Because pride is a deadly sin, Suffolk could have been expected to say "the devil" rather than **the pope.**

64. **in:** i.e., go **in**

70. **otherwhere:** elsewhere

71. **find a:** i.e., **find** this to be **a; unfit:** unsuitable, inappropriate

72. **Health to:** a salutation expressing a wish for someone's prosperity

75. **sad:** unhappy; serious; **Sure:** i.e., surely

And every true heart weeps for 't. All that dare   45
Look into these affairs see this main end,
The French king's sister. Heaven will one day open
The King's eyes, that so long have slept upon
This bold bad man.

SUFFOLK   And free us from his slavery.   50

NORFOLK   We had need pray,
And heartily, for our deliverance,
Or this imperious man will work us all
From princes into pages. All men's honors
Lie like one lump before him, to be fashioned   55
Into what pitch he please.

SUFFOLK   For me, my lords,
I love him not nor fear him; there's my creed.
As I am made without him, so I'll stand,
If the King please. His curses and his blessings   60
Touch me alike: they're breath I not believe in.
I knew him and I know him; so I leave him
To him that made him proud, the Pope.

NORFOLK   Let's in,
And with some other business put the King   65
From these sad thoughts that work too much upon
   him.—
My lord, you'll bear us company?

CHAMBERLAIN   Excuse me;
The King has sent me otherwhere. Besides,   70
You'll find a most unfit time to disturb him.
Health to your Lordships.

NORFOLK   Thanks, my good Lord
   Chamberlain.
          Lord Chamberlain exits; and the King draws
                the curtain and sits reading pensively.

SUFFOLK, ⌜*to Norfolk*⌝
How sad he looks! Sure he is much afflicted.   75

KING
Who's there? Ha?

79. **Who am I, ha:** i.e., don't you know **who I am**

81. **Malice ne'er meant:** i.e., that were never intended as harmful or offensive; **this way:** i.e., in this case

82. **estate:** state

85. **Go to:** an expression of reproof

86. **temporal:** earthly (as opposed to *spiritual*)

88. **The quiet of:** i.e., that which establishes **quiet** in

89. **cure:** remedy (with possible wordplay on **cure** as "spiritual care")

93. **a talker:** i.e., merely **a talker** (Proverbial: "The greatest talkers are the least doers.")

94. **cannot:** i.e., **cannot be found a talker**

95. **I would:** I wish

96. **conference:** conversation

98. **This priest:** i.e., Wolsey

100. **so sick:** i.e., **so sick** with pride; **though for his place:** i.e., even for the offices he holds

103. **have-at-him:** i.e., attack on him

The college of Cardinals. (2.2.115, 119)
From Giovanni Battista Falda,
Nuoua, et essatta pianta del conciaue . . . [1676].

NORFOLK, ⌜*to Suffolk*⌝ Pray God he be not angry.

KING
Who's there, I say? How dare you thrust yourselves
Into my private meditations? Who am I, ha?

NORFOLK
A gracious king that pardons all offenses 80
Malice ne'er meant. Our breach of duty this way
Is business of estate, in which we come
To know your royal pleasure.

KING　　　　　　　　　　　You are too bold.
Go to; I'll make you know your times of business. 85
Is this an hour for temporal affairs, ha?

Enter Wolsey and Campeius, with a commission.

Who's there? My good Lord Cardinal? O my Wolsey,
The quiet of my wounded conscience,
Thou art a cure fit for a king. ⌜*To Campeius.*⌝ You're
　welcome,
Most learnèd reverend sir, into our kingdom. 90
Use us and it.—My good lord, have great care
I be not found a talker.

WOLSEY　　　　　　　Sir, you cannot.
I would your Grace would give us but an hour 95
Of private conference.

KING, ⌜*to Norfolk and Suffolk.*⌝ We are busy. Go.

NORFOLK, ⌜*aside to Suffolk*⌝
This priest has no pride in him?

SUFFOLK, ⌜*aside to Norfolk.*⌝　　　Not to speak of.
I would not be so sick, though for his place. 100
But this cannot continue.

NORFOLK, ⌜*aside to Suffolk*⌝ If it do,
I'll venture one have-at-him.

SUFFOLK, ⌜*aside to Norfolk*⌝　　I another.
　　　　　　　　　　Norfolk and Suffolk exit.

WOLSEY
Your Grace has given a precedent of wisdom 105

107. **voice:** judgment; **Christendom:** the Christian world (See 2.4.223–26 and 3.2.84–87 and note.)

108. **envy:** malice

109. **The Spaniard:** Charles and his court; **blood and favor:** kinship and goodwill; **her:** Queen Katherine

111. **clerks:** clerics, men in holy orders

115. **general tongue:** voice that speaks for all, spokesman

119. **holy conclave:** body of cardinals (See picture, page 78.)

122. **strangers':** foreigners'

124. **by whose virtue: by virtue** of which

127. **unpartial:** impartial

128. **equal:** impartial, just

131. **dear:** i.e., dearly; **that:** i.e., **that** which

132. **less place:** lower status

135. **else:** otherwise

Hitting the mark. (2.1.192)
From Gilles Corrozet, *Hecatongraphie* . . . (1543).

Above all princes in committing freely
Your scruple to the voice of Christendom.
Who can be angry now? What envy reach you?
The Spaniard, tied by blood and favor to her,
Must now confess, if they have any goodness,   110
The trial just and noble; all the clerks—
I mean the learnèd ones in Christian kingdoms—
Have their free voices; Rome, the nurse of judgment,
Invited by your noble self, hath sent
One general tongue unto us, this good man,   115
This just and learnèd priest, Cardinal Campeius,
Whom once more I present unto your Highness.

KING
And once more in mine arms I bid him welcome,
And thank the holy conclave for their loves.
They have sent me such a man I would have wished   120
for.   ⌜*He embraces Campeius.*⌝

CAMPEIUS, ⌜*handing the King a paper*⌝
Your Grace must needs deserve all strangers' loves,
You are so noble. To your Highness' hand
I tender my commission—by whose virtue,
The court of Rome commanding, you, my Lord   125
Cardinal of York, are joined with me their servant
In the unpartial judging of this business.

KING
Two equal men. The Queen shall be acquainted
Forthwith for what you come. Where's Gardiner?

WOLSEY
I know your Majesty has always loved her   130
So dear in heart not to deny her that
A woman of less place might ask by law:
Scholars allowed freely to argue for her.

KING
Ay, and the best she shall have, and my favor
To him that does best. God forbid else. Cardinal,   135

137. **fit:** suitable, ready

144. **In this man's place:** i.e., **secretary** to Henry (line 136)

146. **held:** regarded as

148. **ill:** pernicious, prejudicial

150. **How:** i.e., how say you, what are you saying

151. **will not stick:** are not hesitant; **envied him:** regarded him with dislike

153. **Kept him a foreign man:** i.e., employed him on diplomatic missions abroad; **still:** always

156. **living murmurers:** those alive who complain against constituted authority

157. **There's:** i.e., there are

158. **would needs be:** i.e., insisted upon being; **That good fellow:** i.e., Gardiner

159. **appointment:** direction

160. **near:** i.e., intimate with the king

161. **griped:** clutched at (and then pulled down); **meaner persons:** those of lower status

A fool in motley. (Pro. 16; 1.1.34)
From August Casimir Redel,
Apophtegmata symbolica . . . [n.d.].

Prithee call Gardiner to me, my new secretary.
I find him a fit fellow.　　⌈*Wolsey goes to the door.*⌉

　　　　Enter Gardiner ⌈*to Wolsey.*⌉

WOLSEY, ⌈*aside to Gardiner*⌉
Give me your hand. Much joy and favor to you.
You are the King's now.
GARDINER, ⌈*aside to Wolsey*⌉　　But to be commanded　　140
Forever by your Grace, whose hand has raised me.
KING　Come hither, Gardiner.
　　　　　⌈*The King and Gardiner*⌉ *walk and whisper.*
CAMPEIUS
My lord of York, was not one Doctor Pace
In this man's place before him?
WOLSEY　　　　　　　　Yes, he was.　　145
CAMPEIUS
Was he not held a learnèd man?
WOLSEY　　　　　　　　Yes, surely.
CAMPEIUS
Believe me, there's an ill opinion spread, then,
Even of yourself, Lord Cardinal.
WOLSEY　　　　　　　How? Of me?　　150
CAMPEIUS
They will not stick to say you envied him
And, fearing he would rise—he was so virtuous—
Kept him a foreign man still, which so grieved him
That he ran mad and died.
WOLSEY　　　　　　Heav'n's peace be with him!　155
That's Christian care enough. For living murmurers,
There's places of rebuke. He was a fool,
For he would needs be virtuous. That good fellow
If I command him follows my appointment.
I will have none so near else. Learn this, brother:　160
We live not to be griped by meaner persons.

162. **Deliver this:** i.e., make this known; **modesty:** mildness, moderation

164. **receipt of learning:** i.e., entertaining of scholarly arguments; **Blackfriars:** a Dominican friary that contained a great hall used on occasion for meetings of Parliament (The name **Blackfriars** alludes to the Dominicans' black cloaks. For later theatrical uses of this hall, see "Shakespeare's Theater," page xxxix, above.)

166. **furnished:** equipped, prepared

167. **able:** vigorous, strong

2.3 Anne Bullen pities Katherine, now threatened with divorce. The Lord Chamberlain enters to announce that Henry has created Anne marchioness of Pembroke.

———————

1. **pang:** sharp mental pain; **pinches:** tortures

4. **Pronounce:** report

6. **courses of the sun:** i.e., years

7. **Still:** continually, always

9. **process:** course of time

10. **avaunt:** order to leave; **pity:** i.e., cause for pity

15. **temporal:** worldly, secular (rather than spiritual and eternal)

16. **quarrel:** i.e., quarreler; **Fortune:** See note to 2.2.24–25.

17. **sufferance:** suffering; **panging:** i.e., as painful

20. **stranger:** foreigner

KING, ⌜*to Gardiner*⌝
  Deliver this with modesty to th' Queen.

                              Gardiner exits.
  The most convenient place that I can think of
  For such receipt of learning is Blackfriars.
  There you shall meet about this weighty business.   165
  My Wolsey, see it furnished. O, my lord,
  Would it not grieve an able man to leave
  So sweet a bedfellow? But, conscience, conscience!
  O, 'tis a tender place, and I must leave her.

                              They exit.

Scene 3

Enter Anne Bullen and an old Lady.

ANNE
  Not for that neither. Here's the pang that pinches:
  His Highness having lived so long with her, and she
  So good a lady that no tongue could ever
  Pronounce dishonor of her—by my life,
  She never knew harm-doing!—O, now, after   5
  So many courses of the sun enthroned,
  Still growing in a majesty and pomp, the which
  To leave a thousandfold more bitter than
  'Tis sweet at first t' acquire—after this process,
  To give her the avaunt! It is a pity   10
  Would move a monster.
OLD LADY   Hearts of most hard temper
  Melt and lament for her.
ANNE   O, God's will! Much better
  She ne'er had known pomp; though 't be temporal,   15
  Yet if that quarrel, Fortune, do divorce
  It from the bearer, 'tis a sufferance panging
  As soul and body's severing.
OLD LADY   Alas, poor lady,
  She's a stranger now again!   20

22. **Verily:** in truth

23. **lowly born: born** without rank or status

24. **range:** take one's assigned place; **humble livers:** those of no status; **content:** contentment

25. **perked up:** spruced up, trimmed up; **glist'ring:** glittering

28. **having:** possession

29. **By my troth:** a mild oath (with possible wordplay on **troth** as the promise to marry) **maidenhead:** virginity

31. **Beshrew me:** i.e., curse me, hang me (if I lie)

32. **venture:** risk

33. **For:** in spite of; **spice:** touch, trace, flavor

34. **so fair parts of woman:** i.e., such female beauty **fair:** beautiful **parts:** qualities

36. **Affected:** desired

37. **sooth:** truth

38. **Saving your mincing:** an acerbic rephrasing of the formulaic "**Saving your** honor" **mincing:** affected or elegant speech; or, habit of glossing over unpleasant details

39. **cheveril:** elastic, yielding (**Cheveril** is kid leather.)

44. **threepence bowed:** a bent coin of little value

45. **queen it:** act as **queen** (It has been argued that throughout this scene, there is wordplay on **queen** and *quean*, which means prostitute or strumpet.)

46. **a duchess:** i.e., being **a duchess**

49. **Pluck off a little:** i.e., come down (the social scale) a bit (Literally, **pluck off** means disrobe.)

50. **count:** earl, one rank below a duke

ANNE   So much the more
  Must pity drop upon her. Verily,
  I swear, 'tis better to be lowly born
  And range with humble livers in content
  Than to be perked up in a glist'ring grief   25
  And wear a golden sorrow.

OLD LADY   Our content
  Is our best having.

ANNE   By my troth and maidenhead,
  I would not be a queen.   30

OLD LADY   Beshrew me, I would,
  And venture maidenhead for 't; and so would you,
  For all this spice of your hypocrisy.
  You, that have so fair parts of woman on you,
  Have too a woman's heart, which ever yet   35
  Affected eminence, wealth, sovereignty;
  Which, to say sooth, are blessings; and which gifts,
  Saving your mincing, the capacity
  Of your soft cheveril conscience would receive
  If you might please to stretch it.   40

ANNE   Nay, good troth.

OLD LADY
  Yes, troth, and troth. You would not be a queen?

ANNE
  No, not for all the riches under heaven.

OLD LADY
  'Tis strange. A threepence bowed would hire me,
  Old as I am, to queen it. But I pray you,   45
  What think you of a duchess? Have you limbs
  To bear that load of title?

ANNE   No, in truth.

OLD LADY
  Then you are weakly made. Pluck off a little.
  I would not be a young count in your way   50
  For more than blushing comes to. If your back

52. **vouchsafe:** deign to accept; **this burden:** (1) this title; (2) the weight of the count's body

53. **Ever to get:** i.e., for you **ever to** conceive

57. **little England:** (1) **England** (a comparatively small kingdom); (2) "**Little England** beyond Wales," the name given to the Welsh county of Pembrokeshire because its local population mainly spoke English

58. **emballing:** investing with the ball as an emblem of royalty (with wordplay on *balls* as testicles)

59. **Carnarvanshire:** Caernarfonshire, an impoverished Welsh-speaking county in the north of Wales; **longed:** belonged

60. **Lo:** look

61. **Good morrow:** good morning

62. **conference:** conversation

64. **Not your demand . . . asking:** i.e., it's **not** worth **your asking**

66. **gentle:** suitable for persons of **gentle** (honorable) birth; **becoming:** appropriate for

71. **fair:** beautiful

72. **high note's:** notice by those in **high** position is

74. **Commends . . . you:** i.e., presents his compliments (The phrase **to you** is often deleted by editors to improve the line's metrics.)

75. **purpose:** intend; **flowing:** abundant

76. **Pembroke:** See note to **little England** at line 57 above.

78. **grace:** favor

80. **tender:** offer

81. **nor my prayers:** The word **nor,** which creates a double negative, adds force to the statement.

82. **nor my wishes:** i.e., **nor** are **my wishes**

Cannot vouchsafe this burden, 'tis too weak
Ever to get a boy.

ANNE　　　　　　　How you do talk!
I swear again, I would not be a queen　　　　　　　55
For all the world.

OLD LADY　　　　　In faith, for little England
You'd venture an emballing. I myself
Would for Carnarvanshire, although there longed
No more to th' crown but that. Lo, who comes here?　60

Enter Lord Chamberlain.

CHAMBERLAIN
Good morrow, ladies. What were 't worth to know
The secret of your conference?

ANNE　　　　　　　　　My good lord,
Not your demand; it values not your asking.
Our mistress' sorrows we were pitying.　　　　　65

CHAMBERLAIN
It was a gentle business, and becoming
The action of good women. There is hope
All will be well.

ANNE　　　　　Now, I pray God, amen!

CHAMBERLAIN
You bear a gentle mind, and heav'nly blessings　70
Follow such creatures. That you may, fair lady,
Perceive I speak sincerely, and high note's
Ta'en of your many virtues, the King's Majesty
Commends his good opinion of you to you, and
Does purpose honor to you no less flowing　　75
Than Marchioness of Pembroke, to which title
A thousand pound a year annual support
Out of his grace he adds.

ANNE　　　　　　　　I do not know
What kind of my obedience I should tender.　80
More than my all is nothing, nor my prayers
Are not words duly hallowed, nor my wishes

83. **vanities:** things of no value

85. **return:** i.e., offer in response; **'Beseech:** i.e., I **beseech**

86. **Vouchsafe:** be so good as

90. **approve:** confirm; **fair:** favorable; **conceit:** conception

95. **gem:** ornament; object of priceless worth

96. **lighten:** illuminate; comfort, cheer; **I'll to:** i.e., **I'll** go **to**

99. **this:** i.e., thus

101–2. **nor could / Come . . . late:** i.e., **could** never find the right time   **pat:** opportunely

103. **suit of pounds:** petition for money

105. **compelled fortune:** i.e., good **fortune** forced upon you

106. **open it:** i.e., to petition (but with an allusion to the **fish** opening its **mouth** to feed)

108. **Forty pence:** i.e., I would bet ten groats (the usual amount for a small bet or fee)

111. **mud in Egypt:** i.e., wealth of **Egypt** (which depended on the fertile **mud** left behind by the overflowing Nile)

112. **pleasant:** merry

114. **O'ermount:** rise higher than

115. **pure:** mere, simple

More worth than empty vanities. Yet prayers and
    wishes
Are all I can return. 'Beseech your Lordship,   85
Vouchsafe to speak my thanks and my obedience,
As from a blushing handmaid, to his Highness,
Whose health and royalty I pray for.

CHAMBERLAIN   Lady,
I shall not fail t' approve the fair conceit   90
The King hath of you. (⌈*Aside.*⌉) I have perused her
    well.
Beauty and honor in her are so mingled
That they have caught the King. And who knows yet
But from this lady may proceed a gem   95
To lighten all this isle?—I'll to the King
And say I spoke with you.

ANNE   My honored lord.
                    Lord Chamberlain exits.

OLD LADY   Why, this it is! See, see!
I have been begging sixteen years in court,   100
Am yet a courtier beggarly, nor could
Come pat betwixt too early and too late
For any suit of pounds; and you—O, fate!—
A very fresh fish here—fie, fie, fie upon
This compelled fortune!—have your mouth filled up   105
Before you open it.

ANNE   This is strange to me.

OLD LADY
How tastes it? Is it bitter? Forty pence, no.
There was a lady once—'tis an old story—
That would not be a queen, that would she not,   110
For all the mud in Egypt. Have you heard it?

ANNE
Come, you are pleasant.

OLD LADY   With your theme, I could
O'ermount the lark. The Marchioness of Pembroke?
A thousand pounds a year for pure respect?   115
No other obligation? By my life,

117. **train:** elongated part of robe trailing behind

118. **foreskirt:** the front part of the robe; **By this time:** now

119. **bear a duchess:** be capable of sustaining the title and robes of **a duchess** (though the verb **bear** also suggests sustaining the weight of a man)

122. **particular:** private, personal; **fancy:** fantasy

123. **on 't:** i.e., of it

123–24. **Would . . . jot:** i.e., may I die if this advancement affect my emotions in the least

124. **faints me:** makes me feel faint

127. **deliver:** report

2.4 At the trial, Katherine refuses to have the validity of her marriage judged by the church court, given Wolsey's malice against her. After Katherine departs, Henry clears Wolsey of her accusation that he provoked the king to question the marriage. Henry takes the responsibility himself, and then becomes perturbed at what he sees as the cardinals' delay in resolving his case.

---

0 SD. **sennet:** fanfare of **trumpets** or **cornets** (**Trumpets, sennet, and cornets** suggests some duplication in the stage direction, as is frequent in theatrical manuscripts.) **Vergers:** officials who carry rods before justices; **Scribes:** public functionaries performing secretarial duties; **habit of doctors:** academic robes of **doctors** of laws; **Gentleman . . . pillars:** those who customarily preceded Wolsey in public; **takes place:** sits; **the cloth of state:** canopy

(continued)

That promises more thousands; honor's train
Is longer than his foreskirt. By this time
I know your back will bear a duchess. Say,
Are you not stronger than you were?   120
ANNE   Good lady,
Make yourself mirth with your particular fancy,
And leave me out on 't. Would I had no being
If this salute my blood a jot. It faints me
To think what follows.   125
The Queen is comfortless and we forgetful
In our long absence. Pray do not deliver
What here you've heard to her.
OLD LADY   What do you think me?
                                          They exit.

Scene 4

*Trumpets, sennet, and cornets. Enter two Vergers, with
short silver wands; next them, two Scribes, in the habit of
doctors; after them, the Bishop of Canterbury alone; after
him, the Bishops of Lincoln, Ely, Rochester, and Saint
Asaph; next them, with some small distance, follows a
Gentleman bearing the purse with the great seal, and a
cardinal's hat. Then two Priests, bearing each a silver
cross; then a Gentleman Usher bare-headed, accompanied
with a Sergeant-at-Arms, bearing a silver mace; then two
Gentlemen, bearing two great silver pillars. After them,
side by side, the two Cardinals, ⌈and⌉ two Noblemen with
the sword and mace. The King takes place under the cloth
of state. The two Cardinals sit under him as judges. The
Queen takes place some distance from the King. The
Bishops place themselves on each side the court, in
manner of a consistory; below them the Scribes. The
Lords sit next the Bishops. The rest of the Attendants
⌈including a Crier and the Queen's Gentleman Usher⌉
stand in convenient order about the stage.*

that hangs above a throne; **under:** below; **consistory:** court of judgment, tribunal; bishops' court for ecclesiastical causes; **Crier:** official of a court who makes public announcements

5. **th' authority:** i.e., its **authority; allowed:** acknowledged

18. **stranger:** foreigner

20. **indifferent:** impartial

21. **equal:** equitable, just

24. **put me off:** dismiss me

25. **your good grace:** your favor (The words also suggest "your person," since the king can be called *your Grace.*)

29. **your countenance:** the expression on your face

Fortune with her wheel. (2.2.24–25)
From [John Lydgate,]
The hystorye sege and dystruccyon of Troye [1513].

94

WOLSEY
　Whilst our commission from Rome is read,
　Let silence be commanded.
KING　　　　　　　　　　　　What's the need?
　It hath already publicly been read,
　And on all sides th' authority allowed.
　You may then spare that time.　　　　　　　　　5
WOLSEY　　　　　　　　　　　Be 't so. Proceed.
SCRIBE　Say "Henry King of England, come into the
　court."
CRIER　Henry King of England, come into the court.　10
KING　Here.
SCRIBE　Say "Katherine Queen of England, come into
　the court."
CRIER　Katherine Queen of England, come into the
　court.　　　　　　　　　　　　　　　　　　　15
　　　　The Queen makes no answer, rises out of her
　　　　　chair, goes about the court, comes to the King,
　　　　　　　and kneels at his feet; then speaks.
⌜QUEEN KATHERINE⌝
　Sir, I desire you do me right and justice,
　And to bestow your pity on me; for
　I am a most poor woman and a stranger,
　Born out of your dominions, having here
　No judge indifferent nor no more assurance　　　20
　Of equal friendship and proceeding. Alas, sir,
　In what have I offended you? What cause
　Hath my behavior given to your displeasure
　That thus you should proceed to put me off
　And take your good grace from me? Heaven witness　25
　I have been to you a true and humble wife,
　At all times to your will conformable,
　Ever in fear to kindle your dislike,
　Yea, subject to your countenance, glad or sorry
　As I saw it inclined. When was the hour　　　30
　I ever contradicted your desire,

33. **strove:** i.e., striven
35. **derived:** drawn, brought down
42. **aught:** anything
44. **Against:** toward
50. **wit:** intelligence
51–52. **one / The wisest:** i.e., **the** very **wisest**
52–53. **by many / A year before:** i.e., in **many** years
53. **questioned:** doubted
60. **pleasure:** will
62. **these reverend fathers:** i.e., **the Bishops of Lincoln, Ely, Rochester, and Saint Asaph** (0 SD)
64. **the elect:** i.e., the best (literally, the chosen)
65. **bootless:** to no purpose
66. **longer . . . court:** i.e., **you** wish to delay the work of **the court;** or, **you** entreat **longer** with **the court**

Title page of Raphael Holinshed, . . .
Chronicles . . . (1587).

Or made it not mine too? Or which of your friends
Have I not strove to love, although I knew
He were mine enemy? What friend of mine
That had to him derived your anger did I   35
Continue in my liking? Nay, gave notice
He was from thence discharged? Sir, call to mind
That I have been your wife in this obedience
Upward of twenty years, and have been blessed
With many children by you. If, in the course   40
And process of this time, you can report,
And prove it too, against mine honor aught,
My bond to wedlock or my love and duty
Against your sacred person, in God's name
Turn me away and let the foul'st contempt   45
Shut door upon me, and so give me up
To the sharp'st kind of justice. Please you, sir,
The King your father was reputed for
A prince most prudent, of an excellent
And unmatched wit and judgment. Ferdinand,   50
My father, King of Spain, was reckoned one
The wisest prince that there had reigned by many
A year before. It is not to be questioned
That they had gathered a wise council to them
Of every realm, that did debate this business,   55
Who deemed our marriage lawful. Wherefore I humbly
Beseech you, sir, to spare me till I may
Be by my friends in Spain advised, whose counsel
I will implore. If not, i' th' name of God,
Your pleasure be fulfilled.   60
WOLSEY   You have here, lady,
And of your choice, these reverend fathers, men
Of singular integrity and learning,
Yea, the elect o' th' land, who are assembled
To plead your cause. It shall be therefore bootless   65
That longer you desire the court, as well

67. **quiet:** peace of mind; **rectify:** restore to a normal condition

71. **fit:** appropriate that

76. **pleasure:** wish

79. **We:** royal **we; certain:** i.e., certainly

82. **patient:** calm

85. **Induced:** persuaded; **potent:** strong; **circumstances:** circumstantial evidence

86. **challenge:** objection (usually against a member of a jury in a trial, but here against a **judge** [line 87])

88. **blown this coal:** stirred up this strife

89. **God's dew:** See Shakespeare's *Cymbeline* 5.5.424–25: "The benediction of these covering heavens / Fall on their heads like **dew.**" **quench:** cool, put an end to

96. **stood to:** maintained, been faithful to

97. **gentle:** noble

100. **spleen:** grudge

For your own quiet as to rectify
What is unsettled in the King.

CAMPEIUS   His Grace
Hath spoken well and justly. Therefore, madam, 70
It's fit this royal session do proceed
And that without delay their arguments
Be now produced and heard.

QUEEN KATHERINE   Lord Cardinal,
To you I speak. 75

WOLSEY   Your pleasure, madam.

QUEEN KATHERINE   Sir,
I am about to weep; but thinking that
We are a queen, or long have dreamed so, certain
The daughter of a king, my drops of tears 80
I'll turn to sparks of fire.

WOLSEY   Be patient yet.

QUEEN KATHERINE
I will, when you are humble; nay, before,
Or God will punish me. I do believe,
Induced by potent circumstances, that 85
You are mine enemy, and make my challenge
You shall not be my judge; for it is you
Have blown this coal betwixt my lord and me—
Which God's dew quench! Therefore I say again,
I utterly abhor, yea, from my soul 90
Refuse you for my judge, whom, yet once more,
I hold my most malicious foe and think not
At all a friend to truth.

WOLSEY   I do profess
You speak not like yourself, who ever yet 95
Have stood to charity and displayed th' effects
Of disposition gentle and of wisdom
O'ertopping woman's power. Madam, you do me
 wrong.
I have no spleen against you, nor injustice 100
For you or any. How far I have proceeded,

102. **warranted:** justified, sanctioned

103. **Consistory:** whole body of cardinals presided over by the pope

107. **gainsay my deed:** deny what I have done; **wound:** i.e., impugn (literally, damage as if by piercing)

109. **truth:** integrity

109–11. **If he . . . wrong:** i.e., **if he knows I am** guiltless (**free**) **of** what you have accused me, **he knows** that **I am not free of** the **wrong** you have done me (by accusing me)

113–14. **the which . . . speak in:** i.e., yet **before** the king speaks in reference to this matter

119–20. **humble-mouthed:** i.e., speak as if you were humble

121. **sign:** mark, distinguish, set apart; **place:** high office; **calling:** vocation (as a priest); **in full seeming:** i.e., in a deceptive but entirely convincing appearance

123. **arrogancy:** arrogance; **spleen:** irritable or peevish temper

125. **slightly:** with slight exertion

126. **powers:** powerful people; **retainers:** dependents, followers

127. **Domestics:** household servants

128. **pronounce their office:** declare their function, announce their mode of action (The general sense seems to be that his **words** are transformed into deeds as soon as he speaks them.)

129. **tender:** hold dear; **person's honor:** personal reputation or fame

130. **that again:** so that once more

133. **cause:** case; **'fore:** before

136. **Stubborn:** unyielding; **apt:** ready; inclined

Or how far further shall, is warranted
By a commission from the Consistory,
Yea, the whole Consistory of Rome. You charge me
That I "have blown this coal." I do deny it.   105
The King is present. If it be known to him
That I gainsay my deed, how may he wound,
And worthily, my falsehood, yea, as much
As you have done my truth. If he know
That I am free of your report, he knows   110
I am not of your wrong. Therefore in him
It lies to cure me, and the cure is to
Remove these thoughts from you, the which before
His Highness shall speak in, I do beseech
You, gracious madam, to unthink your speaking   115
And to say so no more.

QUEEN KATHERINE   My lord, my lord,
I am a simple woman, much too weak
T' oppose your cunning. You're meek and humble-
    mouthed;   120
You sign your place and calling, in full seeming,
With meekness and humility, but your heart
Is crammed with arrogancy, spleen, and pride.
You have by fortune and his Highness' favors
Gone slightly o'er low steps, and now are mounted   125
Where powers are your retainers, and your words,
Domestics to you, serve your will as 't please
Yourself pronounce their office. I must tell you,
You tender more your person's honor than
Your high profession spiritual, that again   130
I do refuse you for my judge, and here,
Before you all, appeal unto the Pope
To bring my whole cause 'fore his Holiness,
And to be judged by him.
          She curtsies to the King, and offers to depart.

CAMPEIUS   The Queen is obstinate,   135
Stubborn to justice, apt to accuse it, and

142 SP. GENTLEMAN USHER: See longer note, page 240.

143. **note it:** take notice of it; **keep your way:** keep going

145. **pass on:** continue on your way

149. **Go thy ways:** an indulgent comment on her departure (literally, depart)

151. **naught:** nothing

153. **rare:** splendid, fine

154. **government:** self-control

155. **parts:** qualities

156. **Sovereign:** supreme, most notable; **else:** besides; **speak thee out:** declare or manifest you

159. **Carried herself:** comported or behaved herself

161. **require:** ask, request

165. **satisfied:** compensated, repaid

168. **question on 't:** i.e., inquiry into it; discussion of it

"The spinsters, carders . . . [and] fullers." (1.2.38)
From Johann Amos Comenius, . . .
Orbis sensualium pictus . . . (1700).

Disdainful to be tried by 't. 'Tis not well.
She's going away.
KING   Call her again.
CRIER Katherine, Queen of England, come into the 140
 court.
GENTLEMAN USHER Madam, you are called back.
QUEEN KATHERINE
What need you note it? Pray you, keep your way.
When you are called, return. Now, the Lord help!
They vex me past my patience. Pray you, pass on. 145
I will not tarry; no, nor ever more
Upon this business my appearance make
In any of their courts.
     Queen and her Attendants exit.
KING   Go thy ways, Kate.
That man i' th' world who shall report he has 150
A better wife, let him in naught be trusted,
For speaking false in that. Thou art, alone—
If thy rare qualities, sweet gentleness,
Thy meekness saintlike, wifelike government,
Obeying in commanding, and thy parts 155
Sovereign and pious else, could speak thee out—
The queen of earthly queens. She's noble born,
And like her true nobility she has
Carried herself towards me.
WOLSEY   Most gracious sir, 160
In humblest manner I require your Highness
That it shall please you to declare in hearing
Of all these ears—for where I am robbed and bound,
There must I be unloosed, although not there
At once and fully satisfied—whether ever I 165
Did broach this business to your Highness, or
Laid any scruple in your way which might
Induce you to the question on 't, or ever
Have to you, but with thanks to God for such

170. **spake:** i.e., spoken; **one the least:** i.e., **the very least**

172. **touch:** reproach, blemish

175. **are not to be taught:** i.e., already know

184. **passages:** paths, ways

185. **speak:** i.e., bear witness in favor of

186. **moved:** impelled

188. **mark th' inducement:** consider or give heed to the incentive

191. **on certain:** by reason of some particular

196. **Ere:** before; **determinate:** final

197. **require:** request; **respite:** delay, extension of time

198. **advertise:** inform

200. **Respecting:** with reference to; **dowager:** princess dowager, the title enjoyed by Katherine after the death of her first husband

201. **Sometime:** formerly

203. **a spitting power:** the force of a sharp-pointed rod or spit

205. **mazed:** bewildered, confused

A royal lady, spake one the least word that might 170
Be to the prejudice of her present state,
Or touch of her good person?

KING   My Lord Cardinal,
I do excuse you; yea, upon mine honor,
I free you from 't. You are not to be taught 175
That you have many enemies that know not
Why they are so but, like to village curs,
Bark when their fellows do. By some of these
The Queen is put in anger. You're excused.
But will you be more justified? You ever 180
Have wished the sleeping of this business, never
    desired
It to be stirred, but oft have hindered, oft,
The passages made toward it. On my honor
I speak my good Lord Cardinal to this point 185
And thus far clear him. Now, what moved me to 't,
I will be bold with time and your attention.
Then mark th' inducement. Thus it came; give heed
    to 't:
My conscience first received a tenderness, 190
Scruple, and prick on certain speeches uttered
By th' Bishop of Bayonne, then French ambassador,
Who had been hither sent on the debating
⌜A⌝ marriage 'twixt the Duke of Orleans and
Our daughter Mary. I' th' progress of this business, 195
Ere a determinate resolution, he,
I mean the Bishop, did require a respite
Wherein he might the King his lord advertise
Whether our daughter were legitimate,
Respecting this our marriage with the dowager, 200
Sometime our brother's wife. This respite shook
The bosom of my conscience, entered me,
Yea, with a spitting power, and made to tremble
The region of my breast; which forced such way
That many mazed considerings did throng 205

206. **pressed in:** thrust themselves in (like a crowd, throng, or press of people); **caution:** word of warning; **methought:** it seemed to me

207. **the smile of heaven:** God's favor

210. **Do no more offices of life:** i.e., perform **no more** functions to preserve **life** (with possible word-play on the **offices** or services for the dead)

211. **issue:** offspring

212. **Or:** either

216. **gladded:** gladdened

218. **fail:** death

219. **throe:** spasm of feeling, violent pang of mental anguish; **hulling:** drifting with sails furled

224. **full sick:** entirely **sick; yet:** i.e., is still

225. **By:** i.e., through the agency of

226. **doctors: doctors** of laws (with wordplay on medical **doctors**)

228. **reek:** sweat

229. **moved:** appealed to

231. **spoke:** i.e., spoken

232. **satisfied me:** solved my difficulty

235. **state:** condition; **mighty:** great; **moment:** importance

236. **consequence of dread:** dreadful, fearful **consequence**

236–37. **committed / The ... doubt:** perhaps, distrusted the boldest advice that I had to give (i.e., that the marriage be dissolved)

And pressed in with this caution. First, methought
I stood not in the smile of heaven, who had
Commanded nature that my lady's womb,
If it conceived a male child by me, should
Do no more offices of life to 't than   210
The grave does to th' dead, for her male issue
Or died where they were made, or shortly after
This world had aired them. Hence I took a thought
This was a judgment on me, that my kingdom,
Well worthy the best heir o' th' world, should not   215
Be gladded in 't by me. Then follows that
I weighed the danger which my realms stood in
By this my issue's fail, and that gave to me
Many a groaning throe. Thus hulling in
The wild sea of my conscience, I did steer   220
Toward this remedy whereupon we are
Now present here together. That's to say,
I meant to rectify my conscience, which
I then did feel full sick, and yet not well,
By all the reverend fathers of the land   225
And doctors learnèd. First, I began in private
With you, my Lord of Lincoln. You remember
How under my oppression I did reek
When I first moved you.

LINCOLN   Very well, my liege.   230

KING
I have spoke long. Be pleased yourself to say
How far you satisfied me.

LINCOLN   So please your Highness,
The question did at first so stagger me,
Bearing a state of mighty moment in 't
And consequence of dread, that I committed   235
The daring'st counsel which I had to doubt,
And did entreat your Highness to this course
Which you are running here.

KING   I then moved you,   240

241. **leave:** permission

242. **make this present summons:** i.e., summon **this present** court

244. **by particular consent:** according to the opinion of each of you individually

245. **Under your hands and seals:** i.e., as expressed in writings bearing **your seals**

248. **my allegèd reasons:** i.e., the **reasons** I have advanced

249. **Prove but:** i.e., if you only **prove**

251. **wear our mortal state:** spend the rest of my **mortal** existence

252. **primest:** most excellent

253. **paragoned o':** set forth as the perfect model in

255. **'tis a needful fitness:** it is necessary and appropriate

256. **further day:** a **day** in the future

257. **must be:** i.e., there **must be; motion:** proposal

265. **Break up:** dissolve

266. **set on:** move on, go forward

My Lord of Canterbury, and got your leave
To make this present summons. Unsolicited
I left no reverend person in this court,
But by particular consent proceeded
Under your hands and seals. Therefore go on,   245
For no dislike i' th' world against the person
Of the good queen, but the sharp thorny points
Of my allegèd reasons drives this forward.
Prove but our marriage lawful, by my life
And kingly dignity, we are contented   250
To wear our mortal state to come with her,
Katherine our queen, before the primest creature
That's paragoned o' th' world.

CAMPEIUS   So please your Highness,
The Queen being absent, 'tis a needful fitness   255
That we adjourn this court till further day.
Meanwhile must be an earnest motion
Made to the Queen to call back her appeal
She intends unto his Holiness.

KING, ⌈*aside*⌉   I may perceive   260
These cardinals trifle with me. I abhor
This dilatory sloth and tricks of Rome.
My learnèd and well-belovèd servant Cranmer,
Prithee return. With thy approach, I know,
My comfort comes along.—Break up the court.   265
I say, set on.

                    They exit, in manner as they entered.

HENRY VIII

ACT 3

3.1 Wolsey and Campeius visit Katherine to persuade her to contest the divorce no longer.

---

0 SD. **as at work:** i.e., the actors show the **Queen** and **her women** sewing or doing other handiwork (See picture, page 118.) **as:** i.e., **as** if

2. **Leave:** i.e., **leave** off, stop

3. **Orpheus:** in mythology, a Thracian poet whose music had the power to charm (See picture, page 116.)

7. **sprung:** grew; **as:** i.e., **as** if

11. **lay by:** rested

12–14. **In sweet . . . hearing, die:** i.e., There **is such art in sweet music** that when it is heard, **care** that kills **and grief of heart** either **fall asleep or die.**

16. **An 't . . . Grace:** a polite formula

17. **presence:** i.e., **presence** chamber, where business was conducted

18. **Would they:** do they wish to

A lute. (3.1.1)
From Silvestro Pietrasanta, *Symbola heroica . . .* (1682).

ACT 3

Scene 1

Enter Queen and her Women, as at work.

QUEEN KATHERINE
 Take thy lute, wench. My soul grows sad with troubles.
 Sing, and disperse 'em if thou canst. Leave working.
⌜WOMAN *sings*⌝ *song.*

      Orpheus with his lute made trees
      And the mountaintops that freeze
          Bow themselves when he did sing.   5
      To his music plants and flowers
      Ever sprung, as sun and showers
          There had made a lasting spring.

      Everything that heard him play,
      Even the billows of the sea,   10
          Hung their heads and then lay by.
      In sweet music is such art,
      Killing care and grief of heart
          Fall asleep or, hearing, die.

      Enter a Gentleman.

QUEEN KATHERINE   How now?   15
GENTLEMAN
 An 't please your Grace, the two great cardinals
 Wait in the presence.
QUEEN KATHERINE   Would they speak with me?

113

19. **willed:** wished

20. **Pray:** invite

25. **affairs:** business

26. **But all . . . monks:** Proverbial: "A cowl does **not make** a monk."

28. **part of a housewife:** i.e., performing domestic tasks

29. **all:** entirely a **housewife** (with possible wordplay on *wife*, i.e., to Henry); **against:** in resistance to; **worst:** i.e., **worst** that

31. **May . . . to:** i.e., if you . . . will

35–36. **There's nothing . . . corner:** Proverbial: "Truth seeks no corners."

36. **Would:** i.e., I wish

37. **free:** innocent

38–39. **happy / Above a number:** i.e., happier than many

40. **tried:** judged

41. **Envy:** malice

42. **even:** just

43. **and that . . . wife in:** i.e., concerning my marriage

45–46. **Tanta . . . serenissima:** so great is my integrity of mind toward you, most serene queen (Latin)

48. **truant:** literally, a pupil who, without permission, fails to attend school

GENTLEMAN
    They willed me say so, madam.
QUEEN KATHERINE   Pray their Graces   20
    To come near.   ⌜*Gentleman exits.*⌝
                    What can be their business
    With me, a poor weak woman, fall'n from favor?
    I do not like their coming, now I think on 't.
    They should be good men, their affairs as righteous.   25
    But all hoods make not monks.

        Enter the two Cardinals, Wolsey and Campeius.

WOLSEY   Peace to your Highness.
QUEEN KATHERINE
    Your Graces find me here part of a housewife;
    I would be all, against the worst may happen.
    What are your pleasures with me, reverend lords?   30
WOLSEY
    May it please you, noble madam, to withdraw
    Into your private chamber, we shall give you
    The full cause of our coming.
QUEEN KATHERINE   Speak it here.
    There's nothing I have done yet, o' my conscience,   35
    Deserves a corner. Would all other women
    Could speak this with as free a soul as I do.
    My lords, I care not, so much I am happy
    Above a number, if my actions
    Were tried by ev'ry tongue, ev'ry eye saw 'em,   40
    Envy and base opinion set against 'em,
    I know my life so even. If your business
    Seek me out, and that way I am wife in,
    Out with it boldly. Truth loves open dealing.
WOLSEY *Tanta est erga te mentis integritas, regina*   45
    serenissima—
QUEEN KATHERINE   O, good my lord, no Latin!
    I am not such a truant since my coming

50. **strange:** foreign; **cause:** case
51. **suspicious:** suspect
55. **willing'st:** most deliberate
60. **faith:** loyalty, duty, allegiance
61. **by the way of accusation:** for the purpose of accusing
65. **difference:** The word **difference** could be used to describe disagreements ranging from a simple estrangement to open hostility.
66. **deliver:** declare
67. **free:** magnanimous
71. **still:** always
72. **late:** recent; **censure:** criticism, condemnation
73. **truth:** virtue, integrity; **was:** i.e., went
74. **in a sign:** as **a sign**
79. **suddenly:** without delay, promptly
80. **weight:** importance
81. **wit:** intellect
83. **set:** seated

"Orpheus with his lute." (3.1.3)
From Ovid, . . . *Metamorphoseon* . . . (1565).

As not to know the language I have lived in.
A strange tongue makes my cause more strange, 50
   suspicious.
Pray speak in English. Here are some will thank you,
If you speak truth, for their poor mistress' sake.
Believe me, she has had much wrong. Lord Cardinal,
The willing'st sin I ever yet committed 55
May be absolved in English.

WOLSEY   Noble lady,
I am sorry my integrity should breed—
And service to his Majesty and you—
So deep suspicion, where all faith was meant. 60
We come not by the way of accusation,
To taint that honor every good tongue blesses,
Nor to betray you any way to sorrow—
You have too much, good lady—but to know
How you stand minded in the weighty difference 65
Between the King and you, and to deliver,
Like free and honest men, our just opinions
And comforts to ⌜your⌝ cause.

CAMPEIUS   Most honored madam,
My Lord of York, out of his noble nature, 70
Zeal, and obedience he still bore your Grace,
Forgetting, like a good man, your late censure
Both of his truth and him—which was too far—
Offers, as I do, in a sign of peace,
His service and his counsel. 75

QUEEN KATHERINE, ⌜*aside*⌝   To betray me.—
My lords, I thank you both for your good wills.
You speak like honest men; pray God you prove so.
But how to make you suddenly an answer
In such a point of weight, so near mine honor— 80
More near my life, I fear—with my weak wit,
And to such men of gravity and learning,
In truth I know not. I was set at work

84. **maids:** i.e., ladies-in-waiting; **full:** very

87. **fit:** period, spell

93. **But little:** i.e., **little** (**But** has the general sense of "actually, just, no more nor less than.") **profit:** benefit

96. **desperate:** extremely reckless, utterly careless; **to be honest:** i.e., as **to be** candid, truthful

97. **forsooth:** in truth

98. **weigh out:** measure; or, perhaps, outweigh, counterbalance

99. **grow to:** be an organic or integral part of

102. **would:** wish

105. **main:** principal

108. **o'ertake you:** detect an offense in you, convict you; or, perhaps, get at or surprise you

109. **part away:** depart

112. **Out upon you:** expression of abhorrence or reproach

115. **mistakes:** takes the wrong view of

Women at work. (3.1.0 SD, 28)
From Jan van der Straet,
[. . . *The celebrated Roman women*] (1543).

Among my maids, full little, God knows, looking
Either for such men or such business.   85
For her sake that I have been—for I feel
The last fit of my greatness—good your Graces,
Let me have time and counsel for my cause.
Alas, I am a woman friendless, hopeless.

WOLSEY
Madam, you wrong the King's love with these fears;   90
Your hopes and friends are infinite.

QUEEN KATHERINE   In England
But little for my profit. Can you think, lords,
That any Englishman dare give me counsel,
Or be a known friend, 'gainst his Highness' pleasure,   95
Though he be grown so desperate to be honest,
And live a subject? Nay, forsooth. My friends,
They that must weigh out my afflictions,
They that my trust must grow to, live not here.
They are, as all my other comforts, far hence   100
In mine own country, lords.

CAMPEIUS   I would your Grace
Would leave your griefs and take my counsel.

QUEEN KATHERINE   How, sir?

CAMPEIUS
Put your main cause into the King's protection.   105
He's loving and most gracious. 'Twill be much
Both for your honor better and your cause,
For if the trial of the law o'ertake you,
You'll part away disgraced.

WOLSEY   He tells you rightly.   110

QUEEN KATHERINE
You tell me what you wish for both: my ruin.
Is this your Christian counsel? Out upon you!
Heaven is above all yet; there sits a judge
That no king can corrupt.

CAMPEIUS   Your rage mistakes us.   115

117. **cardinal:** chief (with wordplay on the ecclesiastical rank of **cardinal** and on the term **cardinal virtues** that refers to justice, temperance, prudence, and fortitude)

118. **cardinal sins:** the Seven Deadly Sins: usually, pride, greed, envy, wrath, sloth, gluttony, lechery (with possible wordplay on *card'nal* and *carnal*)

119. **comfort:** At line 68, Wolsey promised to deliver **comforts.**

120. **cordial:** comforting medicine, food, or beverage

121. **lost:** (1) having lost her way; (2) ruined

124. **at once:** all **at once;** one day

126. **a mere distraction:** sheer madness

127. **envy:** malice

129. **professors:** those who openly profess to be Christian

131. **habits:** distinctive attire

133. **has banished me:** i.e., he **has banished me** from

135. **fellowship:** dealing, communication, intercourse

137. **above:** in addition to; **studies:** mental labors

138. **curse:** (1) affliction; (2) accursed person

140. **speak:** describe; **speak** for

145. **Still:** always; **next:** i.e., **next** to

146. **fondness:** affection; foolishness; **superstitious:** idolatrously or extravagantly devoted

QUEEN KATHERINE

  The more shame for you! Holy men I thought you,
  Upon my soul, two reverend cardinal virtues;
  But cardinal sins and hollow hearts I fear you.
  Mend 'em, for shame, my lords. Is this your comfort?
  The cordial that you bring a wretched lady,   120
  A woman lost among you, laughed at, scorned?
  I will not wish you half my miseries;
  I have more charity. But say I warned you:
  Take heed, for heaven's sake, take heed, lest at once
  The burden of my sorrows fall upon you.   125

WOLSEY

  Madam, this is a mere distraction.
  You turn the good we offer into envy.

QUEEN KATHERINE

  You turn me into nothing! Woe upon you
  And all such false professors. Would you have me—
  If you have any justice, any pity,   130
  If you be anything but churchmen's habits—
  Put my sick cause into his hands that hates me?
  Alas, has banished me his bed already,
  His love, too, long ago. I am old, my lords,
  And all the fellowship I hold now with him   135
  Is only my obedience. What can happen
  To me above this wretchedness? All your studies
  Make me a curse like this.

CAMPEIUS   Your fears are worse.

QUEEN KATHERINE

  Have I lived thus long—let me speak myself,   140
  Since virtue finds no friends—a wife, a true one—
  A woman, I dare say without vainglory,
  Never yet branded with suspicion—
  Have I with all my full affections
  Still met the King, loved him next heav'n, obeyed him,   145
  Been, out of fondness, superstitious to him,
  Almost forgot my prayers to content him,

149. **constant woman:** i.e., **woman** faithful

157. **dignities:** high official positions; honorable personal qualities

161. **You have ... hearts:** Proverbial: "Fair face foul heart." (See longer note, page 241.)

166. **Shipwrecked:** shipwrecked

168–70. **the lily ... perish:** See Matthew 6.28 ("Learn how the lilies of the field do grow") and Psalm 103.15–16 ("The days of man are as grass: as a flower of the field, so flourisheth he. For the wind goeth over it, and it is gone, and the place thereof shall know it no more").

172. **ends:** purposes

174. **places:** positions as priests

175. **way:** prescribed course of conduct; path of life; manner; **profession:** i.e., priesthood

179. **carriage:** way of acting; behavior

"The chiding flood." (3.2.244)
From Geoffrey Whitney, *A choice of emblemes . . .* (1586).

And am I thus rewarded? 'Tis not well, lords.
Bring me a constant woman to her husband,
One that ne'er dreamed a joy beyond his pleasure,   150
And to that woman, when she has done most,
Yet will I add an honor: a great patience.

WOLSEY
Madam, you wander from the good we aim at.

QUEEN KATHERINE
My lord, I dare not make myself so guilty
To give up willingly that noble title   155
Your master wed me to. Nothing but death
Shall e'er divorce my dignities.

WOLSEY   Pray hear me.

QUEEN KATHERINE
Would I had never trod this English earth
Or felt the flatteries that grow upon it!   160
You have angels' faces, but heaven knows your hearts.
What will become of me now, wretched lady?
I am the most unhappy woman living.
⌜*To her Women.*⌝ Alas, poor wenches, where are now
    your fortunes?   165
Shipwracked upon a kingdom where no pity,
No friends, no hope, no kindred weep for me,
Almost no grave allowed me, like the lily
That once was mistress of the field and flourished,
I'll hang my head and perish.   170

WOLSEY   If your Grace
Could but be brought to know our ends are honest,
You'd feel more comfort. Why should we, good lady,
Upon what cause, wrong you? Alas, our places,
The way of our profession, is against it.   175
We are to cure such sorrows, not to sow 'em.
For goodness' sake, consider what you do,
How you may hurt yourself, ay, utterly
Grow from the King's acquaintance by this carriage.

184. **even:** unruffled, uniform; **calm:** absolute lack of wind

185. **profess:** i.e., claim to be; **servants:** When used with religious signification, the term might mean **servants** of God or of the church.

189. **doubts:** apprehensions; **false:** counterfeit

191. **it:** i.e., his love; **For:** i.e., as for

193. **studies:** studied efforts

195. **used:** conducted

196. **wit:** intelligence

198. **do my service:** remember me

202. **set footing:** landed

203. **dignities:** high official positions; **so dear:** at such a costly rate

3.2 Courtiers assemble to discuss Wolsey's sudden fall from Henry's favor, Henry's marriage to Anne Bullen, and plans for her coronation. Wolsey enters, unaware of the courtiers but observed by them as he seems troubled in his thoughts. When the king enters and returns to Wolsey some papers that reveal Wolsey's duplicity and greed, the cardinal realizes that he can never restore himself in the king's favor. Wolsey, grieving over his fall and repenting his bad behavior, advises Cromwell about how to secure himself in the king's service.

———————

2. **force them:** urge them, press them home; **a constancy:** persistence

The hearts of princes kiss obedience, 180
So much they love it. But to stubborn spirits
They swell and grow as terrible as storms.
I know you have a gentle, noble temper,
A soul as even as a calm. Pray think us
Those we profess: peacemakers, friends, and servants. 185

CAMPEIUS
Madam, you'll find it so. You wrong your virtues
With these weak women's fears. A noble spirit,
As yours was put into you, ever casts
Such doubts, as false coin, from it. The King loves
you; 190
Beware you lose it not. For us, if you please
To trust us in your business, we are ready
To use our utmost studies in your service.

QUEEN KATHERINE
Do what you will, my lords, and pray forgive me
If I have used myself unmannerly. 195
You know I am a woman, lacking wit
To make a seemly answer to such persons.
Pray do my service to his Majesty.
He has my heart yet and shall have my prayers
While I shall have my life. Come, reverend fathers, 200
Bestow your counsels on me. She now begs
That little thought, when she set footing here,
She should have bought her dignities so dear.

They exit.

Scene 2

*Enter the Duke of Norfolk, Duke of Suffolk, Lord Surrey,
and Lord Chamberlain.*

NORFOLK
If you will now unite in your complaints
And force them with a constancy, the Cardinal

3. **stand under:** bear the burden of; sustain; **omit:** neglect

8. **least:** slightest

9. **Duke:** i.e., of Buckingham

10. **him:** i.e., Wolsey

11. **peers:** nobles

12. **uncontemned:** undespised

13. **Strangely:** coldly; **neglected:** ignored, not treated with proper attention

15. **Out of:** besides, except

16. **speak your pleasures:** say whatever you like

19. **way:** opportunity; **fear:** doubt

20–21. **never attempt / Anything on:** do not try to attack

24. **spell:** enthralling charm; **out:** exhausted, finished

25. **Matter:** cause for action

26–27. **he's settled . . . displeasure:** (1) Wolsey is fixed **in** the king's **displeasure** and not able to extricate himself; (2) the king is fixed **in his displeasure** with Wolsey and will not withdraw from it

32. **In . . . proceedings:** i.e., Wolsey's actions impeding **the divorce**

33. **unfolded:** revealed

36. **practices:** plots, intrigues

Cannot stand under them. If you omit
The offer of this time, I cannot promise
But that you shall sustain more new disgraces   5
With these you bear already.

SURREY   I am joyful
To meet the least occasion that may give me
Remembrance of my father-in-law the Duke,
To be revenged on him.   10

SUFFOLK   Which of the peers
Have uncontemned gone by him, or at least
Strangely neglected? When did he regard
The stamp of nobleness in any person
Out of himself?   15

CHAMBERLAIN   My lords, you speak your pleasures;
What he deserves of you and me I know;
What we can do to him—though now the time
Gives way to us—I much fear. If you cannot
Bar his access to th' King, never attempt   20
Anything on him, for he hath a witchcraft
Over the King in 's tongue.

NORFOLK   O, fear him not.
His spell in that is out. The King hath found
Matter against him that forever mars   25
The honey of his language. No, he's settled,
Not to come off, in his displeasure.

SURREY   Sir,
I should be glad to hear such news as this
Once every hour.   30

NORFOLK   Believe it, this is true.
In the divorce his contrary proceedings
Are all unfolded, wherein he appears
As I would wish mine enemy.

SURREY   How came   35
His practices to light?

SUFFOLK   Most strangely.

SURREY   O, how, how?

39. **miscarried:** got into the wrong hands

42. **stay:** delay

45. **creature:** dependent

48. **work:** produce an effect

49–50. **he coasts / And ... way:** Wolsey moves in a roundabout course.

51–52. **he brings ... death:** He takes action too late. (Proverbial: "**After death** the doctor.") **physic:** medicine

53. **fair:** beautiful

56. **profess:** declare

58. **Trace the conjunction:** mark the marriage (with possible wordplay on the meaning "diagram the position of the planets in the same sign of the zodiac or in adjacent signs"—an astrological determination made on the occasion of an important political event)

62. **Marry:** indeed; **this:** i.e., the news of the **coronation** (line 61), or perhaps of the marriage (which was at first secret); **young:** recent

64. **gallant:** fine-looking; excellent; **complete:** perfect

66. **fall:** drop (with wordplay on **fall** as "give birth")

67. **memorized:** kept alive in memory; made memorable

69. **Digest:** endure, put up with

SUFFOLK
　The Cardinal's letters to the Pope miscarried
　And came to th' eye o' th' King, wherein was read　40
　How that the Cardinal did entreat his Holiness
　To stay the judgment o' th' divorce; for if
　It did take place, "I do," quoth he, "perceive
　My king is tangled in affection to
　A creature of the Queen's, Lady Anne Bullen."　45
SURREY
　Has the King this?
SUFFOLK　　　　　　　　Believe it.
SURREY　　　　　　　　　　　　　Will this work?
CHAMBERLAIN
　The King in this perceives him how he coasts
　And hedges his own way. But in this point　50
　All his tricks founder, and he brings his physic
　After his patient's death: the King already
　Hath married the fair lady.
SURREY　　　　　　　　　　　Would he had!
SUFFOLK
　May you be happy in your wish, my lord,　55
　For I profess you have it.
SURREY　　　　　　　　　　Now, all my joy
　Trace the conjunction!
SUFFOLK　　　　　　　My amen to 't.
NORFOLK　　　　　　　　　　　　All men's.　60
SUFFOLK
　There's order given for her coronation.
　Marry, this is yet but young and may be left
　To some ears unrecounted. But, my lords,
　She is a gallant creature and complete
　In mind and feature. I persuade me, from her　65
　Will fall some blessing to this land which shall
　In it be memorized.
SURREY　　　　　　　　But will the King
　Digest this letter of the Cardinal's?
　The Lord forbid!　70

73. **his:** perhaps, the king's; or, perhaps, Wolsey's

75. **ta'en no leave:** obtained no permission to depart

76. **unhandled:** not dealt with

77. **Is posted:** i.e., has sped off (Literally, *to post* was to travel by relays of horses.)

78. **second:** support; **all his plot:** his whole **plot**

84–87. **He is . . . Christendom:** See longer note, page 241. **is returned in:** has stated by way of a report or verdict

88. **published:** proclaimed

90. **princess dowager:** See note to 2.4.200.

93. **ta'en much pain:** greatly exerted himself (For Cranmer, see picture, page 206.)

101. **packet:** parcel of letters

A jade. (3.2.340)
From Cesare Fiaschi, *Trattato dell'imbrigliare . . . caualli . . .* (1614).

NORFOLK   Marry, amen!
SUFFOLK   No, no.
  There be more wasps that buzz about his nose
  Will make this sting the sooner. Cardinal Campeius
  Is stol'n away to Rome, hath ta'en no leave,   75
  Has left the cause o' th' King unhandled, and
  Is posted as the agent of our cardinal
  To second all his plot. I do assure you
  The King cried "Ha!" at this.
CHAMBERLAIN   Now God incense him,   80
  And let him cry "Ha!" louder.
NORFOLK   But, my lord,
  When returns Cranmer?
SUFFOLK
  He is returned in his opinions, which
  Have satisfied the King for his divorce,   85
  Together with all famous colleges
  Almost in Christendom. Shortly, I believe,
  His second marriage shall be published, and
  Her coronation. Katherine no more
  Shall be called queen, but princess dowager   90
  And widow to Prince Arthur.
NORFOLK   This same Cranmer's
  A worthy fellow, and hath ta'en much pain
  In the King's business.
SUFFOLK   He has, and we shall see him   95
  For it an archbishop.
NORFOLK   So I hear.
SUFFOLK   'Tis so.

  Enter Wolsey and Cromwell, ⌜meeting.⌝

  The Cardinal!
NORFOLK
  Observe, observe; he's moody.   ⌜*They stand aside.*⌝ 100
WOLSEY   The packet, Cromwell;
  Gave 't you the King?

104. **paper:** wrapper

105. **Presently:** immediately

107. **heed:** careful attention

109. **Attend:** wait on

111. **abroad:** out of his **bedchamber** (line 103)

112. **by this:** by now

117. **fair visage:** beautiful face

122. **whet:** sharpen; **to:** against

125. **late:** former

127–28. **This . . . goes:** Proverbial: "To go **out** like a **candle** in snuff." **clear:** brightly **snuff it:** i.e., trim its wick (There may be wordplay here on *bullen* as "peeled hemp stalks," which were used as candlewicks.)

130. **spleeny:** peevish (Since the spleen was also associated with courage, resolution, gaiety, and high spirit, **spleeny** is sometimes thought to have one or more of these meanings.)

131. **Our cause:** Roman Catholicism

132. **hard-ruled:** i.e., stubborn (literally, hard to control or influence)

133. **arch-one:** chief one (with wordplay on *archbishop*)

133–34. **one / Hath:** i.e., **one** who has

CROMWELL   To his own hand, in 's bedchamber.

WOLSEY
  Looked he o' th' inside of the paper?

CROMWELL   Presently   105
  He did unseal them, and the first he viewed,
  He did it with a serious mind; a heed
  Was in his countenance. You he bade
  Attend him here this morning.

WOLSEY   Is he ready   110
  To come abroad?

CROMWELL   I think by this he is.

WOLSEY   Leave me awhile.   *Cromwell exits.*
  ⌐*Aside.*¬ It shall be to the Duchess of Alençon,
  The French king's sister; he shall marry her.
  Anne Bullen? No, I'll no Anne Bullens for him.   115
  There's more in 't than fair visage. Bullen?
  No, we'll no Bullens. Speedily I wish
  To hear from Rome. The Marchioness of Pembroke!

NORFOLK
  He's discontented.   120

SUFFOLK   Maybe he hears the King
  Does whet his anger to him.

SURREY   Sharp enough,
  Lord, for thy justice!

WOLSEY, ⌐*aside*¬
  The late queen's gentlewoman, a knight's daughter,   125
  To be her mistress' mistress? The Queen's queen?
  This candle burns not clear. 'Tis I must snuff it;
  Then out it goes. What though I know her virtuous
  And well-deserving? Yet I know her for
  A spleeny Lutheran, and not wholesome to   130
  Our cause that she should lie i' th' bosom of
  Our hard-ruled king. Again, there is sprung up
  An heretic, an arch-one, Cranmer, one

135. **his oracle:** considered his infallible guide

137–38. **fret the string, / The master-cord on 's heart:** i.e., fray or devour the heartstring, in early anatomy thought to be a tendon or nerve that braced and sustained the heart (with wordplay on the musical meanings of **fret, string,** and **cord**/chord) **on 's:** i.e., of his

139 SD. **reading of a schedule:** i.e., **reading** an official list (of Wolsey's assets and expenses)

141. **To his own portion:** i.e., for himself; **expense:** spending

150. **straight:** straightaway, at once

152. **anon:** instantly

153. **against:** toward

156. **mutiny:** contention, struggle

158. **required:** demanded; **wot you:** do you know

159. **on my conscience:** a mild oath

160. **Forsooth:** in truth; **importing:** making known, signifying

161. **several:** individual, particular; **parcels:** items; **plate:** utensils for domestic use, often of silver or gold

162. **stuffs:** fabrics

163. **proud rate:** magnificent value

163–64. **outspeaks ... subject:** i.e., describes more than **a subject** should possess

Hath crawled into the favor of the King
And is his oracle.   135
NORFOLK   He is vexed at something.
SURREY
I would 'twere something that would fret the string,
The master-cord on 's heart.
SUFFOLK   The King, the King!

*Enter King, reading of a schedule, ⌜with Lovell
and Attendants.⌝*

KING
What piles of wealth hath he accumulated   140
To his own portion! And what expense by th' hour
Seems to flow from him! How i' th' name of thrift
Does he rake this together? ⌜*Seeing the nobles.*⌝ Now,
    my lords,
Saw you the Cardinal?   145
NORFOLK, ⌜*indicating Wolsey*⌝   My lord, we have
Stood here observing him. Some strange commotion
Is in his brain. He bites his lip, and starts,
Stops on a sudden, looks upon the ground,
Then lays his finger on his temple, straight   150
Springs out into fast gait, then stops again,
Strikes his breast hard, and anon he casts
His eye against the moon. In most strange postures
We have seen him set himself.
KING   It may well be   155
There is a mutiny in 's mind. This morning
Papers of state he sent me to peruse,
As I required, and wot you what I found?
There—on my conscience, put unwittingly—
Forsooth, an inventory, thus importing   160
The several parcels of his plate, his treasure,
Rich stuffs and ornaments of household, which
I find at such proud rate that it outspeaks
Possession of a subject.

167. **withal:** with

170. **he should still:** i.e., he would be allowed to continue to

172. **below the moon:** earthly, secular, rather than spiritual

173 SD. **whispers:** i.e., **whispers** to

177. **stuff:** matter of thought (with wordplay on the **stuffs** listed in the **inventory** [line 160], wordplay that continues with **inventory, steal, audit, husband**)

178. **graces:** virtues

180. **leisure:** deliberation; **span:** space of time

182. **ill:** poor; **husband:** household manager (Wordplay on Henry's ironic take on his relations with Katherine is implied in line 183. It has been argued that Henry uses the wordplay to mock Wolsey's judging Henry as a bad **husband** to Katherine and opposing his marriage to Anne.)

185. **holy offices:** ceremonial services, religious observances, divine services or worship

189. **amongst my brethren mortal:** i.e., a **mortal** human being

190. **tendance:** attention

193. **lend:** give, afford

197. **words are no deeds:** Proverbial: "Saying is one thing, doing another." (The **words/deeds** dichotomy dominates lines 191–99.)

NORFOLK   It's heaven's will!   165
  Some spirit put this paper in the packet
  To bless your eye withal.
KING, ⌈*studying Wolsey*⌉   If we did think
  His contemplation were above the earth
  And fixed on spiritual object, he should still   170
  Dwell in his musings, but I am afraid
  His thinkings are below the moon, not worth
  His serious considering.
                    King takes his seat, whispers Lovell,
                              who goes to the Cardinal.
WOLSEY   Heaven forgive me!
  Ever God bless your Highness.   175
KING   Good my lord,
  You are full of heavenly stuff and bear the inventory
  Of your best graces in your mind, the which
  You were now running o'er. You have scarce time
  To steal from spiritual leisure a brief span   180
  To keep your earthly audit. Sure, in that
  I deem you an ill husband, and am glad
  To have you therein my companion.
WOLSEY   Sir,
  For holy offices I have a time; a time   185
  To think upon the part of business which
  I bear i' th' state; and Nature does require
  Her times of preservation, which perforce
  I, her frail son, amongst my brethren mortal,
  Must give my tendance to.   190
KING   You have said well.
WOLSEY
  And ever may your Highness yoke together,
  As I will lend you cause, my doing well
  With my well saying.
KING   'Tis well said again,   195
  And 'tis a kind of good deed to say well.
  And yet words are no deeds. My father loved you;

198–99. **with his deed . . . upon you:** Henry VII appointed Wolsey royal chaplain and later dean of Lincoln.

199. **had my office:** i.e., became king

200. **next:** nearest; **not alone:** not only

201. **home:** i.e., to you

202. **pared:** reduced; **havings:** possessions

205. **increase:** advance

207. **prime:** first; **state:** government

208. **pronounce:** declare

209. **withal:** in addition

210. **bound:** under obligations of duty and gratitude

211. **graces:** favors

213. **studied purposes:** i.e., efforts (literally, deliberate intentions or aims); **which:** i.e., the **royal graces** (Some editors see **which** as referring instead to Wolsey's efforts to **requite** the king.)

216. **filed:** kept pace; **ends:** objectives

217. **so, that:** only to the extent **that**

220. **undeserver:** unworthy person

221. **allegiant:** loyal

227–28. **The honor . . . act of it:** i.e., **the honor of** being **loyal** is the reward of loyalty (Proverbial: "Virtue is its own reward.")

229. **foulness:** i.e., ugliness, repulsiveness (of disloyalty)

He said he did, and with his deed did crown
His word upon you. Since I had my office
I have kept you next my heart, have not alone   200
Employed you where high profits might come home,
But pared my present havings to bestow
My bounties upon you.

WOLSEY, ⌜*aside*⌝   What should this mean?

SURREY, ⌜*aside*⌝
The Lord increase this business!   205

KING   Have I not made you
The prime man of the state? I pray you tell me
If what I now pronounce you have found true;
And, if you may confess it, say withal
If you are bound to us or no. What say you?   210

WOLSEY
My sovereign, I confess your royal graces,
Showered on me daily, have been more than could
My studied purposes requite, which went
Beyond all man's endeavors. My endeavors
Have ever come too short of my desires,   215
Yet ⌜filed⌝ with my abilities. Mine own ends
Have been mine so, that evermore they pointed
To th' good of your most sacred person and
The profit of the state. For your great graces
Heaped upon me, poor undeserver, I   220
Can nothing render but allegiant thanks,
My prayers to heaven for you, my loyalty,
Which ever has and ever shall be growing
Till death—that winter—kill it.

KING   Fairly answered.   225
A loyal and obedient subject is
Therein illustrated. The honor of it
Does pay the act of it, as, i' th' contrary,
The foulness is the punishment. I presume
That, as my hand has opened bounty to you,   230
My heart dropped love, my power rained honor, more

233. **function:** action, activity; **of your power:** i.e., within **your power**

234. **notwithstanding ... duty:** perhaps, in spite of **your bond of duty** (to Rome or to the priesthood); or, perhaps, over and above **your bond of duty** (to me)

235. **in love's particular:** i.e., out of personal affection, in the personal devotion of friendship

239. **mine own, that am, have, and will be:** i.e., my good, present, past, and future (This difficult line is often emended.)

244. **chiding flood:** brawling torrent (See picture, page 122.)

245. **break:** i.e., stem, hold back (literally, dash in pieces)

249. **open 't:** lay it bare

251. **after:** afterward

256. **chafèd:** angered

257. **galled:** vexed

258. **makes him nothing:** i.e., destroys him

261. **undone:** ruined; **accompt:** account

On you than any, so your hand and heart,
Your brain, and every function of your power
Should—notwithstanding that your bond of duty
As 'twere in love's particular—be more   235
To me, your friend, than any.

WOLSEY   I do profess
That for your Highness' good I ever labored
More than mine own, that am, have, and will be—
Though all the world should crack their duty to you   240
And throw it from their soul, though perils did
Abound as thick as thought could make 'em, and
Appear in forms more horrid—yet my duty,
As doth a rock against the chiding flood,
Should the approach of this wild river break,   245
And stand unshaken yours.

KING   'Tis nobly spoken.—
Take notice, lords: he has a loyal breast,
For you have seen him open 't.
                              ⌜*He hands Wolsey papers.*⌝
                                   Read o'er this,   250
And after, this; and then to breakfast with
What appetite you have.
                    King exits, frowning upon the Cardinal;
                         the nobles throng after him smiling
                              and whispering, ⌜*and exit.*⌝

WOLSEY   What should this mean?
What sudden anger's this? How have I reaped it?
He parted frowning from me, as if ruin   255
Leaped from his eyes. So looks the chafèd lion
Upon the daring huntsman that has galled him,
Then makes him nothing. I must read this paper—
I fear, the story of his anger.
                              ⌜*He reads one of the papers.*⌝
                                   'Tis so.   260
This paper has undone me. 'Tis th' accompt
Of all that world of wealth I have drawn together

263. **popedom:** papacy (According to John Foxe's *Book of Martyrs,* Wolsey, in his desire to be named pope, distributed bribes.)

264. **fee:** bribe

265. **Fit:** suitable; **cross:** contrarious, perverse

268. **device:** stratagem, contrivance

270. **take right:** has the intended result

271. **bring me off:** rescue me

274. **writ:** i.e., wrote

276. **full meridian:** i.e., culmination, **full** splendor (Literally, the point at which a star or the sun attains its highest altitude.)

278. **exhalation:** meteor (See picture below.)

280. **pleasure:** will

282. **presently:** at once

287. **commission:** warrant

289. **cross:** contradict; oppose

291. **do it:** i.e., **carry authority** (lines 287–88)

"A bright exhalation." (3.2.278)
From Hartmann Schedel, *Liber chronicorum* [1493].

For mine own ends—indeed, to gain the popedom
And fee my friends in Rome. O negligence,
Fit for a fool to fall by! What cross devil   265
Made me put this main secret in the packet
I sent the King? Is there no way to cure this?
No new device to beat this from his brains?
I know 'twill stir him strongly; yet I know
A way, if it take right, in spite of fortune   270
Will bring me off again.   ⌈*He looks at another paper.*⌉
                    What's this? "To th' Pope"?
The letter, as I live, with all the business
I writ to 's Holiness. Nay then, farewell!
I have touched the highest point of all my greatness,   275
And from that full meridian of my glory
I haste now to my setting. I shall fall
Like a bright exhalation in the evening
And no man see me more.

*Enter to Wolsey the Dukes of Norfolk and Suffolk, the
    Earl of Surrey, and the Lord Chamberlain.*

NORFOLK
  Hear the King's pleasure, cardinal, who commands   280
      you
  To render up the great seal presently
  Into our hands, and to confine yourself
  To Asher House, my Lord of Winchester's,
  Till you hear further from his Highness.   285
WOLSEY   Stay.
  Where's your commission, lords? Words cannot carry
  Authority so weighty.
SUFFOLK   Who dare cross 'em,
  Bearing the King's will from his mouth expressly?   290
WOLSEY
  Till I find more than will or words to do it—
  I mean your malice—know, officious lords,
  I dare and must deny it. Now I feel

294. **envy:** malice

296. **it:** malice; **sleek:** oily, specious; **wanton:** merciless

297. **everything:** i.e., **everything** that

299. **Christian warrant:** justification by **Christian** principles or example (This bitter sarcasm continues in the word **rewards** [i.e., punishments] in line 300.)

300. **fit:** appropriate

303. **place:** official position of Lord Chancellor; **honors:** titles

305. **letters patents: letters** from a sovereign conferring an office or title

310. **Within these forty hours:** i.e., less than **forty hours** ago (**Forty** was used indefinitely, usually to express a large number. Here it seems to mean a smaller number.)

313. **scarlet sin:** a reference to Wolsey's cardinal's robes and perhaps an allusion to Isaiah 1.18: "Though your sins were as crimson, they shall be made white as snow; though they were red like scarlet, they shall be as wool."

316. **parts:** qualities, abilities

317. **Weighed:** equaled in value; **Plague of:** may a pestilence take

319. **his succor:** i.e., where I could be of help to him (See 2.1.52–57.)

320. **gav'st:** ascribed to

324. **credit:** reputation

327. **end:** death

Of what coarse metal you are molded, envy;
How eagerly you follow my disgraces,   295
As if it fed you, and how sleek and wanton
You appear in everything may bring my ruin.
Follow your envious courses, men of malice;
You have Christian warrant for 'em, and no doubt
In time will find their fit rewards. That seal   300
You ask with such a violence, the King,
Mine and your master, with his own hand gave me;
Bade me enjoy it, with the place and honors,
During my life; and to confirm his goodness,
Tied it by letters patents. Now, who'll take it?   305

SURREY
The King that gave it.

WOLSEY   It must be himself, then.

SURREY
Thou art a proud traitor, priest.

WOLSEY   Proud lord, thou liest.
Within these forty hours Surrey durst better   310
Have burnt that tongue than said so.

SURREY   Thy ambition,
Thou scarlet sin, robbed this bewailing land
Of noble Buckingham, my father-in-law.
The heads of all thy brother cardinals,   315
With thee and all thy best parts bound together,
Weighed not a hair of his. Plague of your policy!
You sent me Deputy for Ireland,
Far from his succor, from the King, from all
That might have mercy on the fault thou gav'st him,   320
Whilst your great goodness, out of holy pity,
Absolved him with an ax.

WOLSEY   This, and all else
This talking lord can lay upon my credit,
I answer, is most false. The Duke by law   325
Found his deserts. How innocent I was
From any private malice in his end,

328. **cause:** case

333. **Dare mate:** i.e., I **dare** rival or vie with

336. **long coat:** clerical robe; **protects you:** i.e., shields you from the challenge your words invite

337. **else:** otherwise

339. **fellow:** person of no esteem or worth

340. **jaded:** driven off as if we were jades (broken-down horses) See picture, page 130. **scarlet:** the color of the cardinal's robes

341. **his Grace:** i.e., Wolsey

342. **dare:** dazzle; **larks:** birds that could be captured when dazzled by a mirror or piece of bright cloth (For a specific allusion here, see longer note, page 241.)

346. **gleaning:** gathering

347. **extortion:** undue exercise of authority

349. **writ:** i.e., wrote

353. **issues:** children, especially sons and heirs

354. **he:** i.e., Wolsey; **gentlemen:** a rank far lower than that of their noble fathers

355. **articles:** distinct charges in an accusation

357. **sacring bell:** small bell rung to summon people (after the Reformation) either to attend morning prayers or to receive communion during a church service; **brown wench:** See longer note to line 342, page 241.

359. **methinks:** it seems to me

361. **hand:** possession

362. **thus much:** i.e., but I can say this **much**

His noble jury and foul cause can witness.—
If I loved many words, lord, I should tell you
You have as little honesty as honor,   330
That in the way of loyalty and truth
Toward the King, my ever royal master,
Dare mate a sounder man than Surrey can be,
And all that love his follies.

SURREY   By my soul,   335
Your long coat, priest, protects you; thou shouldst feel
My sword i' th' life blood of thee else.—My lords,
Can you endure to hear this arrogance?
And from this fellow? If we live thus tamely,
To be thus jaded by a piece of scarlet,   340
Farewell, nobility. Let his Grace go forward
And dare us with his cap, like larks.

WOLSEY   All goodness
Is poison to thy stomach.

SURREY   Yes, that goodness   345
Of gleaning all the land's wealth into one,
Into your own hands, card'nal, by extortion;
The goodness of your intercepted packets
You writ to th' Pope against the King. Your goodness,
Since you provoke me, shall be most notorious.—   350
My Lord of Norfolk, as you are truly noble,
As you respect the common good, the state
Of our despised nobility, our issues,
Whom, if he live, will scarce be gentlemen,
Produce the grand sum of his sins, the articles   355
Collected from his life.—I'll startle you
Worse than the sacring bell when the brown wench
Lay kissing in your arms, Lord Cardinal.

WOLSEY
How much, methinks, I could despise this man,
But that I am bound in charity against it!   360

NORFOLK
Those articles, my lord, are in the King's hand;
But thus much, they are foul ones.

365. **truth:** steadfast allegiance

368. **shall:** i.e., **shall** come

372. **dare:** meet defiantly; **objections:** accusations

373. **want:** lack

374. **Have at you:** an exclamation used by a fighter as he begins his attack

376. **wrought:** contrived; **legate:** representative of the pope, armed with his authority

377. **maimed the jurisdiction of:** i.e., rendered powerless

378. **writ:** wrote

379. **ego et rex meus:** I and my king (Latin)

380. **still:** always

384. **Emperor:** Holy Roman Emperor Charles V; **made bold:** ventured, presumed so far as

386. **commission:** body of persons charged with some official function

387. **Gregory de Cassado:** English ambassador to the papal court

388. **allowance:** permission

389. **Ferrara:** a city-state in central Italy

390. **mere:** sheer

391. **Your . . . coin:** See picture, page 150.

392. **innumerable:** countless; **substance:** wealth

393. **got:** gotten, obtained

WOLSEY   So much fairer
  And spotless shall mine innocence arise
  When the King knows my truth.   365
SURREY   This cannot save you.
  I thank my memory I yet remember
  Some of these articles, and out they shall.
  Now, if you can blush and cry "Guilty," cardinal,
  You'll show a little honesty.   370
WOLSEY   Speak on, sir.
  I dare your worst objections. If I blush,
  It is to see a nobleman want manners.
SURREY
  I had rather want those than my head. Have at you:
  First, that without the King's assent or knowledge,   375
  You wrought to be a legate, by which power
  You maimed the jurisdiction of all bishops.
NORFOLK
  Then, that in all you writ to Rome, or else
  To foreign princes, *"ego et rex meus"*
  Was still inscribed, in which you brought the King   380
  To be your servant.
SUFFOLK   Then, that without the knowledge
  Either of king or council, when you went
  Ambassador to the Emperor, you made bold
  To carry into Flanders the great seal.   385
SURREY
  Item, you sent a large commission
  To Gregory de Cassado, to conclude,
  Without the King's will or the state's allowance,
  A league between his Highness and Ferrara.
SUFFOLK
  That out of mere ambition you have caused   390
  Your holy hat to be stamped on the King's coin.
SURREY
  Then, that you have sent innumerable substance—
  By what means got I leave to your own conscience—

394–95. **To furnish . . . dignities:** i.e., as bribes in a bid for the papacy **furnish:** supply **dignities:** high official positions

395. **mere:** utter; **undoing:** destruction

397. **of you:** about you

400. **'Tis virtue:** i.e., it is virtuous not to **press** him

401. **open:** exposed

407. **legative:** as papal legate

408. **compass:** scope; **praemunire:** See longer note, page 242.

409. **sued:** enforced

410. **tenements:** buildings, dwellings

411. **Chattels:** personal possessions

412. **Out of the King's protection:** i.e., made an outlaw; **my charge:** the duty entrusted to me

414. **For:** i.e., as **for**

421. **state:** condition

423. **honors:** (1) glories; (2) titles

425. **easy:** comfortable; **full:** most

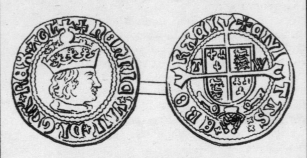

A Wolsey half groat. (3.2.390-91)
From Edward Hawkins,
The silver coins of England . . . (1841).

To furnish Rome and to prepare the ways
You have for dignities, to the mere undoing   395
Of all the kingdom. Many more there are
Which, since they are of you, and odious,
I will not taint my mouth with.

CHAMBERLAIN   O, my lord,
Press not a falling man too far! 'Tis virtue.   400
His faults lie open to the laws; let them,
Not you, correct him. My heart weeps to see him
So little of his great self.

SURREY   I forgive him.

SUFFOLK
Lord Cardinal, the King's further pleasure is—   405
Because all those things you have done of late
By your power legative within this kingdom
Fall into th' compass of a *praemunire*—
That therefore such a writ be sued against you,
To forfeit all your goods, lands, tenements,   410
⌈Chattels,⌉ and whatsoever, and to be
Out of the King's protection. This is my charge.

NORFOLK
And so we'll leave you to your meditations
How to live better. For your stubborn answer
About the giving back the great seal to us,   415
The King shall know it and, no doubt, shall thank
    you.
So, fare you well, my little good Lord Cardinal.

WOLSEY
So, farewell to the little good you bear me.
                              All but Wolsey exit.
Farewell? A long farewell to all my greatness!   420
This is the state of man: today he puts forth
The tender leaves of hopes; tomorrow blossoms
And bears his blushing honors thick upon him;
The third day comes a frost, a killing frost,
And when he thinks, good easy man, full surely   425

428. **wanton:** playful; **bladders:** i.e., inflated **bladders,** to keep them afloat

433. **rude:** rough, violent

434. **Vain pomp and glory of this world:** During the Church of England's baptismal ceremony the sponsors are asked "Dost thou forsake . . . the **vain pomp and glory of** the **world?**"

435. **I feel . . . opened:** Acts 16.14: "whose heart the Lord opened."

435–36. **O, how . . . favors:** Psalm 118.9: "It is better to trust in the Lord than to have confidence in princes."

438. **aspect:** look, glance; **their ruin:** i.e., the **ruin** they cause

439. **have:** (1) bring about; (2) experience

440. **Lucifer:** the brightest of the archangels, who, out of pride, challenged God for supremacy and was cast into hell forever (Isaiah 14.12: "How art thou fallen from heaven, **O Lucifer,** son of the morning.")

441 SD. **amazed:** bewildered, stunned

446. **an:** if

451. **I know myself now:** See note to 2.2.26.

452. **dignities:** high official positions

His greatness is a-ripening, nips his root,
And then he falls, as I do. I have ventured,
Like little wanton boys that swim on bladders,
This many summers in a sea of glory,
But far beyond my depth. My high-blown pride   430
At length broke under me and now has left me,
Weary and old with service, to the mercy
Of a rude stream that must forever hide me.
Vain pomp and glory of this world, I hate you.
I feel my heart new opened. O, how wretched   435
Is that poor man that hangs on princes' favors!
There is betwixt that smile we would aspire to,
That sweet aspect of princes, and their ruin,
More pangs and fears than wars or women have;
And when he falls, he falls like Lucifer,   440
Never to hope again.

          Enter Cromwell, standing amazed.

                    Why, how now, Cromwell?
CROMWELL
  I have no power to speak, sir.
WOLSEY   What, amazed
  At my misfortunes? Can thy spirit wonder   445
  A great man should decline? Nay, an you weep,
  I am fall'n indeed.
CROMWELL   How does your Grace?
WOLSEY   Why, well.
  Never so truly happy, my good Cromwell.   450
  I know myself now, and I feel within me
  A peace above all earthly dignities,
  A still and quiet conscience. The King has cured me—
  I humbly thank his Grace—and from these shoulders,
  These ruined pillars, out of pity, taken   455
  A load would sink a navy: too much honor.
  O, 'tis a burden, Cromwell, 'tis a burden
  Too heavy for a man that hopes for heaven.

459. **right:** proper

460. **methinks:** it seems to me

463. **weak-hearted:** fainthearted

465. **heaviest:** most distressing

466. **displeasure:** trouble, unpleasant relation

474. **run his course:** died; **sleeps in blessings:** has been granted salvation

475. **orphans' tears:** The Lord Chancellor was the general guardian of minors.

478. **Installed:** invested in the office of

481. **long:** i.e., **long** ago

482. **in open:** openly, in public

483. **voice:** common talk

Bevis fighting Asparte. (1.1.44)
From John Ashton, *Romances of chivalry . . .* (1887).

CROMWELL
  I am glad your Grace has made that right use of it.
WOLSEY
  I hope I have. I am able now, methinks,   460
  Out of a fortitude of soul I feel,
  To endure more miseries and greater far
  Than my weak-hearted enemies dare offer.
  What news abroad?
CROMWELL   The heaviest and the worst   465
  Is your displeasure with the King.
WOLSEY   God bless him.
CROMWELL
  The next is that Sir Thomas More is chosen
  Lord Chancellor in your place.
WOLSEY   That's somewhat sudden.   470
  But he's a learnèd man. May he continue
  Long in his Highness' favor and do justice
  For truth's sake and his conscience, that his bones,
  When he has run his course and sleeps in blessings,
  May have a tomb of orphans' tears wept on him.   475
  What more?
CROMWELL   That Cranmer is returned with welcome,
  Installed Lord Archbishop of Canterbury.
WOLSEY
  That's news indeed.
CROMWELL   Last, that the Lady Anne,   480
  Whom the King hath in secrecy long married,
  This day was viewed in open as his queen,
  Going to chapel, and the voice is now
  Only about her coronation.
WOLSEY
  There was the weight that pulled me down.   485
    O Cromwell,
  The King has gone beyond me. All my glories
  In that one woman I have lost forever.

490. **noble troops:** crowds of attendants of **noble** rank

495. **true:** loyal

498. **hopeful:** promising

499. **use:** opportunity

510. **play the woman:** i.e., weep

513. **dull:** inanimate; cheerless

516. **sounded:** i.e., measured (The literal meaning of *to sound*—to measure the depth of a body of water using a line and sinker or some comparable device—is continued in the words **"all the depths and shoals."**)

517. **wrack:** ruin, downfall

519. **Mark:** observe

520. **charge thee:** exhort you authoritatively

521. **By . . . angels:** See note to line 440.

522. **The image of his maker:** Genesis 1.26: "God said, Let us make **man** in our **image." win:** gain

The water Spagnell.

A spaniel. (5.2.195)
From Edward Topsell,
The historie of foure-footed beastes . . . (1607).

No sun shall ever usher forth mine honors,
Or gild again the noble troops that waited   490
Upon my smiles. Go, get thee from me, Cromwell.
I am a poor fall'n man, unworthy now
To be thy lord and master. Seek the King;
That sun, I pray, may never set! I have told him
What and how true thou art. He will advance thee;   495
Some little memory of me will stir him—
I know his noble nature—not to let
Thy hopeful service perish too. Good Cromwell,
Neglect him not. Make use now, and provide
For thine own future safety.   500
CROMWELL, ⌈*weeping*⌉   O, my lord,
Must I then leave you? Must I needs forgo
So good, so noble, and so true a master?
Bear witness, all that have not hearts of iron,
With what a sorrow Cromwell leaves his lord.   505
The King shall have my service, but my prayers
Forever and forever shall be yours.
WOLSEY, ⌈*weeping*⌉
Cromwell, I did not think to shed a tear
In all my miseries, but thou hast forced me,
Out of thy honest truth, to play the woman.   510
Let's dry our eyes. And thus far hear me, Cromwell,
And when I am forgotten, as I shall be,
And sleep in dull cold marble, where no mention
Of me more must be heard of, say I taught thee;
Say Wolsey, that once trod the ways of glory   515
And sounded all the depths and shoals of honor,
Found thee a way, out of his wrack, to rise in,
A sure and safe one, though thy master missed it.
Mark but my fall and that that ruined me.
Cromwell, I charge thee, fling away ambition!   520
By that sin fell the angels; how can man, then,
The image of his maker, hope to win by it?

523. **Love thyself last:** Philippians 2.3: "In meekness of mind every man esteem other better than himself." **cherish . . . thee:** Luke 6.27–28: "**Love** your enemies; do well to them which **hate** you."

525. **Still . . . peace:** Romans 12.18: "As much as in you is, have **peace** with all men." **Still:** always

526. **envious:** malicious

527. **ends:** objectives

532. **robe:** clerical habit

537. **naked:** defenseless

Falling from the tree of Fortune. (2.3.14–18)
From *Fortunes tennis-ball:*
a warning to . . . nursers of pride . . . (1640).

Love thyself last; cherish those hearts that hate thee.
Corruption wins not more than honesty.
Still in thy right hand carry gentle peace   525
To silence envious tongues. Be just, and fear not.
Let all the ends thou aim'st at be thy country's,
Thy God's, and truth's. Then if thou fall'st, O Cromwell,
Thou fall'st a blessèd martyr.
Serve the King. And, prithee, lead me in.   530
There take an inventory of all I have
To the last penny; 'tis the King's. My robe
And my integrity to heaven is all
I dare now call mine own. O Cromwell, Cromwell,
Had I but served my God with half the zeal   535
I served my king, He would not in mine age
Have left me naked to mine enemies.

CROMWELL
Good sir, have patience.

WOLSEY   So I have. Farewell,
The hopes of court! My hopes in heaven do dwell.   540

                              They exit.

HENRY VIII

ACT 4

4.1 The procession returns from Anne's coronation, which is then described by a gentleman who was in attendance.

———

1. **well met:** an expression of welcome
3. **stand:** position
5. **all my business:** i.e., the whole errand on which I've come; or, perhaps, **all** that concerns me at the moment
10. **at full:** fully, completely; **royal minds:** generous **minds;** loyalty to the king
11. **rights:** due; **forward:** ready, eager
12. **shows:** large-scale displays, such as masques or processions
13. **sights:** spectacles
15. **better:** more favorably; **taken:** accepted; interpreted

An hautboy. (1.4.0, 83; 4.1.40 SDD)
From Balthasar Küchler, *Repraesentatio der fürstlichen Auffzug vnd Ritterspil* . . . [1611].

ACT 4

Scene 1

*Enter two Gentlemen, meeting one another, ⌜the First
Gentleman carrying a paper.⌝*

FIRST GENTLEMAN
  You're well met once again.
SECOND GENTLEMAN   So are you.
FIRST GENTLEMAN
  You come to take your stand here and behold
  The Lady Anne pass from her coronation?
SECOND GENTLEMAN
  'Tis all my business. At our last encounter,   5
  The Duke of Buckingham came from his trial.
FIRST GENTLEMAN
  'Tis very true. But that time offered sorrow,
  This general joy.
SECOND GENTLEMAN 'Tis well. The citizens
  I am sure have shown at full their royal minds,
  As, let 'em have their rights, they are ever forward   10
  In celebration of this day with shows,
  Pageants, and sights of honor.
FIRST GENTLEMAN   Never greater,
  Nor, I'll assure you, better taken, sir.   15
SECOND GENTLEMAN
  May I be bold to ask what that contains,
  That paper in your hand?
FIRST GENTLEMAN   Yes, 'tis the list

19–20. those . . . coronation: According to the account in Holinshed's *Chronicles,* "the king caused . . . proclamations to be made that all men that claimed to . . . execute any office [perform any service] at the . . . coronation . . . should put their grant [promise] . . . before Charles **duke of Suffolk**."

22. High Steward: an officer appointed only for the coronation, at which he presides

23. Earl Marshal: a high officer who manages or arranges great ceremonies

25. beholding: beholden, obliged

27. her business: the matter concerning her

30. order: rank, status (i.e., bishops or other learned clergy)

31. late: recent

32. lay: resided

33. cited: summoned officially

34. not appearance: failure to appear

35. main assent: general judicial concurrence

37. late: former; **of none effect:** void, invalid

38. was removed: has been moved

40 SD. Hautboys . . . trumpets: In the Folio, this stage direction is massed in a single stage direction with those that here appear separately through 67 SD. (See "An Introduction to This Text," page lii.) **flourish:** fanfare

41. close: near

41 SD. purse: See note to 1.1.135 SD. **mace:** scepter or staff of office; **Garter:** i.e., **Garter** King of Arms, one of three chief heralds of the College of Arms; **gilt:** gilded, or covered with a thin layer of gold

42. royal: splendid; **train:** procession

Of those that claim their offices this day
By custom of the coronation.   20
The Duke of Suffolk is the first, and claims
To be High Steward; next, the Duke of Norfolk,
He to be Earl Marshal. You may read the rest.
⌈*He offers him the paper.*⌉

⌈SECOND⌉ GENTLEMAN
    I thank you, sir. Had I not known those customs,
    I should have been beholding to your paper.   25
    But I beseech you, what's become of Katherine,
    The Princess Dowager? How goes her business?

FIRST GENTLEMAN
    That I can tell you too. The Archbishop
    Of Canterbury, accompanied with other
    Learnèd and reverend fathers of his order,   30
    Held a late court at Dunstable, six miles off
    From Ampthill, where the Princess lay, to which
    She was often cited by them, but appeared not;
    And, to be short, for not appearance and
    The King's late scruple, by the main assent   35
    Of all these learnèd men she was divorced,
    And the late marriage made of none effect;
    Since which she was removed to Kymmalton,
    Where she remains now sick.

SECOND GENTLEMAN   Alas, good lady!   40
            Hautboys. A lively flourish of trumpets.
    The trumpets sound. Stand close. The Queen is coming.

*Then, ⌈enter⌉ two Judges; Lord Chancellor, with purse
and mace before him. Choristers singing. Music.
⌈Enter⌉ Mayor of London, bearing the mace. Then
Garter, in his coat of arms, and on his head he wore a
gilt copper crown.*

A royal train, believe me! These I know.

42 SD. **demi-coronal:** half-circle of gold or gems; **Collars of S's:** ornamental chains consisting of a series of S's either joined together side by side or fastened in a row upon a band or ribbon

46 SD. **estate:** state

51 SD. **four of the Cinque-ports:** i.e., representatives from **four of** a group of five **ports** on the southeast coast of England; **in her hair:** i.e., with **her hair** let down, in the custom of a bride

55. **all the Indies:** i.e., the East and the West **Indies,** both fabled as regions of great wealth

56. **strains:** clasps tightly in his arms

59. **cloth of honor:** canopy

61. **happy:** fortunate; **all:** i.e., **all** who

King Richard III. (1.2.226; 2.1.128)
From John Taylor, *All the workes of . . .* (1630).

⌜*Enter*⌝ *Marques Dorset, bearing a scepter of gold; on his
head a demi-coronal of gold. With him, the Earl of
Surrey, bearing the rod of silver with the dove, crowned
with an earl's coronet. Collars of S's.*

Who's that that bears the scepter?
FIRST GENTLEMAN   Marques Dorset,
  And that the Earl of Surrey with the rod.   45
SECOND GENTLEMAN
  A bold brave gentleman.

    ⌜*Enter*⌝ *Duke of Suffolk, in his robe of estate, his
coronet on his head, bearing a long white wand, as High
Steward. With him, the Duke of Norfolk, with the rod of
Marshalship, a coronet on his head. Collars of S's.*

                        That should be
  The Duke of Suffolk.
FIRST GENTLEMAN   'Tis the same: High Steward.
SECOND GENTLEMAN
  And that my Lord of Norfolk?   50
FIRST GENTLEMAN   Yes.

⌜*Enter*⌝ *a canopy, borne by four of the Cinque-ports,
under it the Queen in her robe, in her hair, richly
adorned with pearl, crowned. On each side her, the
Bishops of London and Winchester.*

SECOND GENTLEMAN   Heaven bless thee!
  Thou hast the sweetest face I ever looked on.—
  Sir, as I have a soul, she is an angel.
  Our king has all the Indies in his arms,   55
  And more, and richer, when he strains that lady.
  I cannot blame his conscience.
FIRST GENTLEMAN   They that bear
  The cloth of honor over her are four barons
  Of the Cinque-ports.   60
SECOND GENTLEMAN
  Those men are happy, and so are all are near her.

61 SD. **Enter the Old Duchess:** See longer note, page 242.

66. **falling ones:** meteors (with wordplay on the women's **falling** from chastity)

68. **broiling:** subjected to great heat

69. **th' Abbey:** Westminster **Abbey,** site of Anne's coronation

71. **mere:** utter; **rankness:** excess; foul smell; **their:** i.e., the crowd's

77. **speak:** describe

Men in doublets. (4.1.90)
From [Robert Greene,]
A quip for an vpstart courtier . . . (1620).

⌈*Enter*⌉ *the Old Duchess of Norfolk, in a coronal of*
gold wrought with flowers, bearing the Queen's train.
Certain Ladies or Countesses, with plain circlets of gold
without flowers.

I take it she that carries up the train
Is that old noble lady, Duchess of Norfolk.

FIRST GENTLEMAN
It is, and all the rest are countesses.

SECOND GENTLEMAN
Their coronets say so. These are stars indeed.   65

⌈FIRST GENTLEMAN⌉
And sometimes falling ones.

SECOND GENTLEMAN   No more of that.
          ⌈*The Coronation procession exits, having*
passed⌉ *over the stage in order and state, and then*
          a great flourish of trumpets.

          Enter a third Gentleman.

FIRST GENTLEMAN
God save you, sir. Where have you been broiling?

THIRD GENTLEMAN
Among the crowd i' th' Abbey, where a finger
Could not be wedged in more. I am stifled   70
With the mere rankness of their joy.

SECOND GENTLEMAN   You saw
The ceremony?

THIRD GENTLEMAN   That I did.

FIRST GENTLEMAN   How was it?   75

THIRD GENTLEMAN
Well worth the seeing.

SECOND GENTLEMAN   Good sir, speak it to us!

THIRD GENTLEMAN
As well as I am able. The rich stream
Of lords and ladies, having brought the Queen

80. **fell off:** withdrew

83–84. **opposing . . . people:** openly placing **the beauty of her person** directly before **the people**

85. **goodliest:** i.e., most beautiful

88. **shrouds:** ropes forming part of the standing rigging of a ship

90. **Doublets:** close-fitting jackets worn by men (See picture, page 168.)

92. **Great-bellied:** pregnant (See picture, page 172.)

93. **rams:** battering **rams**

94. **press:** crowd

97. **piece:** length of cloth

99. **modest:** moderate

102. **bowed her:** i.e., **bowed**

104. **makings:** i.e., trappings, accoutrements (**Makings of a queen** means, literally, materials of which **a queen** is made)

105. **As:** i.e., namely; **Edward Confessor's crown:** i.e., the **crown** of **Edward** the **Confessor,** saint and king of England (1042–66)

106. **The rod . . . peace:** Holinshed: "**the rod** of ivory with the dove"

108. **music:** musicians

109. **Te Deum:** a hymn that begins "We praise thee, O God"; **parted:** departed

110. **full state:** great pomp and solemnity; great train

113. **more:** longer

To a prepared place in the choir, fell off   80
A distance from her, while her Grace sat down
To rest awhile, some half an hour or so,
In a rich chair of state, opposing freely
The beauty of her person to the people.
Believe me, sir, she is the goodliest woman   85
That ever lay by man, which when the people
Had the full view of, such a noise arose
As the shrouds make at sea in a stiff tempest—
As loud and to as many tunes. Hats, cloaks,
Doublets, I think, flew up, and had their faces   90
Been loose, this day they had been lost. Such joy
I never saw before. Great-bellied women
That had not half a week to go, like rams
In the old time of war, would shake the press
And make 'em reel before 'em. No man living   95
Could say "This is my wife there," all were woven
So strangely in one piece.
SECOND GENTLEMAN   But what followed?
THIRD GENTLEMAN
At length her Grace rose, and with modest paces
Came to the altar, where she kneeled and saintlike   100
Cast her fair eyes to heaven and prayed devoutly,
Then rose again and bowed her to the people.
When by the Archbishop of Canterbury
She had all the royal makings of a queen—
As, holy oil, Edward Confessor's crown,   105
The rod, and bird of peace, and all such emblems—
Laid nobly on her; which performed, the choir,
With all the choicest music of the kingdom,
Together sung *Te Deum.* So she parted,
And with the same full state paced back again   110
To York Place, where the feast is held.
FIRST GENTLEMAN   Sir,
You must no more call it "York Place"; that's past,

117. **lately:** recently

118. **fresh:** i.e., as if new; not faded or worn; active

121. **the one of Winchester:** i.e., **Gardiner**

122. **preferred:** promoted

125. **held:** regarded as

129. **friend:** i.e., **friend** who

134. **Master o' th' Jewel House:** The **master** of the king's **Jewel House** was in charge of the crown jewels and other royal valuables. (For **Cromwell** [line 131], see picture, page 216.)

141. **Something:** to some extent

A "great-bellied" woman with her midwife. (4.1.92)
From James Wolveridge, *Speculum matricis* . . . (1671).

For since the Cardinal fell, that title's lost.
'Tis now the King's and called "Whitehall." 115

THIRD GENTLEMAN   I know it,
But 'tis so lately altered that the old name
Is fresh about me.

SECOND GENTLEMAN What two reverend bishops
Were those that went on each side of the Queen? 120

THIRD GENTLEMAN
Stokeley and Gardiner, the one of Winchester,
Newly preferred from the King's secretary,
The other London.

SECOND GENTLEMAN He of Winchester
Is held no great good lover of the Archbishop's, 125
The virtuous Cranmer.

THIRD GENTLEMAN   All the land knows that.
However, yet there is no great breach. When it comes,
Cranmer will find a friend will not shrink from him.

SECOND GENTLEMAN
Who may that be, I pray you? 130

THIRD GENTLEMAN   Thomas Cromwell,
A man in much esteem with th' King, and truly
A worthy friend. The King has made him
Master o' th' Jewel House,
And one already of the Privy Council. 135

SECOND GENTLEMAN
He will deserve more.

THIRD GENTLEMAN   Yes, without all doubt.
Come, gentlemen, you shall go my way,
Which is to th' court, and there you shall be my
   guests, 140
Something I can command. As I walk thither,
I'll tell you more.

BOTH   You may command us, sir.

They exit.

4.2 The dying Princess Dowager Katherine and her attendant Griffith provide contrasting accounts of the character of the newly dead Wolsey. The sleeping Katherine is then granted a vision of eternal paradise. She wakes to be visited by an ambassador from her nephew, the Emperor Charles. She appeals to the ambassador to intercede with Henry on behalf of her daughter and her attendants, and exits to die.

---

3. **loaden branches: branches** loaded with leaves, fruit, ice, or snow

4. **leave:** abandon; **Reach:** i.e., bring me

5. **ease:** comfort, absence of pain

10. **Out of:** on account of

12. **happily:** appropriately

14. **Well:** i.e., **he died well** (lines 11–12); **voice:** common talk

15. **stout:** brave

17. **sorely:** severely; **tainted:** corrupted; guilty; **answer:** defense against the charges on which he was arrested

21. **easy roads:** moderate spells of riding

23. **convent:** body of monks

27. **for charity:** i.e., as an act of Christian love

28. **eagerly:** harshly, fiercely

Scene 2

Enter Katherine Dowager, sick, led between Griffith, her
gentleman usher, and Patience, her woman.

GRIFFITH
  How does your Grace?
KATHERINE   O Griffith, sick to death.
  My legs like loaden branches bow to th' earth,
  Willing to leave their burden. Reach a chair.
                                    ⌜*She sits.*⌝
  So. Now, methinks, I feel a little ease.   5
  Didst thou not tell me, Griffith, as thou ledst me,
  That the great child of honor, Cardinal Wolsey,
  Was dead?
GRIFFITH   Yes, madam, but I ⌜think⌝ your Grace,
  Out of the pain you suffered, gave no ear to 't.   10
KATHERINE
  Prithee, good Griffith, tell me how he died.
  If well, he stepped before me happily
  For my example.
GRIFFITH   Well, the voice goes, madam;
  For after the stout Earl Northumberland   15
  Arrested him at York and brought him forward,
  As a man sorely tainted, to his answer,
  He fell sick suddenly and grew so ill
  He could not sit his mule.
KATHERINE   Alas, poor man!   20
GRIFFITH
  At last, with easy roads, he came to Leicester,
  Lodged in the abbey, where the reverend abbot
  With all his convent honorably received him;
  To whom he gave these words: "O Father Abbot,
  An old man, broken with the storms of state,   25
  Is come to lay his weary bones among you.
  Give him a little earth, for charity."
  So went to bed, where eagerly his sickness

32. **sorrows:** lamentations

36. **speak:** describe

38. **stomach:** pride; obstinacy; malice

39. **suggestion:** underhand dealing; incitement to evil; false representation

40. **Tied:** brought into bondage; **Simony:** buying and selling of clerical positions

41. **th' presence:** the king's presence chamber, where state business was conducted

42. **double:** deceitful; ambiguous

44. **pitiful:** i.e., (seemingly) compassionate, tender

47. **Of his own body:** i.e., in his sexual morality; **ill:** reprehensible

50–51. **Men's . . . water:** Proverbial: "Injuries are written **in brass,** but benefits **in water."**

52. **speak his good:** describe **his good** qualities

54. **else:** otherwise

56. **stock:** ancestry

59. **Exceeding:** i.e., exceedingly; **fair-spoken:** courteous, smooth-tongued

60. **Lofty:** haughty

61. **sought him:** Holinshed: **"sought** his friendship"

62. **unsatisfied:** i.e., insatiable; **getting:** accumulating wealth

Pursued him still; and three nights after this,
About the hour of eight, which he himself   30
Foretold should be his last, full of repentance,
Continual meditations, tears, and sorrows,
He gave his honors to the world again,
His blessèd part to heaven, and slept in peace.

KATHERINE
So may he rest. His faults lie gently on him!   35
Yet thus far, Griffith, give me leave to speak him,
And yet with charity. He was a man
Of an unbounded stomach, ever ranking
Himself with princes; one that by suggestion
Tied all the kingdom. Simony was fair play.   40
His own opinion was his law. I' th' presence
He would say untruths, and be ever double
Both in his words and meaning. He was never,
But where he meant to ruin, pitiful.
His promises were, as he then was, mighty,   45
But his performance, as he is now, nothing.
Of his own body he was ill, and gave
The clergy ill example.

GRIFFITH   Noble madam,
Men's evil manners live in brass; their virtues   50
We write in water. May it please your Highness
To hear me speak his good now?

KATHERINE   Yes, good Griffith;
I were malicious else.

GRIFFITH   This cardinal,   55
Though from an humble stock, undoubtedly
Was fashioned to much honor. From his cradle
He was a scholar, and a ripe and good one:
Exceeding wise, fair-spoken, and persuading;
Lofty and sour to them that loved him not,   60
But, to those men that sought him, sweet as summer.
And though he were unsatisfied in getting,
Which was a sin, yet in bestowing, madam,

64–65. **Ever . . . you:** i.e., the two colleges he built in your cities **witness** to his **princely** generosity

66. **one of which:** i.e., the college in **Ipswich**

67. **good:** goodness; **did:** made, created

68. **The other:** i.e., the college he founded in **Oxford** (line 66), which became Christ Church College (Its quadrangle remains **unfinished.**)

69. **art:** scholarship; **still so rising:** i.e., its reputation constantly growing greater (with wordplay on **rising** because the college was never fully raised or constructed) **still:** always

72. **felt:** became conscious of

75. **fearing:** revering

77. **speaker:** proclaimer, celebrator

80. **Whom:** i.e., him **whom**

81. **religious:** scrupulous, exact; **modesty:** moderation, clemency

83. **set me lower:** arrange for me to recline more

85. **sad:** mournful; **note:** tune

86. **my knell:** i.e., the song heralding my death (literally, the sound of a bell rung solemnly immediately after a death)

89. **Softly:** quietly

89 SD. **tripping:** dancing; **bays:** bay leaves, emblems of triumph, usually worn by conquerors or poets; **vizards:** masks; **palm:** In Revelation 7.9, those praising God carry palms. **congee:** bow in courtesy; **changes:** rounds in dancing; **other next:** i.e., **next; in their dancing:** i.e., still **dancing** (For **vizards,** see picture, page 180.)

He was most princely. Ever witness for him
Those twins of learning that he raised in you,   65
Ipswich and Oxford, one of which fell with him,
Unwilling to outlive the good that did it;
The other, though unfinished, yet so famous,
So excellent in art, and still so rising,
That Christendom shall ever speak his virtue.   70
His overthrow heaped happiness upon him,
For then, and not till then, he felt himself,
And found the blessedness of being little.
And, to add greater honors to his age
Than man could give him, he died fearing God.   75

KATHERINE
After my death I wish no other herald,
No other speaker of my living actions,
To keep mine honor from corruption
But such an honest chronicler as Griffith.
Whom I most hated living, thou hast made me,   80
With thy religious truth and modesty,
Now in his ashes honor. Peace be with him!—
Patience, be near me still, and set me lower.
I have not long to trouble thee.—Good Griffith,
Cause the musicians play me that sad note   85
I named my knell, whilst I sit meditating
On that celestial harmony I go to.
                    Sad and solemn music.

GRIFFITH
She is asleep. Good wench, let's sit down quiet,
For fear we wake her. Softly, gentle Patience.
                    ⌈*They sit.*⌉

The Vision.

*Enter, solemnly tripping one after another, six
Personages clad in white robes, wearing on their
heads garlands of bays, and golden vizards on their
faces, branches of bays or palm in their hands. They*

98. **thousand:** i.e., a **thousand**
103. **fancy:** imagination
104. **music:** musicians; **leave:** cease
105. **heavy:** tedious
106. **note:** perceive

Vizards. (4.2.89 SD)
From Guillaume de La Perrière,
Le théâtre des bons engins . . . [1539?].

*first congee unto her, then dance; and, at certain
changes, the first two hold a spare garland over her
head, at which the other four make reverent curtsies.
Then the two that held the garland deliver the same
to the other next two, who observe the same order in
their changes and holding the garland over her head;
which done, they deliver the same garland to the last
two, who likewise observe the same order. At which,
as it were by inspiration, she makes in her sleep
signs of rejoicing and holdeth up her hands to
heaven; and so, in their dancing, vanish, carrying
the garland with them.*

> *The music continues.*

KATHERINE, ⌈*waking*⌉

Spirits of peace, where are you? Are you all gone, 90
And leave me here in wretchedness behind you?

GRIFFITH

Madam, we are here.

KATHERINE   It is not you I call for.
Saw you none enter since I slept?

GRIFFITH   None, madam. 95

KATHERINE

No? Saw you not, even now, a blessed troop
Invite me to a banquet, whose bright faces
Cast thousand beams upon me, like the sun?
They promised me eternal happiness
And brought me garlands, Griffith, which I feel 100
I am not worthy yet to wear. I shall, assuredly.

GRIFFITH

I am most joyful, madam, such good dreams
Possess your fancy.

KATHERINE   Bid the music leave.
They are harsh and heavy to me.   *Music ceases.* 105

PATIENCE, ⌈*aside to Griffith*⌉   Do you note
How much her Grace is altered on the sudden?

109. **earthy cold:** i.e., **cold** as earth (as if her body were already dead and turning into earth, which, as one of the four elements, was associated with **cold**); **Mark:** observe

110. **going:** dying

112. **An 't like your Grace:** a minimally polite form of address

113. **saucy:** insolent, presumptuous

114. **reverence:** respect, deference

115. **to blame:** blameworthy, guilty

116. **lose:** fail to maintain; **wonted:** accustomed

117. **Go to:** an expression of remonstrance

119. **staying:** waiting

121. **Admit:** allow

122. **fellow:** person of no worth

125. **should be:** i.e., are, must **be**

127. **Your servant:** a form of greeting

129. **strangely:** unfavorably; extremely

CARLO V·IMP·

Charles V, the Holy Roman Emperor.
(1.1.207; 2.2.30–31, 109)
From [Pompilio Totti,]
Ritratti et elogii di capitani illustri . . . (1635).

How long her face is drawn? How pale she looks,
And of an earthy cold? Mark her eyes.
GRIFFITH, ⌜*aside to Patience*⌝
　　She is going, wench. Pray, pray.　　　　　　　　110
PATIENCE　　　　　　　　Heaven comfort her!

Enter a Messenger.

MESSENGER, ⌜*to Katherine*⌝
　　An 't like your Grace—
KATHERINE　　　　　　You are a saucy fellow.
　　Deserve we no more reverence?
GRIFFITH, ⌜*to Messenger*⌝　　　You are to blame,　115
　　Knowing she will not lose her wonted greatness,
　　To use so rude behavior. Go to. Kneel.
MESSENGER, ⌜*kneeling*⌝
　　I humbly do entreat your Highness' pardon.
　　My haste made me unmannerly. There is staying
　　A gentleman sent from the King to see you.　　120
KATHERINE
　　Admit him entrance, Griffith.　　⌜*Messenger rises.*⌝
　　　　　　　　　　But this fellow
　　Let me ne'er see again.　　　　*Messenger exits.*

Enter Lord Capuchius.

　　　　　　　　If my sight fail not,
　　You should be Lord Ambassador from the Emperor,　125
　　My royal nephew, and your name Capuchius.
CAPUCHIUS
　　Madam, the same. Your servant.
KATHERINE　　　　　　O my lord,
　　The times and titles now are altered strangely
　　With me since first you knew me. But I pray you,　130
　　What is your pleasure with me?
CAPUCHIUS　　　　　　Noble lady,
　　First, mine own service to your Grace; the next,
　　The King's request that I would visit you,

136. **commendations:** compliments, greetings

140. **physic:** medicine; **had:** would have

151. **Most willing:** i.e., I am **most willing** to do so

153. **model:** image; **daughter:** i.e., Katherine's and Henry's **daughter,** Mary

155. **breeding:** upbringing, education

162. **both my fortunes:** i.e., my good fortune as queen, and my bad as princess dowager

164. **now:** i.e., at the point of death

Two-faced Fortune turning her wheel.
From Giovanni Boccaccio, *A treatise . . . shewing . . . the falles of . . . princes . . .* (1554).

Who grieves much for your weakness, and by me 135
Sends you his princely commendations,
And heartily entreats you take good comfort.

KATHERINE
O, my good lord, that comfort comes too late;
'Tis like a pardon after execution.
That gentle physic given in time had cured me. 140
But now I am past all comforts here but prayers.
How does his Highness?

CAPUCHIUS   Madam, in good health.

KATHERINE
So may he ever do, and ever flourish,
When I shall dwell with worms, and my poor name 145
Banished the kingdom.—Patience, is that letter
I caused you write yet sent away?

PATIENCE   No, madam.
⌜*She presents a paper to Katherine, who gives*
                              it to Capuchius.⌝

KATHERINE
Sir, I most humbly pray you to deliver
This to my lord the King— 150

CAPUCHIUS   Most willing, madam.

KATHERINE
In which I have commended to his goodness
The model of our chaste loves, his young daughter—
The dews of heaven fall thick in blessings on her!—
Beseeching him to give her virtuous breeding— 155
She is young and of a noble, modest nature;
I hope she will deserve well—and a little
To love her for her mother's sake that loved him,
Heaven knows how dearly. My next poor petition
Is that his noble Grace would have some pity 160
Upon my wretched women, that so long
Have followed both my fortunes faithfully,
Of which there is not one, I dare avow—
And now I should not lie—but will deserve,

166. **honesty:** chastity; **decent:** modest, proper; **carriage:** behavior

167. **right:** altogether

168. **sure:** i.e., surely; **happy:** fortunate

169. **men:** male attendants and servants

174. **able:** suitable

179. **last right:** final justice (with wordplay on Roman Catholic *last rites*, Holy Communion and Extreme Unction administered to the dying)

181. **fashion:** form

184. **long:** i.e., longtime

188. **must to:** i.e., **must** go **to**

190. **used:** treated

191. **maiden flowers:** i.e., **flowers** that are emblems of chastity

193. **lay me forth:** stretch me out and prepare me for burial

195. **can:** i.e., **can** say or **can** do

we dzum that domes day now at hand:
Doth call all soldiers to deathes band.

A figure in a burial shroud. (4.2.193)
From [Richard Day,]
A booke of christian prayers . . . (1578).

For virtue and true beauty of the soul, 165
For honesty and decent carriage,
A right good husband. Let him be a noble;
And sure those men are happy that shall have 'em.
The last is for my men—they are the poorest,
But poverty could never draw 'em from me— 170
That they may have their wages duly paid 'em,
And something over to remember me by.
If heaven had pleased to have given me longer life
And able means, we had not parted thus.
These are the whole contents. And, good my lord, 175
By that you love the dearest in this world,
As you wish Christian peace to souls departed,
Stand these poor people's friend, and urge the King
To do me this last right.
CAPUCHIUS   By heaven, I will, 180
Or let me lose the fashion of a man!
KATHERINE
I thank you, honest lord. Remember me
In all humility unto his Highness.
Say his long trouble now is passing
Out of this world. Tell him in death I blessed him, 185
For so I will. Mine eyes grow dim. Farewell,
My lord.—Griffith, farewell.—Nay, Patience,
You must not leave me yet. I must to bed;
Call in more women. When I am dead, good wench,
Let me be used with honor. Strew me over 190
With maiden flowers, that all the world may know
I was a chaste wife to my grave. Embalm me,
Then lay me forth. Although unqueened, yet like
A queen and daughter to a king inter me.
I can no more. 195
                    They exit, leading Katherine.

HENRY VIII

ACT 5

5.1 The new archbishop of Canterbury, Cranmer, is under attack because his religious beliefs seem heretical. The king, after receiving news that Anne is in labor, summons Cranmer, assures him of royal support, and gives him a ring to show the Privy Council if need be. The king is then told of the birth of his daughter.

---

3. **necessities:** necessary acts
4. **repair:** restore, renew
8. **Whither:** i.e., where are you going
10. **primero:** a gambling card game
12. **must:** i.e., **must** go
13. **take my leave:** say goodbye
15. **An if:** i.e., **if**
16. **offense:** (1) breach of trust; (2) imposition on my part
17. **touch:** brief statement, hint
18. **at midnight:** i.e., in the middle of the night

A christening ceremony. (5.3.38; 5.4.0 SD)
From [Richard Day,]
A booke of christian prayers . . . (1578).

ACT 5

Scene 1

*Enter Gardiner, Bishop of Winchester, a Page with a
torch before him, met by Sir Thomas Lovell.*

GARDINER
  It's one o'clock, boy, is 't not?
PAGE   It hath struck.
GARDINER
  These should be hours for necessities,
  Not for delights; times to repair our nature
  With comforting repose, and not for us   5
  To waste these times.—Good hour of night, Sir
    Thomas.
  Whither so late?
LOVELL   Came you from the King, my lord?
GARDINER
  I did, Sir Thomas, and left him at primero   10
  With the Duke of Suffolk.
LOVELL   I must to him too,
  Before he go to bed. I'll take my leave.
GARDINER
  Not yet, Sir Thomas Lovell. What's the matter?
  It seems you are in haste. An if there be   15
  No great offense belongs to 't, give your friend
  Some touch of your late business. Affairs that walk,
  As they say spirits do, at midnight have
  In them a wilder nature than the business
  That seeks dispatch by day.   20

191

22. **durst commend:** would dare to entrust

23. **work:** business, doing

25. **in great extremity:** near death; **feared:** i.e., it is **feared**

28. **heartily:** with genuine sincerity

29. **Good time:** i.e., to be born; **stock:** tree (bearing **the fruit** of line 27)

30. **grubbed up:** torn out by the roots (and thus destroyed)

31. **Methinks:** it seems to me

32. **Cry the amen:** assent

37. **way:** i.e., religious persuasion

43. **remarked:** noted, conspicuous

44. **that of the Jewel House:** i.e., Master **of the Jewel House** (See 4.1.133–34 and note.)

44–45. **Master / O' th' Rolls:** official in charge of all scrolls, patents, and grants bearing the great seal, and all records of the Court of Chancery, the highest court next to the House of Lords

46. **Stands:** i.e., he **stands; gap:** entry; **trade:** path; **of more preferments:** to **more** promotions

47. **time:** course of events; **Th' Archbishop:** i.e., Cranmer (See picture, page 206.)

51. **are that:** i.e., are those who

54. **Incensed:** urged; **Council:** i.e., Privy **Council**

LOVELL   My lord, I love you,
And durst commend a secret to your ear
Much weightier than this work. The Queen's in
    labor—
They say in great extremity—and feared   25
She'll with the labor end.
GARDINER   The fruit she goes with
I pray for heartily, that it may find
Good time and live; but for the stock, Sir Thomas,
I wish it grubbed up now.   30
LOVELL   Methinks I could
Cry the amen, and yet my conscience says
She's a good creature and, sweet lady, does
Deserve our better wishes.
GARDINER   But, sir, sir,   35
Hear me, Sir Thomas. You're a gentleman
Of mine own way. I know you wise, religious;
And let me tell you, it will ne'er be well,
'Twill not, Sir Thomas Lovell, take 't of me,
Till Cranmer, Cromwell—her two hands—and she   40
Sleep in their graves.
LOVELL   Now, sir, you speak of two
The most remarked i' th' kingdom. As for Cromwell,
Besides that of the Jewel House, is made Master
O' th' Rolls and the King's secretary; further, sir,   45
Stands in the gap and trade of more preferments,
With which the ⌜time⌝ will load him. Th' Archbishop
Is the King's hand and tongue, and who dare speak
One syllable against him?
GARDINER   Yes, yes, Sir Thomas, 50
There are that dare, and I myself have ventured
To speak my mind of him. And indeed this day,
Sir—I may tell it you, I think—I have
Incensed the lords o' th' Council that he is—
For so I know he is, they know he is—   55

56. **arch:** chief (with wordplay on ***arch****bishop*)
57. **moved:** stirred up, roused
58. **broke with:** i.e., disclosed their views to
60. **fell:** destructive; **mischiefs:** evils
61. **reasons:** arguments
62. **board:** meeting
63. **He:** Cranmer; **convented:** summoned for trial or examination; **rank:** highly offensive; gross
66. **rest:** remain
71. **fancy's:** imagination is, i.e., attention is
73. **deliver to:** tell
75. **her:** i.e., Anne's
79. **crying out:** i.e., in labor (See picture below.)
80. **suff'rance:** suffering
83. **quit:** deliver; **burden:** that which is borne in the womb, a child

A woman "in labor." (5.1.23–24)
From Jakob Rüff,
De conceptu et generatione hominis . . . (1580).

A most arch heretic, a pestilence
That does infect the land; with which they, moved,
Have broken with the King, who hath so far
Given ear to our complaint, of his great grace
And princely care foreseeing those fell mischiefs   60
Our reasons laid before him, hath commanded
Tomorrow morning to the Council board
He be convented. He's a rank weed, Sir Thomas,
And we must root him out. From your affairs
I hinder you too long. Goodnight, Sir Thomas.   65

LOVELL
Many good nights, my lord. I rest your servant.
                              Gardiner and Page exit.

          Enter King and Suffolk.

KING
Charles, I will play no more tonight.
My mind's not on 't; you are too hard for me.

SUFFOLK
Sir, I did never win of you before.

KING   But little, Charles,   70
Nor shall not when my fancy's on my play.—
Now, Lovell, from the Queen what is the news?

LOVELL
I could not personally deliver to her
What you commanded me, but by her woman
I sent your message, who returned her thanks   75
In the great'st humbleness, and desired your Highness
Most heartily to pray for her.

KING   What sayst thou, ha?
To pray for her? What, is she crying out?

LOVELL
So said her woman, and that her suff'rance made   80
Almost each pang a death.

KING   Alas, good lady!

SUFFOLK
God safely quit her of her burden, and

84. **travail:** labor and pain of childbirth; **gladding:** making glad

88. **estate:** state

95. **what follows:** i.e., what's next; what's your news

101. **attends:** awaits

104. **happily:** fortunately

105. **Avoid:** leave, vacate; **gallery:** long room designed for taking indoor walks

106. **I have said: I have** spoken

A man in the stocks. (5.3.83–84)
From August Casimir Redel,
Apophtegmata symbolica . . . [n.d.].

With gentle travail, to the gladding of
Your Highness with an heir!   85

KING   'Tis midnight, Charles.
Prithee, to bed, and in thy prayers remember
Th' estate of my poor queen. Leave me alone,
For I must think of that which company
Would not be friendly to.   90

SUFFOLK   I wish your Highness
A quiet night, and my good mistress will
Remember in my prayers.

KING   Charles, good night.
                                        Suffolk exits.

                Enter Sir Anthony Denny.

Well, sir, what follows?   95

DENNY
Sir, I have brought my lord the Archbishop,
As you commanded me.

KING   Ha! Canterbury?

DENNY
Ay, my good lord.

KING   'Tis true. Where is he, Denny?   100

DENNY
He attends your Highness' pleasure.

KING   Bring him to us.
                                        ⌜*Denny exits.*⌝

LOVELL, ⌜*aside*⌝
This is about that which the Bishop spake.
I am happily come hither.

                Enter Cranmer and Denny.

KING
Avoid the gallery.   *Lovell seems to stay.*   105
                    Ha! I have said. Be gone!
What!   *Lovell and Denny exit.*

108. **Wherefore:** why

109. **aspect of terror:** terrifying expression or look

113. **attend:** heed

116. **walk a turn:** i.e., take a walk

120. **right:** very

122. **grievous:** serious

123. **of you:** i.e., about you

125. **moved:** prompted

127. **freedom:** ease, lack of encumbrance; **purge yourself:** establish your innocence

129. **answer:** reply to clear yourself

131. **Tower:** See note to 1.1.243 and picture, page 214. **a brother of us:** i.e., my close associate

132. **fits:** is appropriate that

136. **right:** very; **occasion:** opportunity

137. **throughly:** thoroughly; **winnowed:** subjected to a process like the winnowing of grain, in which one's worthless elements are blown away; **chaff:** husks

138. **corn:** grains, seeds

139. **stands under:** is exposed to; **calumnious:** slanderous, defamatory

142. **is:** i.e., are

CRANMER, ⌈*aside*⌉ I am fearful. Wherefore frowns he thus?
  'Tis his aspect of terror. All's not well.

KING
  How now, my lord? You do desire to know   110
  Wherefore I sent for you.

CRANMER, ⌈*kneeling*⌉   It is my duty
  T' attend your Highness' pleasure.

KING   Pray you arise,
  My good and gracious Lord of Canterbury.   115
  Come, you and I must walk a turn together.
  I have news to tell you. Come, come, give me your
    hand.   ⌈*Cranmer rises.*⌉
  Ah, my good lord, I grieve at what I speak,
  And am right sorry to repeat what follows.   120
  I have, and most unwillingly, of late
  Heard many grievous—I do say, my lord,
  Grievous—complaints of you, which, being
    considered,
  Have moved us and our Council that you shall   125
  This morning come before us, where I know
  You cannot with such freedom purge yourself
  But that, till further trial in those charges
  Which will require your answer, you must take
  Your patience to you and be well contented   130
  To make your house our Tower. You a brother of us,
  It fits we thus proceed, or else no witness
  Would come against you.

CRANMER, ⌈*kneeling*⌉   I humbly thank your
    Highness,   135
  And am right glad to catch this good occasion
  Most throughly to be winnowed, where my chaff
  And corn shall fly asunder. For I know
  There's none stands under more calumnious tongues
  Than I myself, poor man.   140

KING   Stand up, good Canterbury!
  Thy truth and thy integrity is rooted

144. **by my halidom:** a mild oath (literally, **by my** holiness or sanctity)

145. **manner:** kind; **looked:** i.e., expected that

149. **endurance:** hardship, imprisonment

151. **good:** virtue

153. **my person:** myself; **weigh not:** do not ascribe any value to

154. **Being . . . vacant:** i.e., if it is empty of **truth and honesty** (line 151); **nothing:** not at all

155. **What:** whatever

157. **state:** condition

159. **practices:** plots

160. **bear the same proportion:** i.e., be as many and as great; **ever:** always

161. **o' th' question:** i.e., in the dispute; **carries:** i.e., carry

162. **due:** right; **At what ease:** i.e., how easily

165. **potently:** powerfully

166. **Ween you of:** do you expect

167. **in:** i.e., in the matter of; **witness:** evidence, testimony; **master:** i.e., Christ (Matthew 26.59–60: "Now the chief priests and the elders and all the whole council sought false **witness** against Jesus, to put him to death . . . , and . . . at the last came two false witnesses.")

169. **naughty:** wicked; **Go to:** an expression of remonstrance

170. **You take . . . danger:** i.e., you regard a **leap** from **a precipice** as if it were of **no danger**

171. **woo:** court, invite

173. **or I:** i.e., **or** else **I**

174. **trap:** i.e., **trap** that

176. **way:** opportunity

In us, thy friend. Give me thy hand. Stand up.
⌜*Cranmer rises.*⌝
Prithee, let's walk. Now by my halidom,
What manner of man are you? My lord, I looked   145
You would have given me your petition that
I should have ta'en some pains to bring together
Yourself and your accusers and to have heard you
Without endurance further.

CRANMER   Most dread liege,   150
The good I stand on is my truth and honesty.
If they shall fail, I with mine enemies
Will triumph o'er my person, which I weigh not,
Being of those virtues vacant. I fear nothing
What can be said against me.   155

KING   Know you not
How your state stands i' th' world, with the whole
    world?
Your enemies are many and not small; their practices
Must bear the same proportion, and not ever   160
The justice and the truth o' th' question carries
The due o' th' verdict with it. At what ease
Might corrupt minds procure knaves as corrupt
To swear against you? Such things have been done.
You are potently opposed, and with a malice   165
Of as great size. Ween you of better luck,
I mean in perjured witness, than your master,
Whose minister you are, whiles here he lived
Upon this naughty earth? Go to, go to.
You take a precipice for no leap of danger   170
And woo your own destruction.

CRANMER   God and your Majesty
Protect mine innocence, or I fall into
The trap is laid for me.

KING   Be of good cheer.   175
They shall no more prevail than we give way to.

179. **commit you:** i.e., to the Tower
181. **vehemency:** vehemence, force
188. **truehearted:** loyal, honest, sincere
194. **tidings:** news
196. **shade:** protect
205. **your visitation:** i.e., you to visit
205–6. **to be . . . stranger:** wishes you to meet this newcomer

Guy fights to free all Englands feares,
With Colbrond, Gyant Dane:

Sir Guy of Warwick fights Colbrand,
the giant Dane. (5.3.23)
From [Samuel Rowlands,]
The famous historie, of Guy Earle of Warwick [1609].

Keep comfort to you, and this morning see
You do appear before them. If they shall chance,
In charging you with matters, to commit you,
The best persuasions to the contrary   180
Fail not to use, and with what vehemency
Th' occasion shall instruct you. If entreaties
Will render you no remedy, this ring
Deliver them, and your appeal to us
There make before them.   ⌜*He gives Cranmer a ring.*⌝ 185
    ⌜*Aside.*⌝ Look, the good man weeps!
He's honest, on mine honor! God's blest mother,
I swear he is truehearted, and a soul
None better in my kingdom.—Get you gone,
And do as I have bid you.   *Cranmer exits.* 190
                    He has strangled
His language in his tears.
⌜LOVELL⌝ (*within*)   Come back! What mean you?

Enter Old Lady, ⌜*followed by Lovell.*⌝

OLD LADY
  I'll not come back! The tidings that I bring
  Will make my boldness manners.—Now, good angels 195
  Fly o'er thy royal head and shade thy person
  Under their blessèd wings!
KING   Now by thy looks
  I guess thy message. Is the Queen delivered?
  Say "Ay, and of a boy."   200
OLD LADY   Ay, ay, my liege,
  And of a lovely boy. The God of heaven
  Both now and ever bless her! 'Tis a girl
  Promises boys hereafter. Sir, your queen
  Desires your visitation, and to be   205
  Acquainted with this stranger. 'Tis as like you
  As cherry is to cherry.

210. **marks:** A mark was equivalent to eight ounces of silver.

211. **By this light:** a mild oath

212. **groom:** servant of inferior position

216. **put it to the issue:** force a decision to be made

5.2 Cranmer suffers the public humiliation of being locked out of a Privy Council meeting. Allowed in, he is then threatened with confinement in prison. He quells this threat by showing the king's ring. The king then enters and orders his councillors to reconcile themselves to Cranmer and asks him to be godfather to the royal newborn.

---

0 SD. **Footboys:** boy attendants, page boys; **attend:** wait

2. **That:** i.e., who; **prayed:** begged

4. **fast:** locked

6. **Sure:** i.e., surely

KING   Lovell.
LOVELL   Sir.
KING
  Give her an hundred marks. I'll to the Queen.   210
                                    King exits.
OLD LADY
  An hundred marks? By this light, I'll ha' more.
  An ordinary groom is for such payment.
  I will have more or scold it out of him.
  Said I for this the girl was like to him?
  I'll have more or else unsay 't. And now,   215
  While 'tis hot, I'll put it to the issue.
                        ⌜*Old*⌝ *Lady exits,* ⌜*with Lovell.*⌝

                        Scene 2

Enter Cranmer, Archbishop of Canterbury. ⌜*(Pages,
Footboys, Grooms, and other servants attend at the
                  Council door.)*⌝

CRANMER
  I hope I am not too late, and yet the gentleman
  That was sent to me from the Council prayed me
  To make great haste.   *⌜He tries the door.⌝*
                    All fast? What means this? Ho!
  Who waits there?   5

                    Enter Keeper.

                    Sure you know me!
KEEPER   Yes, my lord,
  But yet I cannot help you.
CRANMER   Why?
KEEPER
  Your Grace must wait till you be called for.   10
CRANMER   So.

13. **happily:** fortunately

14. **understand it:** learn of it; **presently:** immediately

18. **sound:** make known (with possible wordplay on **sound** as *probe,* as a physician does a wound)

19. **of purpose laid:** devised on **purpose**

20. **turn:** change; **hearts:** minds

21. **quench:** destroy, crush

22. **else:** otherwise

23. **lackeys:** footmen; **pleasures:** wills

24. **fulfilled:** obeyed; **attend:** wait

28. **many a day:** often, on many days (used ironically)

29. **Body o' me:** a mild oath

32. **holds his state:** i.e., occupies a place appropriate to his exalted position (ironic); maintains his dignity; **pursuivants:** messengers, attendants

37. **parted:** shared; **honesty:** respect

THOMAS CRAMMERVS

Thomas Cranmer, Archbishop of Canterbury.
From Henry Holland, *Herωologia* . . . [1620].

Enter Doctor Butts.

BUTTS, ⌜*aside*⌝
  This is a ⌜piece⌝ of malice. I am glad
  I came this way so happily. The King
  Shall understand it presently.   *Butts exits.*
CRANMER, ⌜*aside*⌝   'Tis Butts,   15
  The King's physician. As he passed along
  How earnestly he cast his eyes upon me!
  Pray heaven he sound not my disgrace. For certain
  This is of purpose laid by some that hate me—
  God turn their hearts! I never sought their malice—   20
  To quench mine honor. They would shame to make me
  Wait else at door, a fellow councillor,
  'Mong boys, grooms, and lackeys. But their pleasures
  Must be fulfilled, and I attend with patience.

Enter the King and Butts at a window above.

BUTTS
  I'll show your Grace the strangest sight.   25
KING   What's that,
    Butts?
BUTTS
  I think your Highness saw this many a day.
KING
  Body o' me, where is it?
BUTTS   There, my lord: 30
  The high promotion of his Grace of Canterbury,
  Who holds his state at door, 'mongst pursuivants,
  Pages, and footboys.
KING   Ha! 'Tis he indeed.
  Is this the honor they do one another?   35
  'Tis well there's one above 'em yet. I had thought
  They had parted so much honesty among 'em—
  At least good manners—as not thus to suffer

39. **place:** office in the service of the crown
40. **dance attendance:** stand waiting
41. **post:** courier; **packets:** parcels of letters
43. **close:** closed, shut
44. **anon:** soon
44 SD. **state:** canopy, such as usually hangs above a throne; **Lord Chancellor:** See longer note, page 242. **above him:** closer to the privileged upper end of the table than his
45. **Speak to:** comment on; **business:** action that commands our attention
49. **had knowledge:** i.e., been informed
52. **Without:** outside
59. **present:** moment, time
60–62. **But we all . . . angels:** a combination of proverbs: **"Flesh** is **frail"** and **"men are** not **angels." capable / Of:** susceptible to **flesh:** sensual appetites and inclinations

A French dandy. (1.3.37-38)
From Cesare Vecellio, *Habiti antichi et moderni . . .* (1598).

A man of his place, and so near our favor,
To dance attendance on their Lordships' pleasures,   40
And at the door, too, like a post with packets.
By holy Mary, Butts, there's knavery!
Let 'em alone, and draw the curtain close.
We shall hear more anon.   ⌈*They draw the curtain.*⌉

A council table brought in with chairs and stools and
placed under the state. Enter Lord Chancellor, places
himself at the upper end of the table on the left hand, a
seat being left void above him, as for Canterbury's seat.
    Duke of Suffolk, Duke of Norfolk, Surrey, Lord
Chamberlain, Gardiner seat themselves in order on each
      side, Cromwell at lower end as secretary.

CHANCELLOR
   Speak to the business, Master Secretary.   45
   Why are we met in council?
CROMWELL   Please your honors,
   The chief cause concerns his Grace of Canterbury.
GARDINER
   Has he had knowledge of it?
CROMWELL   Yes.   50
NORFOLK, ⌈*to Keeper*⌉   Who waits there?
KEEPER
   Without, my noble lords?
GARDINER   Yes.
KEEPER   My lord Archbishop,
   And has done half an hour, to know your pleasures.   55
CHANCELLOR
   Let him come in.
KEEPER, ⌈*at door*⌉   Your Grace may enter now.
           Cranmer approaches the council table.
CHANCELLOR
   My good lord Archbishop, I'm very sorry
   To sit here at this present and behold
   That chair stand empty. But we all are men,   60

63. **want:** lack; **that:** i.e., who

64. **misdemeaned . . . little:** misbehaved badly

69. **Divers:** various; opposed to what is right

73. **Pace . . . hands:** i.e., do not lead them by hand as they amble

74. **stubborn:** hard, rigid

75. **manage:** training; **suffer:** allow

76. **easiness:** kindness, indulgence; **pity:** clemency, mercy

78. **physic:** medical treatment, medicine

79. **taint:** corrupting influence

80. **late:** recent

81. **upper Germany:** location of the Peasants' War (1524–25), which pitted Luther's supporters against Catholics; **dearly:** at a high price or great cost

82. **Yet:** i.e., and still

83. **progress:** journey

85. **study:** deliberate effort

86. **course:** line or path

87. **one way:** i.e., in a single direction; **end:** goal

89. **a single heart:** a sincere **heart** free of duplicity

90. **more stirs:** is **more** active

91. **place:** official position

In our own natures frail, and capable
Of our flesh—few are angels—out of which frailty
And want of wisdom you, that best should teach us,
Have misdemeaned yourself, and not a little,
Toward the King first, then his laws, in filling 65
The whole realm, by your teaching and your
   chaplains'—
For so we are informed—with new opinions,
Divers and dangerous, which are heresies
And, not reformed, may prove pernicious. 70

GARDINER
Which reformation must be sudden too,
My noble lords; for those that tame wild horses
Pace 'em not in their hands to make 'em gentle,
But stop their mouths with stubborn bits, and spur 'em
Till they obey the manage. If we suffer, 75
Out of our easiness and childish pity
To one man's honor, this contagious sickness,
Farewell, all physic. And what follows then?
Commotions, uproars, with a general taint
Of the whole state, as of late days our neighbors, 80
The upper Germany, can dearly witness,
Yet freshly pitied in our memories.

CRANMER
My good lords, hitherto, in all the progress
Both of my life and office, I have labored,
And with no little study, that my teaching 85
And the strong course of my authority
Might go one way and safely; and the end
Was ever to do well. Nor is there living—
I speak it with a single heart, my lords—
A man that more detests, more stirs against, 90
Both in his private conscience and his place,
Defacers of a public peace than I do.
Pray heaven the King may never find a heart

96. **the best:** i.e., the most virtuous

97. **case of justice:** perhaps, **case** brought here for judicial proceedings; or, perhaps, cause in which **justice** should be sought

98. **Be what they will:** i.e., whoever they are

99. **urge:** bring forward allegations

102. **by that virtue:** consequently

103. **My lord:** i.e., Cranmer; **moment:** importance

104. **short:** brief

105. **And our consent:** i.e., to which we have consented

111. **pass:** proceed

113. **end:** purpose

114. **undoing:** destruction

116. **modesty:** moderation, clemency

119. **make:** have; **do conscience:** have **conscience,** have scruples

121. **modest:** moderate

122. **sectary:** adherent of a heretical sect

123. **painted gloss:** (1) false or feigned show or semblance; (2) specious explanation or comment; **discovers:** reveals

With less allegiance in it! Men that make
Envy and crookèd malice nourishment   95
Dare bite the best. I do beseech your Lordships
That, in this case of justice, my accusers,
Be what they will, may stand forth face to face
And freely urge against me.

SUFFOLK   Nay, my lord,   100
That cannot be. You are a councillor,
And by that virtue no man dare accuse you.

GARDINER
My lord, because we have business of more moment,
We will be short with you. 'Tis his Highness' pleasure,
And our consent, for better trial of you   105
From hence you be committed to the Tower,
Where, being but a private man again,
You shall know many dare accuse you boldly—
More than, I fear, you are provided for.

CRANMER
Ah, my good Lord of Winchester, I thank you.   110
You are always my good friend. If your will pass,
I shall both find your Lordship judge and juror,
You are so merciful. I see your end:
'Tis my undoing. Love and meekness, lord,
Become a churchman better than ambition.   115
Win straying souls with modesty again;
Cast none away. That I shall clear myself,
Lay all the weight you can upon my patience,
I make as little doubt as you do conscience
In doing daily wrongs. I could say more,   120
But reverence to your calling makes me modest.

GARDINER
My lord, my lord, you are a sectary.
That's the plain truth. Your painted gloss discovers,
To men that understand you, words and weakness.

126. **sharp:** harsh

127. **faulty:** guilty of wrongdoing; censurable

129. **load:** oppress

131. **cry your Honor mercy:** beg your pardon (for what I am about to say); **worst:** with least justification

132. **table:** i.e., council

135. **sound:** orthodox or theologically correct; loyal

138. **honest:** honorable, held in honor

140. **bold:** audacious

142. **bold:** shameless

148. **voices:** judgments, expressed opinions

149. **conveyed:** taken, conducted

154. **must needs to:** i.e., have to go to **needs:** of necessity, necessarily

The Tower

The Tower of London. (1.1.243; 5.1.131)
From Claes Jansz Visscher,
Londinum florentissima Britanniae urbs . . . [c. 1625].

CROMWELL
  My Lord of Winchester, you're a little,   125
  By your good favor, too sharp. Men so noble,
  However faulty, yet should find respect
  For what they have been. 'Tis a cruelty
  To load a falling man.
GARDINER   Good Master Secretary—   130
  I cry your Honor mercy—you may worst
  Of all this table say so.
CROMWELL   Why, my lord?
GARDINER
  Do not I know you for a favorer
  Of this new sect? You are not sound.   135
CROMWELL   Not sound?
GARDINER
  Not sound, I say.
CROMWELL   Would you were half so honest!
  Men's prayers then would seek you, not their fears.
GARDINER
  I shall remember this bold language.   140
CROMWELL   Do.
  Remember your bold life too.
⌜CHANCELLOR⌝   This is too much!
  Forbear, for shame, my lords.
GARDINER   I have done.   145
CROMWELL   And I.
⌜CHANCELLOR, *to Cranmer*⌝
  Then thus for you, my lord: it stands agreed,
  I take it, by all voices, that forthwith
  You be conveyed to th' Tower a prisoner,
  There to remain till the King's further pleasure   150
  Be known unto us.—Are you all agreed, lords?
ALL
  We are.
CRANMER Is there no other way of mercy
  But I must needs to th' Tower, my lords?

160. **Receive him:** take him into custody

161. **safe:** secured

162. **Stay:** wait

165. **grips:** clutches

169. **right:** genuine

170–71. **When . . . ourselves:** See Proverbs 26.27: "He that rolleth a **stone,** it shall return unto him."

173. **suffer:** allow

174. **vexed:** afflicted

176. **in value with him:** i.e., valued by him

177. **fairly out on 't:** fully **out** of it, i.e., the mistreatment of Cranmer

178. **My mind gave me:** i.e., I suspected that

179. **tales:** mischievous gossip; **informations:** accusations by informants

181. **envy at:** begrudge

182. **You . . . you:** See Ecclesiasticus 28.12: "If thou blow the spark, it shall burn." **have at you:** i.e., watch out (a warning before an attack)

Thomas Cromwell.
From Henry Holland, *Herωologia* . . . [1620].

GARDINER   What other   155
  Would you expect? You are strangely troublesome.
  Let some o' th' guard be ready there.

                    Enter the Guard.

CRANMER   For me?
  Must I go like a traitor thither?
GARDINER   Receive him,   160
  And see him safe i' th' Tower.
CRANMER   Stay, good my lords,
  I have a little yet to say. Look there, my lords.
                        ⌜*He holds out the ring.*⌝
  By virtue of that ring, I take my cause
  Out of the grips of cruel men and give it   165
  To a most noble judge, the King my master.
CHAMBERLAIN
  This is the King's ring.
SURREY   'Tis no counterfeit.
SUFFOLK
  'Tis the right ring, by heaven! I told you all,
  When we first put this dangerous stone a-rolling,   170
  'Twould fall upon ourselves.
NORFOLK   Do you think, my lords,
  The King will suffer but the little finger
  Of this man to be vexed?
CHAMBERLAIN   'Tis now too certain.   175
  How much more is his life in value with him!
  Would I were fairly out on 't!
CROMWELL   My mind gave me,
  In seeking tales and informations
  Against this man, whose honesty the devil   180
  And his disciples only envy at,
  You blew the fire that burns you. Now, have at you!

    Enter King, frowning on them; takes his seat.

183. **bound:** obliged

186. **the Church:** i.e., the good of **the Church**

187. **aim:** goal

188. **dear:** heartfelt, loving; **respect:** care, attention

190. **cause:** case; **betwixt:** between; **her:** i.e., the Church

191. **sudden:** impromptu; **commendations:** compliments

194. **They:** the **commendations** (line 191)

196. **win:** persuade, prevail upon

198. **bloody:** bloodthirsty

201. **that:** i.e., who

202. **starve:** die a lingering death

203. **place:** seat at the Privy Council table; high official position

207. **had thought I had had:** Editors in the past often removed one or more **"had."**

213. **shame:** disgrace; **commission:** authoritative direction; delegated judicial authority

215. **try him:** put him on trial (with wordplay at line 218 on the meaning "afflict him")

GARDINER
    Dread sovereign, how much are we bound to heaven
    In daily thanks, that gave us such a prince,
    Not only good and wise, but most religious;   185
    One that in all obedience makes the Church
    The chief aim of his honor, and to strengthen
    That holy duty out of dear respect,
    His royal self in judgment comes to hear
    The cause betwixt her and this great offender.   190

KING
    You were ever good at sudden commendations,
    Bishop of Winchester. But know I come not
    To hear such flattery now, and in my presence
    They are too thin and base to hide offenses.
    To me you cannot reach. You play the spaniel,   195
    And think with wagging of your tongue to win me;
    But whatsoe'er thou tak'st me for, I'm sure
    Thou hast a cruel nature and a bloody.—
    Good man, sit down.   ⌜*Cranmer takes his seat.*⌝
                     Now let me see the proudest   200
    He, that dares most, but wag his finger at thee.
    By all that's holy, he had better starve
    Than but once think ⌜this⌝ place becomes thee not.

SURREY
    May it please your Grace—

KING   No, sir, it does not please   205
    me.
    I had thought I had had men of some understanding
    And wisdom of my Council, but I find none.
    Was it discretion, lords, to let this man,
    This good man—few of you deserve that title—   210
    This honest man, wait like a lousy footboy
    At chamber door? And one as great as you are?
    Why, what a shame was this! Did my commission
    Bid you so far forget yourselves? I gave you
    Power as he was a councillor to try him,   215

218. **to the utmost: to the** uttermost extreme or limit; **mean:** opportunity

221. **like:** please

224. **faith:** sincerity

225. **purgation:** clearing himself from accusation

230. **beholding:** obliged, indebted

235. **suit:** petition, supplication

236. **wants:** lacks

237. **answer for her:** stand sponsor **for her;** speak in behalf of her

241. **spare:** avoid the expense of; **spoons:** A spoon was a traditional gift to a child at its baptism.

St. Paul's Cathedral. (5.3.16)
From Claes Jansz Visscher,
Londinum florentissima Britanniae urbs . . . [c. 1625].

Not as a groom. There's some of you, I see,
More out of malice than integrity,
Would try him to the utmost, had you mean,
Which you shall never have while I live.

CHANCELLOR   Thus far,   220
My most dread sovereign, may it like your Grace
To let my tongue excuse all. What was purposed
Concerning his imprisonment was rather,
If there be faith in men, meant for his trial
And fair purgation to the world than malice,   225
I'm sure, in me.

KING   Well, well, my lords, respect him.
Take him, and use him well; he's worthy of it.
I will say thus much for him: if a prince
May be beholding to a subject, I   230
Am, for his love and service, so to him.
Make me no more ado, but all embrace him.
Be friends, for shame, my lords.
                              ⌜*They embrace Cranmer.*⌝
                         My Lord of Canterbury,
I have a suit which you must not deny me: 235
That is, a fair young maid that yet wants baptism.
You must be godfather and answer for her.

CRANMER
The greatest monarch now alive may glory
In such an honor. How may I deserve it,
That am a poor and humble subject to you?   240

KING   Come, come, my lord, you'd spare your spoons.
       You shall have two noble partners with you: the
       old Duchess of Norfolk and Lady Marquess Dor-
       set. Will these please you?—
Once more, my lord of Winchester, I charge you,   245
Embrace and love this man.

GARDINER   With a true heart
And brother-love I do it.   ⌜*He embraces Cranmer.*⌝

250. **confirmation:** act of corroboration

252. **voice:** rumor, report

254. **shrewd turn:** malicious act

256. **made a Christian:** i.e., christened

257. **made you one, lords, one remain:** i.e., **made you** united, **lords, remain** united

258. **So:** i.e., thus, in that way

5.3 A porter and his assistant fight to control the crowd determined to view the royal daughter's christening.

———

0 SD. **within:** offstage

1. **leave:** cease; **anon:** soon

2. **Parish Garden:** i.e., Paris Garden, an arena for noisy bull- and bearbaiting; **rude:** ignorant; boisterous

3. **gaping:** bawling, shouting

4–5. **I . . . larder:** i.e., **I** work in the palace **larder** (meat closet)

7. **roar:** behave in a noisy and riotous manner

7–8. **crab-tree staves:** cudgels from the proverbially hard wood of the crab apple tree

8. **These:** the cudgels now being used

10. **ale and cakes:** customary fare at church festivals

15. **May Day morning:** by custom a festive occasion

16. **Paul's:** St. **Paul's** Cathedral, by far the largest building in London (See picture, page 220.)

17. **be hanged:** i.e., go to the devil

CRANMER, ⌜*weeping*⌝   And let heaven
  Witness how dear I hold this confirmation.   250

KING
  Good man, those joyful tears show thy true ⌜heart.⌝
  The common voice, I see, is verified
  Of thee, which says thus: "Do my Lord of Canterbury
  A shrewd turn, and he's your friend forever."—
  Come, lords, we trifle time away. I long   255
  To have this young one made a Christian.
  As I have made you one, lords, one remain.
  So I grow stronger, you more honor gain.

                           They exit.

Scene 3

Noise and tumult within. Enter Porter and his Man,
⌜*carrying cudgels.*⌝

PORTER You'll leave your noise anon, you rascals! Do
  you take the court for Parish Garden? You rude
  slaves, leave your gaping!

⌜ONE,⌝ (*within*) Good Master Porter, I belong to th'
  larder.   5

PORTER Belong to th' gallows and be hanged, you rogue!
  Is this a place to roar in?—Fetch me a dozen crab-
  tree staves, and strong ones. These are but switches
  to 'em.—I'll scratch your heads! You must be seeing
  christenings? Do you look for ale and cakes here,   10
  you rude rascals?

PORTER'S MAN
  Pray, sir, be patient. 'Tis as much impossible—
  Unless we sweep 'em from the door with cannons—
  To scatter 'em as 'tis to make 'em sleep
  On May Day morning, which will never be.   15
  We may as well push against Paul's as stir 'em.

PORTER How got they in, and be hanged?

21. **made no spare:** left none unharmed; or, exercised no moderation

23. **Samson, Sir Guy, Colbrand:** famous strong men (See longer note, page 243, and picture, page 202.)

26. **cuckold or cuckold-maker:** i.e., husband or wife (A **cuckold** is a man whose wife is unfaithful.)

27. **see a chine:** i.e., eat meat (A **chine** is the animal backbone with the adjoining flesh.)

28. **And . . . her:** This line has not been satisfactorily explained. See longer note, page 243.

30. **presently:** immediately

31. **close:** shut

34. **Moorfields:** a recreation area north of the city, used for training by the militia; **muster:** assemble as an army

35. **Indian:** probably alluding to American Indians, who were put on exhibition in London; **great tool:** large penis

37. **fry of fornication:** swarm of bastards

40. **spoons:** See note to 5.2.241.

42. **brazier:** brass worker, who works in high heat

43. **dog days:** hottest **days** of the year (associated with the period of the rising of the Dog Star in August)

44. **under the line:** at the equator

45. **penance:** i.e., suffering in the fires of purgatory; **fire-drake:** fiery meteor; fiery dragon

46. **discharged:** (1) cleared; (2) fired off

47. **mortar-piece:** short cannon with a large bore

48. **blow:** blast; **haberdasher's wife: wife** of a **haberdasher,** a maker of hats and caps

(continued)

224

PORTER'S MAN
  Alas, I know not. How gets the tide in?
  As much as one sound cudgel of four foot—
  You see the poor remainder—could distribute,   20
  I made no spare, sir.
PORTER   You did nothing, sir.
PORTER'S MAN
  I am not Samson, nor Sir Guy, nor Colbrand,
  To mow 'em down before me; but if I spared any
  That had a head to hit, either young or old,   25
  He or she, cuckold or cuckold-maker,
  Let me ne'er hope to see a chine again—
  And that I would not for a cow, God save her!
⌐ONE,⌐ (*within*) Do you hear, Master Porter?
PORTER I shall be with you presently, good master   30
  puppy.— Keep the door close, sirrah.
PORTER'S MAN What would you have me do?
PORTER What should you do but knock 'em down by
  th' dozens? Is this Moorfields to muster in? Or have
  we some strange Indian with the great tool come to   35
  court, the women so besiege us? Bless me, what a
  fry of fornication is at door! On my Christian conscience, this one christening will beget a thousand;
  here will be father, godfather, and all together.
PORTER'S MAN The spoons will be the bigger, sir. There is   40
  a fellow somewhat near the door—he should be a
  brazier by his face, for, o' my conscience, twenty of
  the dog days now reign in 's nose. All that stand
  about him are under the line; they need no other
  penance. That fire-drake did I hit three times on the   45
  head, and three times was his nose discharged
  against me. He stands there like a mortar-piece, to
  blow us. There was a haberdasher's wife of small
  wit near him that railed upon me till her pinked
  porringer fell off her head for kindling such a   50
  combustion in the state. I missed the meteor once

49. **wit:** intelligence; **railed upon me:** abused me verbally; **pinked:** ornamentally perforated or slashed

50. **porringer:** hat resembling a small basin

51. **meteor:** i.e., red-faced **brazier** (line 42)

52. **Clubs:** traditional cry to draw apprentices from their work to join a fight

53. **truncheoners:** cudgel bearers

54. **succor:** aid; **the hope o' th' Strand:** merchants' apprentices **hope:** those who give **hope** or promise for the future **Strand:** a street of fine merchants' houses and shops

55. **was quartered:** resided; **fell on:** attacked

55–56. **made good my place:** carried out my duty

56. **to th' broomstaff to:** to close quarters with **broomstaff:** broomstick

58. **loose shot:** marksmen not attached to a company (a military term)

59. **pibbles:** pebbles; **fain:** obliged

60. **win the work:** literally, capture the fort

64–65. **tribulation of Tower Hill, limbs of Limehouse:** two rough crowds, one associated with public executions on **Tower Hill,** the other with **Limehouse,** a Thames dockyard east of London (See longer note, page 243.)

66. **Limbo Patrum:** i.e., prison (literally, "limbo of the fathers" [Latin], a place bordering hell where, in Roman Catholic theology, dwell the just people who died before the coming of Christ or who never were baptized)

68. **running banquet of two beadles:** i.e., public whipping **running banquet:** literally, light refreshment or dessert **beadles:** parish constables

(continued)

and hit that woman, who cried out "Clubs!" when I
might see from far some forty truncheoners draw to
her succor, which were the hope o' th' Strand, where
she was quartered. They fell on; I made good my   55
place. At length they came to th' broomstaff to me;
I defied 'em still, when suddenly a file of boys behind 'em, loose shot, delivered such a shower of
pibbles that I was fain to draw mine honor in and
let 'em win the work. The devil was amongst 'em, I   60
think, surely.

PORTER   These are the youths that thunder at a playhouse and fight for bitten apples, that no audience
but the tribulation of Tower Hill or the limbs of
Limehouse, their dear brothers, are able to   65
endure. I have some of 'em in *Limbo Patrum*, and
there they are like to dance these three days, besides
the running banquet of two beadles that is to come.

Enter Lord Chamberlain.

CHAMBERLAIN
Mercy o' me, what a multitude are here!
They grow still too. From all parts they are coming,   70
As if we kept a fair here! Where are these porters,
These lazy knaves?—You've made a fine hand, fellows!
There's a trim rabble let in. Are all these
Your faithful friends o' th' suburbs? We shall have
Great store of room, no doubt, left for the ladies,   75
When they pass back from the christening!

PORTER   An 't please
    your Honor,
We are but men, and what so many may do,
Not being torn a-pieces, we have done.   80
An army cannot rule 'em.

CHAMBERLAIN   As I live,
If the King blame me for 't, I'll lay you all
By th' heels, and suddenly, and on your heads

72. **fine hand:** great success (sarcastic)

73. **trim:** nice, fine (sarcastic)

74. **suburbs:** outlying and disreputable parts of the city

75. **Great store:** i.e., a **great** deal (sarcastic)

76. **pass back:** return

77. **An 't:** if it

79. **so many:** i.e., the two of us

81. **rule:** control

83–84. **lay you all / By th' heels:** arrest you; put you in the stocks (See picture, page 196.)

84. **suddenly:** without delay

85. **round:** large

86. **baiting of bombards:** drinking liquor from leather jugs

87. **service:** i.e., your duty for your master

90. **break:** make an opening; **press:** crowd; **find a way out:** i.e., discover a way

91. **troop:** royal company; **pass:** move forward; **fairly:** i.e., comfortably

92. **Marshalsea:** prison in Southwark; **hold you play:** keep you occupied

95. **close up:** i.e., out of the way

96. **camlet:** silk garment

97. **peck:** throw; **pales:** fences; **else:** otherwise

5.4 At Princess Elizabeth's christening, Cranmer prophesies a magnificent reign for the future Queen Elizabeth I and an equally successful one for her successor King James I.

———————

(continued)

Clap round fines for neglect. You're lazy knaves,   85
And here you lie baiting of bombards, when
You should do service.   ⌜*Trumpets.*⌝
                    Hark, the trumpets sound!
They're come already from the christening.
Go break among the press, and find a way out   90
To let the troop pass fairly, or I'll find
A Marshalsea shall hold you play these two months.

PORTER
Make way there for the Princess!

PORTER'S MAN   You great fellow,
Stand close up, or I'll make your head ache.   95

PORTER
You i' th' camlet, get up o' th' rail!
I'll peck you o'er the pales else.

                                        They exit.

Scene 4

Enter Trumpets, sounding. Then two Aldermen, Lord
Mayor, Garter, Cranmer, Duke of Norfolk with his
marshal's staff, Duke of Suffolk, two Noblemen bearing
great standing bowls for the christening gifts; then four
Noblemen bearing a canopy, under which the Duchess
of Norfolk, godmother, bearing the child richly habited
in a mantle, etc., train borne by a Lady. Then follows the
Marchioness Dorset, the other godmother, and Ladies.
The troop pass once about the stage, and Garter speaks.

GARTER   Heaven, from thy endless goodness, send
    prosperous life, long, and ever happy, to the high
    and mighty princess of England, Elizabeth.

            Flourish. Enter King and Guard.

CRANMER, ⌜*kneeling*⌝
    And to your royal Grace and the good queen,

0 SD. **Trumpets:** trumpeters; **Garter:** See note to 4.1.41 SD. **standing . . . gifts:** In Holinshed, the princess is given two gold "**standing** cups," or **bowls** with supporting bases. **richly habited:** splendidly dressed; **mantle:** infant's outer robe; **train:** elongated back part of the **mantle; troop:** company; **pass:** proceed

5. **partners:** i.e., fellow godparents; **pray: pray** that

6. **lady:** i.e., baby princess that

18. **gossips:** godparents to my child; **prodigal:** extravagant (in your christening gifts)

24. **still:** always

29. **pattern:** model, example to be followed; **with her:** at the same time as she

30. **succeed:** come after; **Saba:** i.e., the Queen of Sheba, who visited Solomon to verify his reputation for wisdom (1 Kings 10.1–10)

33. **mold up:** go to form; **piece:** masterpiece

35. **still:** ever more and more

37. **Her own:** i.e., **her own** people

38. **beaten corn:** windbeaten wheat or other grain

My noble partners and myself thus pray   5
All comfort, joy, in this most gracious lady
Heaven ever laid up to make parents happy
May hourly fall upon you!
KING   Thank you, good lord
    Archbishop.   10
What is her name?
CRANMER   Elizabeth.
KING   Stand up, lord.
               ⌜*Cranmer stands.*⌝
With this kiss take my blessing. ⌜*King kisses infant.*⌝
                God protect thee,   15
Into whose hand I give thy life.
CRANMER   Amen.
KING, ⌜*to the two godmothers*⌝
My noble gossips, you've been too prodigal.
I thank you heartily; so shall this lady
When she has so much English.   20
CRANMER   Let me speak, sir,
For heaven now bids me; and the words I utter
Let none think flattery, for they'll find 'em truth.
This royal infant—heaven still move about her!—
Though in her cradle, yet now promises   25
Upon this land a thousand thousand blessings,
Which time shall bring to ripeness. She shall be—
But few now living can behold that goodness—
A pattern to all princes living with her
And all that shall succeed. Saba was never   30
More covetous of wisdom and fair virtue
Than this pure soul shall be. All princely graces
That mold up such a mighty piece as this is,
With all the virtues that attend the good,
Shall still be doubled on her. Truth shall nurse her;   35
Holy and heavenly thoughts still counsel her.
She shall be loved and feared. Her own shall bless her;
Her foes shake like a field of beaten corn

42. **Under his own vine:** Biblical: Micah 4.4: "But they shall sit every man **under his vine** . . . , and none shall make them afraid"; Isaiah 65.21–2: "and they shall plant vineyards, and **eat** the fruit of them. They . . . shall not plant, and another **eat**."

44. **God . . . known:** a possible allusion to the Protestant religion, celebrated under Elizabeth

45. **read:** learn

46. **those:** i.e., **the perfect ways of honor; greatness:** eminent rank; **blood:** lineage, descent

47. **sleep:** i.e., die

48. **bird of wonder:** wondrous **bird; maiden phoenix:** a mythical bird that is reborn from the ashes of its own death by fire, and **maiden** because it does not reproduce sexually (See picture, page 238.)

50. **great in admiration:** greatly wondered at

51. **she:** Elizabeth, who dies a **virgin** (line 69); **one:** King James I, whom Elizabeth names as her successor

52. **cloud of darkness:** i.e., mortal life

55. **terror:** the quality of causing dread

60. **new nations:** perhaps a reference to the colony of Virginia

61. **mountain cedar:** Biblical: Psalm 92.12–13: "The righteous shall flourish like a palm tree, and shall grow **like a cedar** in Lebanon."

66. **An agèd princess:** See picture, page 234.

67. **deed:** good **deed**

68. **Would:** i.e., I wish

And hang their heads with sorrow. Good grows with
    her.   40
In her days every man shall eat in safety
Under his own vine what he plants and sing
The merry songs of peace to all his neighbors.
God shall be truly known, and those about her
From her shall read the perfect ⌜ways⌝ of honor   45
And by those claim their greatness, not by blood.
Nor shall this peace sleep with her; but, as when
The bird of wonder dies, the maiden phoenix,
Her ashes new create another heir
As great in admiration as herself,   50
So shall she leave her blessedness to one,
When heaven shall call her from this cloud of darkness,
Who from the sacred ashes of her honor
Shall starlike rise as great in fame as she was
And so stand fixed. Peace, plenty, love, truth, terror, 55
That were the servants to this chosen infant,
Shall then be his, and like a vine grow to him.
Wherever the bright sun of heaven shall shine,
His honor and the greatness of his name
Shall be, and make new nations. He shall flourish, 60
And like a mountain cedar reach his branches
To all the plains about him. Our children's children
Shall see this and bless heaven.
KING   Thou speakest wonders.
CRANMER
She shall be to the happiness of England   65
An agèd princess; many days shall see her,
And yet no day without a deed to crown it.
Would I had known no more! But she must die,
She must, the saints must have her; yet a virgin,
A most unspotted lily, shall she pass   70
To th' ground, and all the world shall mourn her.

74. **made me now a man:** i.e., **now** ensured my success
75. **get:** (1) beget; (2) gain
80. **beholding:** beholden, obliged
84. **sick:** disappointed, vexed
85. **'Has:** i.e., he has; **stay:** cease work
86. **holiday:** printed by many editors as "holy day"

Queen Elizabeth I, "a pattern to all princes." (5.4.29)
From *A booke containing . . .
proclamations . . .* (c. 1603-04).

KING   O lord
     Archbishop,
Thou hast made me now a man. Never before
This happy child did I get anything.   75
This oracle of comfort has so pleased me
That when I am in heaven I shall desire
To see what this child does and praise my Maker.—
I thank you all.—To you, my good lord mayor
And you, good brethren, I am much beholding.   80
I have received much honor by your presence,
And you shall find me thankful. Lead the way, lords.
You must all see the Queen, and she must thank you;
She will be sick else. This day, no man think
'Has business at his house, for all shall stay.   85
This little one shall make it holiday.
                                        They exit.

5. **naught:** worthless

5–6. **to hear ... witty:** a reference to the many satirical city comedies that mocked ordinary citizens

7. **that:** i.e., so that

8. **expected good:** i.e., anticipated approval; **like:** likely

10. **construction:** interpretation

13. **ill hap:** bad luck

14. **hold:** refrain, **hold** back; **clap:** applaud

Queen Katherine of Aragon.
By George Perfect Harding after an unknown artist (1843).
From the Folger Library Collection.

⌈*Enter Epilogue*⌉

EPILOGUE
'Tis ten to one this play can never please
All that are here. Some come to take their ease
And sleep an act or two—but those, we fear,
We've frighted with our trumpets; so, 'tis clear,
They'll say 'tis naught—others, to hear the city   5
Abused extremely and to cry "That's witty!"—
Which we have not done neither—that I fear
All the expected good we're like to hear
For this play at this time is only in
The merciful construction of good women,   10
For such a one we showed 'em. If they smile
And say 'twill do, I know within a while
All the best men are ours; for 'tis ill hap
If they hold when their ladies bid 'em clap.
⌈*He exits.*⌉

A phoenix. (5.4.48)
From Geoffrey Whitney, *A choice of emblemes* . . . (1586).

Longer Notes

1.1.262. **Michael Hopkins:** The monk who served as Buckingham's confessor and who allegedly fed him stories to whet his appetite for the kingship is named three times in the Folio text of *Henry VIII*, once as **Michael Hopkins,** once (at 1.2.169) as **Nicholas Henton,** and once as simply **Hopkins** (at 2.1.28). Holinshed calls this monk "Nicholas Hopkins." Editors since the early eighteenth century have tended to change the monk's name at 1.1.262 to "Nicholas Hopkins" to accord with Holinshed, and have tended to allow the second naming, **Nicholas Henton,** to stand, adding explanatory notes that account for the discrepancy in one of two ways. Both explanations refer to Holinshed's description of the monk as "one Nicholas Hopkins, a monk of an house of the Chartreux order, beside Bristow, called Henton, sometime his confessor." Editors have read this passage as saying (1) that Henton was an alias used by Hopkins, and that Shakespeare in turn used the alias to refer to the monk in 1.2; or (2) that Henton is the name of the "Chartreux" monastery, and that Shakespeare either misread Holinshed or deliberately called the monk after the name of his monastery. We have allowed the Folio names to stand.

1.3.41. **cum privilegio:** *Cum privilegio ad imprimendum solum* [with the exclusive right to print] is a Latin formula that appears on the title pages of books when publishers have a monopoly on them. This formula announces a unique privilege that a publisher enjoys—the right to be the only one who can publish the book in which it appears. However, in the context of the play's dialogue, the formula takes a sarcastic turn. Rather than signaling privileged exclusivity, it instead specifies the exclusion of the affected young courtiers from the English court.

1.4.128. **kiss:** There is evidence that at the end of a dance, the man customarily kissed the woman. Shakespeare's contemporary Nicholas Breton wrote a poem that includes the lines "Dancers, besides, may claim a kiss of right, / After the dance is ended, and before." Henry's line claiming a kiss may refer to this custom as he, in effect, apologizes for not having kissed Anne after dancing with her earlier (98 SD).

2.1.70 SD. **Sir Walter Sands:** This historical figure was called Lord Sands in the first act of the play. His apparent demotion in Act 2 comes about because the action represented in 2.1 in fact occurred before that represented in 1.3–4. The rank of this character, then, who rose from the position of knight to that of "Lord Sands," is, in the play, keyed to his rank at the time of the historical action represented. When Buckingham was arrested in 1521, Sir William Sands (as he is named in Holinshed) was still a knight. By the time Henry met Anne Bullen, Sands had been made a noble.

2.4.142 SP. GENTLEMAN USHER: Some editors identify this speaker with the character Griffith, who appears in 4.2, where he is identified in a stage direction as *"her* [i.e., Katherine's] *gentleman usher."* Such identification is based on Holinshed's *Chronicles;* there Griffith is given a speech very much like the one at line 142: "With that (quoth maister Griffith) Madame, you be called againe." However, the play's text does not identify the speaker of line 142 as Griffith, and there is so little to the speech that it provides in itself nothing to connect the gentleman usher who delivers it to the much more fully developed character Griffith of 4.2. Therefore we have not made the connection by identifying the gentleman usher of 2.4 as Griffith.

3.1.161. **You have . . . hearts:** There may be a reference in these lines to the legend that St. Gregory called the Anglo-Saxons *"non Angli sed angeli"* (not Angles but angels). Then, according to Camden, an English historian of Shakespeare's time, Gregory went on to regret that "the foul fiend should be Lord of such fair folk."

3.2.84–87. **He is . . . Christendom:** This sentence has been interpreted by editors in more than one way: (1) Cranmer has reported **opinions** that he has gathered abroad concerning the king's divorce, and these have **satisfied the king** and **the colleges** (at this time staffed by learned clerics); (2) Cranmer has reported the **opinions** of **the colleges** abroad regarding the divorce, which have confirmed his own opinion and **satisfied the king.** The first interpretation puts the least strain on the language of the passage, while the second is closer to what some authorities of Shakespeare's day recorded as actual historical events.

3.2.342. **larks:** Gordon McMullan has recently suggested that this reference to **larks** is also an allusion to Wolsey's mistress Joan Lark, sister to his chaplain. Wolsey's failure to preserve his vow of chastity was, like the identity of his mistress, well known in his own time. Joan Lark is characterized at line 357 as a **brown wench,** that is, as a woman of no social standing, because upper-class women were careful to preserve the whiteness of their complexions against the effects of sun and wind.

3.2.408. **praemunire:** i.e., *praemunire facias*. This Latin legal term was more than a century old by the reign of Henry VIII, the time in which this play is set. Initially it referred to a writ by which a person could be charged for appealing to a foreign court (especially a papal court) in an action involving an English subject and hence relevant to the king's court. The meaning of the term changed after Henry VIII declared himself head of the church in England, a declaration he had not yet made when Wolsey fell. The term thereafter referred to a writ to summon a person charged with asserting papal jurisdiction in England, thereby denying the ecclesiastical supremacy of the sovereign. The second meaning was in force when this play was written. It is difficult to know just which meaning might have been given the term by an audience watching this play in 1613. Presumably, individuals would understand it differently, according to their own varying knowledge of history and legal terminology.

4.1.61 SD. **Enter the Old Duchess:** It may be noted that some ten lines of dialogue separate the Gentlemen's first comment about Anne's entrance from their first comment on the duchess of Norfolk, who bears Anne's train. This particular feature of the play's dialogue may capture Holinshed's observation that "the queen's train . . . was very long."

5.2.44 SD. **Lord Chancellor:** At 3.2.468–69, Cromwell tells Wolsey that Sir Thomas More has replaced him in this office. In the present scene, though, the play is silent about the office holder. It has been suggested that the official is not brought on as More to avoid the intrusion of a personality, and More's is so large a personality that his represented presence certainly could unduly complicate the audience's response.

5.3.23. Samson, Sir Guy, Colbrand: Judges 15.15 tells of **Samson** killing a thousand in battle; the medieval romance *Guy of Warwick* tells of the knight's battles against Saracens and against the Danish giant **Colbrand.**

5.3.28. And . . . her: Since the phrase **not for a cow** also occurs in the manuscript play *The Tell-tale*, it might have been a common expression. However, its meaning has not been determined.

5.3.64–65. tribulation of Tower Hill, limbs of Limehouse: These phrases may be figurative names for two troublemaking gangs, or the word **tribulation** may simply mean "troublemakers" and **limbs** may echo the popular phrase "limb of Satan," meaning a mischievous wicked person.

Textual Notes

The reading of the present text appears to the left of the square bracket. Unless otherwise noted, the reading to the left of the bracket is from **F,** the First Folio text (upon which this edition is based). The earliest sources of readings not in **F** are indicated as follows: **F2** is the Second Folio of 1632; **F3** is the Third Folio of 1663–64; **F4** is the Fourth Folio of 1685; **Ed.** is an earlier editor of Shakespeare, beginning with Rowe in 1709. No sources are given for emendations of punctuation or for corrections of obvious typographical errors, like turned letters that produce no known word. **SD** means stage direction; **SP** means speech prefix; *uncorr.* means the first or uncorrected state of the First Folio; *corr.* means the second or corrected state of the First Folio; ~ stands in place of a word already quoted before the square bracket; ʌ indicates the omission of a punctuation mark.

Prologue 1. SP PROLOGUE] Ed.; *THE PROLOGVE* F 19. besides] F (beside)
  1.1 39. censure.] ~, F 43. seenʌ] ~, F 49. All] Ed.; *Buc.* All F 53. SP BUCKINGHAM Who] Ed.; who F 55. as] F4; *Nor.* As F 56. SP NORFOLK One] Ed.; One F 73. web,] ~. F 73. he] Ed.; O F 74. way—] ~ʌ F 80–81. that? . . . hell,] ~, . . . ~? F 91. council out,] ~, ~ʌ F 134. it] ir F 135. advise] F (aduice) 135. SD *Buckingham, and Buckingham*] Buckham, and Buckingham F 136 *and hereafter except for* 2.2.105–55; 2.4.61–160; 3.1.27–31, 90–110; 3.2.323, 363–419. SP WOLSEY] Ed.; *Car.* F 147. chafed] F (chaff'd) 183.

245

July] *Inly* F   197. rinsing] F (wrenching)   230. SD
three] *theee* F   268. lord] Ed.; Lords F   269. SD *They
exit.*] F (*Exe.*)

1.2   0. SD *Nobles . . . Cardinal*] Ed.; *Nobles, and Sir
Thomas Louell* F   5. Buckingham's;] ~, F   8. SD *Enter
the Queen Katherine, ushered by the Duke of Norfolk,*]
Ed.; *vsher'd by the Duke of Norfolke. Enter the Queene,
Norfolke* F   8. SD *Suffolk*] *Snffolke* F   9 *and hereafter until* 4.2. SP QUEEN KATHERINE] Ed.; *Queen.* F   10.
SD *He . . . him.*] 2 *lines earlier in* F, *immediately following*
1.2.8 SD "*State,*" *as* "*takes her vp, kisses and placeth her by
him.*"   15. Majesty.] ~∧ F   17. nor] F *corr.;* no F *uncorr.*
44. Wherein?] F *corr.;* ~; F *uncorr.*   44. taxation?] F *corr.;*
~. F *uncorr.*   58. They] F *corr.;* hey F *uncorr.*   59. or] er F
72. mouths.] ~, F   75. did;] ~: F *corr.;* ~, F *uncorr.*   106.
precedent] F (President)   124. SD *Secretary*] F (*Secret.*)
188. confession's] Ed.; Commissions F   194. gain] F4;
omit F   207. him] Ed.; this F   232. prison?] ~. F

1.3   0. SD *Lord*] F (*L.*) *twice*   1 *and hereafter in this
scene.* SP CHAMBERLAIN] Ed.; *L. Ch.* F   3 *and hereafter
in this scene.* SP SANDS] Ed.; *L. San.* F   15. Or] Ed.; A F
18. SD *Enter . . . Lovell.*] 2 *lines later in* F   41. *privilegio*] *Pruiilegio* F   41. *oui*] Ed.; F (wee)   74. lord.] ~, F
74. 'Has] F (Ha's)   74. wherewithal. In him,] ~∧~~; F

1.4   1. SP GUILFORD] Ed.; *S. Hen. Guilf.* F   7. SD
Lord] F (*L.*) *twice*   14, 81, 131. banquet] F (banket)   39.
gentlemen] Gntlemen F   64. SD *Drum . . . discharged.*]
1 *line earlier in* F   96. SD *The masquers . . . Bullen.*] This
ed.; *Choose Ladies, King and An. Bullen.* F   105. and]
aud F   107. SD *Whisper . . . masquers.*] 1 *line earlier in*
F, *as* "*Whisper.*"

2.1   1. Whither] F (Whether)   14. for 't] F (fort)
30. prophecies?] ~. F   52. attainder] F (Attendure)
55. Lest] F (Least)   70. SD *Enter . . . etc.*] 2 *lines earlier
in* F   80. 'T has] F (T'has)   81. Christian] This Ed.;
Christians F   136. Eighth] F (Eight)

2.2   28. For,] ~∧ F   43. true:] ~∧ F   100. sick,] ~∧ F   103. one∧] ~; F   103. have-at-him] F (haue at him)   105. precedent] F (President)   125. commanding,] ~. F   142. SD *The . . . whisper.*] F (*Walkes and whispers.*)

2.3   9. process,] ~. F   16. quarrel,] ~. F   98. SD *Lord . . . exits.*] *1/2 line earlier in* F   129. me?] ~ === F

2.4   10, 14–15. come into the court] F (&c.)   99. wrong.] ~∧ F   119. cunning] eunning F   130. spiritual,] ~. F   140. Queen] F (Q)   183. hindered, oft,] ~, ~∧ F   194. A] Ed.; And F   201. Sometime] F (Sometimes)   219. throe] F (throw)   226, 263. learnèd] F (learn'd)   230. SP LINCOLN] Ed.; *B. Lin.* F   242. summons. Unsolicited∧] ~∧~. F   264. return. With thy approach,] ~, ~~~: F

3.1   24. coming, . . . on 't.] ~; . . . ~, F   26. SD *Campeius*] F (*Campian*)   30. reverend] F (reuerent)   32. chamber,] ~; F   58. should] shoul F   68. your] F2; our F   93. profit.] ~∧ F   97. forsooth.] ~, F   98. afflictions] affllictions F   168. me,] ~? F   188. was∧] ~, F   194. me∧] ~; F   195. unmannerly.] ~, F

3.2   108. bade] F (bad)   137. that] F (y̆)   139. SD *Enter . . . Attendants.*] *3 lines earlier in* F   158. found?] ~∧ F   181. audit.] ~, F   182. glad] gald F   216. filed] Ed.; fill'd F   287. commission, lords?] ~? ~, F   294. coarse metal] F (course Mettle)   411. Chattels] Ed.; Castles F   419. SD *All . . . exit.*] *1 line earlier in* F   518. missed] F (mist)   527. country's] F (Countries)

4.1   24. SP SECOND GENTLEMAN] Ed.; I F   41. SD *Then . . . crown.*] This Ed.; The Order of the Coronation. I *A liuely Flourish of Trumpets.* 2 *Then, two Iudges.* 3 *Lord* Chancellor, *with Purse and Mace before him.* 4 Quirristers *singing.* Musicke. 5 Maior of London, *bearing the Mace. Then* Garter, *in his Coate of Armes, and on his head he wore a Gilt Copper Crowne.* 6 Marquesse

Dorset, *bearing a Scepter of Gold, on his head, a Demy Coronall of Gold. With him, the Earle of* Surrey, *bearing the Rod of Siluer with the Doue, Crowned with an Earles Coronet. Collars of Esses.* 7 Duke of Suffolke, *in his Robe of Estate, his Coronet on his head, bearing a long white Wand, as High Steward. With him, the Duke of* Norfolke, *with the Rod of Marshalship, a Coronet on his head. Collars of Esses.* 8 A Canopy, *borne by foure of the* Cinque-Ports, *vnder it the Queene in her Robe, in her haire, richly adorned with Pearle, Crowned. On each side her, the Bishops of* London, *and* Winchester. 9 *The* Olde Dutchesse of Norfolke, *in a Coronall of Gold, wrought with Flowers bearing the Queenes Traine.* 10 *Certaine* Ladies *or* Countesses, *with plaine Circlets of Gold, without Flowers. Exeunt, first passing ouer the Stage in Order and State, and then, A great Flourish of Trumpets.* F 66. SP FIRST GENTLEMAN] Ed.; *omit* F 69. crowd] crow'd F 80, 107. choir] F (Quire) 81. sat] F (sate) 94. press] F (prease)

4.2 9. think] F2; thanke F 21. roads] F (Rodes) 23. convent] F (Couent) 89. SD *congee*] F (*Conge*) 89. SD *reuerent*] F (*reuerend*) 119. haste] F (hast)

5.1 15. haste] F (hast) 44. Besides] F (Beside) 47. time] F4; Lime F 53. you, I think—] ~) ~~∧ F 66. SD *Gardiner . . . exit.*] *1 line earlier in* F 94. SD *Enter Sir Anthony Denny.*] *1 line later in* F 144. halidom] F (Holydame) 170. precipice] F (Precepit) 171. woo] F (woe) 193. SP LOVELL] Ed.; *Gent.* F 193. SD *Enter . . . Lovell.*] *1 line earlier in* F 194 *and hereafter.* SP OLD LADY] Ed.; *Lady* F

5.2 5. SD *Enter Keeper.*] *1/2 line later in* F 11. SD *Enter . . . Butts.*] *1 line earlier in* F 12. piece] F2; Peere F 15. Butts,] ~. F 16. physician.] ~, F 32. pursuivants] F (Purseuants) 69. heresies∧] ~; F 95. nourishment∧] ~; F 111. friend.] ~, F 127. faulty] faultly F 143, 147. SP CHANCELLOR] Ed.; *Cham.* F

169. 'Tis] 'Ts F   194. offenses.] ~, F   197. for,] ~; F
203. this] F4; his F   230. subject,] ~; F   248. brother-
love] ~; ~ F   251. heart] F2; hearts F

5.3   4, 29. SP ONE] Ed.; *omit* F   4, 29. Master] F
(M.)   16. Paul's] F (Powles)   38. thousand;] ~, F   54.
Strand] F (Strond)   90. press] F (preasse)   90. a way]
F (away)

5.4   0. SD *Lord*] F (*L.*) F   0. SD *etc.*] F (*&c.*)   45.
ways] F4; way F   50. herself,] ~. F   74. man.] ~, F
86. holiday] F (Holy-day)

Epilogue   1. SP EPILOGUE] Ed.; THE EPILOGVE F
4. trumpets] *Tumpets* F   8. hear∧] ~. F

The Famous History of the Life of
King HENRY the Eight.

THE PROLOGUE.

I Come no more to make you Laugh, Things now,
That beare a Weighty, and a Serious Brow,
Sad, high, and working, full of State and awe:
Such Noble Scoenes, as draw the Eye to flow
We now present. Those that can Pitty, heere
May (if they thinke it well) let fall a Teare,
The Subiect will deserue it. Such as giue
Their Money out of hope they may beleeue,
May heere finde Truth too. Those that come to see
Onely a show or two, and so agree,
The Play may passe: If they be still, and willing,
Ile vndertake may see away their shilling
Richly in two short houres. Onely they
That come to heare a Merry, Bawdy Play,
A noyse of Targets: Or to see a Fellow
In a long Motley Coate, garded with Yellow,

Will be deceyu'd. For gentle Hearers, know
To ranke our chosen Truth with such a show
As Foole, and Fight is, beside forfeyting
Our owne Braines, and the Opinion that we bring
To make that onely true, we now intend,
Will leaue vs neuer an vnderstanding Friend.
Therefore, for Goodnesse sake, and as you are knowne
The First and Happiest Hearers of the Towne,
Be sad, as we would make ye. Thinke ye see
The very Persons of our Noble Story,
As they were Liuing: Thinke you see them Great,
And follow'd with the generall throng, and sweat
Of thousand Friends: Then, in a moment, see
How soone this Mightinesse, meets Misery:
And if you can be merry then, Ile say,
A Man may weepe vpon his Wedding day.

Actus Primus. Scœna Prima.

*Enter the Duke of Norfolke at one doore. At the other,
the Duke of Buckingham, and the Lord
Abergauenny.*

Buckingham.

GOod morrow, and well met. How haue ye done
Since last we saw in France?

Norf. I thanke your Grace:
Healthfull, and euer since a fresh Admirer
Of what I saw there.

Buck. An vntimely Ague
Staid me a Prisoner in my Chamber, when
Those Sunnes of Glory, those two Lights of Men
Met in the vale of Andren.

Nor. 'Twixt Guynes and Arde,
I was then present, saw them salute on Horsebacke,
Beheld them when they lighted, how they clung
In their Embracement, as they grew together,
Which had they,
What foure Thron'd ones could haue weigh'd
Such a compounded one?

Buck. All the whole time
I was my Chambers Prisoner.

Nor. Then you lost
The view of earthly glory: Men might say
Till this time Pompe was single, but now married
To one aboue it selfe. Each following day
Became the next dayes master, till the last
Made former Wonders, it's. To day the French,
All Clinquant all in Gold, like Heathen Gods
Shone downe the English; and to morrow, they
Made Britaine, India: Euery man that stood,
Shew'd like a Mine. Their Dwarfish Pages were
As Cherubins, all gilt: the Madams too,
Not vs'd to toyle, did almost sweat to beare
The Pride vpon them, that their very labour
Was to them, as a Painting. Now this Maske
Was cry'de incomparable; and th'ensuing night
Made it a Foole, and Begger. The two Kings
Equall in lustre, were now best, now worst
As presence did present them: Him in eye,
Still him in praise, and being present both,
'Twas said they saw but one, and no Discerner
Durst wagge his Tongue in censure, when these Sunnes
(For so they phrase 'em) by their Heralds challeng'd
The Noble Spirits to Armes, they did performe

Beyond

t 3

Appendix on Authorship

Henry VIII was first published, together with thirty-five other plays, in 1623 in the book we now call the Shakespeare First Folio. Until Edmond Malone did so in 1790, no one suggested that the play was the work of anyone else but Shakespeare; and until James Spedding made the argument in 1850, no one attempted to attribute parts of it to John Fletcher, Shakespeare's successor as principal dramatist of the King's Men. Since Spedding, a number of different scholars, using different methods, have attempted to discriminate between those parts of the play to be credited to Shakespeare and those to be credited to Fletcher. These scholars have arrived at no consensus, although all who see the play as jointly authored have agreed that the collaborators who wrote the play included Shakespeare and Fletcher. Opinion has continued to fluctuate about whether the play is a work of collaboration or is solely Fletcher's or is solely Shakespeare's, with belief in collaborative authorship currently in the ascendant.

While we do not consider the play solely Fletcher's, we do not think it impossible or even improbable that Fletcher's hand may be represented in the play. It is conservatively estimated that at least half the plays from the public theater of Shakespeare's time were collaborative efforts. Shakespeare is known to have collaborated with Fletcher on *The Two Noble Kinsmen*, published as a quarto with both dramatists' names on the title page in 1634. We respect the labor expended and skill exhibited by attribution scholars; at the same time, we take seriously the limitations that they acknowledge necessarily attend their efforts. On this basis we simply set aside the question of whether Fletcher wrote some of *Henry VIII* and contest neither those who have argued for collaboration nor those who have claimed the play for Shakespeare.

We treat the play in the same way as the others published in the Shakespeare First Folio, referring to it for convenience as a Shakespeare play. In doing so, we fully recognize that the theater is always the location of collaborative creation, not just among named dramatists but also among members of acting companies and their employees and associates. We are aware of documentary evidence of other hands reaching into dramatic manuscripts in the course of their annotation or transcription, and we suspect that Shakespeare's words could not possibly have commanded in their own time the same reverence they have subsequently been accorded. Such circumstances attach to all the Shakespeare printed plays that have come down to us. In calling *Henry VIII* Shakespeare's, then, we simply acknowledge its inclusion in the 1623 First Folio and its acceptance as Shakespeare's among scholars, theater practitioners, and lovers of Shakespeare for most of the past four hundred years.

Henry VIII:
A Modern Perspective

Barbara A. Mowat

On June 29, 1613, *Henry VIII* was performed at the Globe theater in what was probably one of its first performances. When the production reached the fourth scene, cannons were set off to signal Henry's entrance; the cannons sparked a fire in the thatch of the roof, and, according to Sir Henry Wotton, the audience was so "attentive to the show" that they ignored the smoke, and the theater burned to the ground. Wotton also remarked on the spectacular costuming and staging of the play, at that time called—by some, at least—"All Is True": "The King's Players had a new Play, called *All is true*, representing some principal pieces of the Reign of *Henry* the *8th*, which was set forth with many extraordinary Circumstances of Pomp and Majesty."[1] While the rest of the letter makes it clear that Wotton was most interested in the production's "Pomp and Majesty," his comment on the play as "representing . . . principal pieces" is perhaps more significant, in that it calls immediate attention to what has later been perceived as the play's odd dramatic structure.

For more than two centuries after its opening, *Henry VIII* was loved for its spectacle and its sonorous, heart-rending speeches, and it was considered one of Shakespeare's more attractive theater pieces. But beginning in the nineteenth century, critics found the design of the play inexplicably defective. As Wotton had pointed out, the play presents a sequence of "principal pieces" from a sixteen-year portion of Henry's reign, "pieces" that include Henry's divorce from Katherine of Aragon, his marriage to Anne Bullen, and the birth and christening of the infant Elizabeth. Other pieces center on events involving the powerful Cardinal Wolsey, the duke of Buckingham, and Archbishop Cranmer. Nineteenth-century scholars and critics remarked that while it might have been possible for these incidents to have been shaped into a coherent, meaningful drama, the play instead is mere disjointed spectacle with a plotline that puts the audience in an impossible position. As James Spedding argued in 1850, it encourages us through the first four acts to sympathize deeply with Katherine and to see Henry's desire for Anne as "the mere caprice of passion"; then, in Act 4, Katherine goes offstage to die, and the audience, in the remainder of the play, is supposed to rejoice in the coronation of Katherine's rival Anne and in the birth of Anne's daughter, Elizabeth. Cranmer's speech that concludes the play—a prophecy about the reign of Elizabeth—crowns Henry's passion "with all felicity, present and to come," wrote Spedding, and the audience is made "to entertain as a theme of joy and compensatory satisfaction" this happy outcome of Henry's lust and Katherine's suffering. Spedding concluded that the play's "principal defect, which is the incoherence of the general design," could be accounted for only by assuming that the play "was written partly by Shakspere, partly by Fletcher, with assistance probably of some third hand."[2] Algernon Swinburne, who in the face of Spedding's almost universally accepted hypothesis continued to argue for Shakespeare's sole authorship, shared Spedding's despair over the play's design, calling *Henry VIII*, because of its structure, "possibly the hardest problem" facing the serious student of Shakespeare.[3]

For scholars today, the design of *Henry VIII* seems no longer to provoke despair, in part because many have found explanations that, for them, answer Spedding's allegations about the "incoherence of the [play's] general design." Their defenses of the play's structure fall into two camps, one of which finds in the play a pattern we might call "providential." Some in this group see the play as religious or patriotic; some see it as resembling a masque, others a romance. All of them, though, share a fundamental belief that the play is structured as a kind of comic parabola, a progression of events leading to the play's significant moment: the birth and christening of Elizabeth and Cranmer's prophetic vision—a vision of the new Golden Age when the royal infant will grow up to be a "pattern to all princes" and of an England in which, under Queen Elizabeth, "every man shall eat in safety / Under his own vine what he plants and sing / The merry songs of peace to all his neighbors" (5.4.29, 41–43). For most providential-design critics, the hero of the play is England itself, and the play is, in structure, a comedy.[4]

An opposing group of critics views the design as quite other: no comic parabola but a tragic "wheel of Fortune" pattern. They argue that the play focuses our attention and our sympathy on three of Henry's victims in turn—Buckingham, Katherine, and Wolsey—and that the unifying design of the play is a series of linked circles, a repeated pattern of rises and falls on Fortune's wheel, a pattern that the still moment of Elizabeth's christening interrupts only briefly.[5] For the providential-design critics, the play is a celebration not to be darkened by protracted sympathy for history's victims; for those in the "wheel of Fortune" group, the play is a lament for the suffering and mutability of falling men, and of fallen man, brightened at best momentarily by Cranmer's vision of England as a new Eden.

Interestingly—and paradoxically—considerable evidence supports both sets of critics. Both the providential design and the wheel of Fortune design seem carefully structured into the play, and each is carefully called to the attention of the audience. The design that leads toward the high point of Elizabeth's birth, for instance, is part of the structural fabric of the play. Two prophecies about Anne Bullen—that she will bring forth a jewel to give light to the whole nation, that from her will fall a blessing to England—are strategically placed in Acts 2 and 3 to remind us of the providential significance of Henry's desire for Anne and to point our expectations toward Elizabeth's birth and christening. The language of these two prophecies, as well as their import, are of a piece with the prophecy by Cranmer with which the play concludes. Together, these three foretellings form a pattern that supports a reading of the play as a celebration of the Tudor myth—the dominant sixteenth-century narrative explaining English history as shaped by God to bring Elizabeth to the English throne. It is hard to argue that an audience in 1613 would have been ignorant of Anne's role as mother of the babe of promise, or that the prophecies, placed as they are, would have failed to remind the audience that the fruit of Henry's union with Anne was the Elizabethan Golden Age.

The role of Providence in shaping the grand design that produced Queen Elizabeth is called to our attention in more subtle ways as well. While the playwright draws heavily on the history of the period as recorded in Holinshed's _Chronicles_,[6] he also changes historical fact—shifting chronology, inventing incidents—so that key events appear to have been directly guided by heaven's will. The manner of Wolsey's fall, for instance, is an invention so deliberately improbable that, in its exquisite timing, we are almost forced to see the hand of God. Wolsey, the prime mover in instigating the divorce proceedings, had been a necessary figure in the providential scheme. But his opposition to Henry's desire to marry Anne Bullen led Wolsey to begin to block forward progress, and Providence therefore needed to get him out of the way. Thus, in the play's representation of history, Wolsey at precisely the right moment betrayed himself by sending to Henry not one but *two* self-incriminating documents in a single packet. The incident—modeled on a "mishap" featuring Thomas Ruthall, bishop of Durham, in the reign of Henry's father[7]—is entirely fictional as applied to Wolsey and is most uncharacteristic of the careful archbishop presented elsewhere in the play. As Wolsey stands self-betrayed, he says to himself,

> O negligence,
> Fit for a fool to fall by! What cross devil
> Made me put this main secret in the packet
> I sent the King?
>
> (3.2.264–67)

Norfolk's reading of the event is to the point: "It's heaven's will! / Some spirit put this paper in the packet / To bless" Henry's eyes (165–67) and thereby, we might add, to push the action of history toward the improbable sequence of events culminating in Elizabeth's legitimate birth. Wolsey's ruin is swift, complete, and timely. The play shows Providence busily removing an unwanted character in order to make room for the much more tractable Archbishop Cranmer—all at the perfect moment, and all in order to bring us, the play, and history to that happy tableau of Henry, Cranmer, and the royal infant.

Yet Fortune, too, shapes events in this play; and, again, the resulting design—the wheel of Fortune design—seems quite deliberate. As such critics as Frank Kermode have pointed out, Shakespeare shows us Buckingham, Wolsey, and Katherine at the top of Fortune's wheel; as it turns for each of them, bringing them to disgrace and to death, each is given a speech in which the fall from greatness is lamented, and the audience is told the moral of the victim's tale.[8] In structure, in language, and in pathos, each of these "falls" would have presented to a Jacobean audience a familiar, if old-fashioned, pattern—that of *de casibus* tragedy, a form most often associated with medieval stories of falls from greatness.[9] This wheel of Fortune pattern clearly governs the stories of Buckingham, Wolsey, and Katherine as the play presents them. Their farewell speeches themselves suffice to tie the characters to this familiar form. Wolsey describes it quite specifically, using the apparent rising and falling motion of the sun or a star to image his trajectory:

> I have touched the highest point of all my greatness,
> And from that full meridian of my glory
> I haste now to my setting. I shall fall
> Like a bright exhalation in the evening
> And no man see me more.
>
> (3.2.275–79)

Buckingham goes to his death reflecting on the fall that ends his life: "The last hour / Of my long weary life is come upon me. / Farewell. And when you would say something that is sad, / Speak how I fell" (2.1.152–56). And Katherine, too, voices the poignancy of her life's failure, describing herself as

> Shipwracked upon a kingdom where no pity,
> No friends, no hope, no kindred weep for me,
> Almost no grave allowed me, like the lily
> That once was mistress of the field and flourished,
> I'll hang my head and perish.
>
> (3.1.166–70)

As if their speeches were not enough to point to the wheel of Fortune pattern, the play again alters history to fit their stories more snugly into the familiar design. The impact of Wolsey's wheel of Fortune fall, for example, is heightened by the play's compression of a year of history into a few moments. In a single scene— the one in which the nefarious packet exposes his double-dealing—the great cardinal, all-powerful when the scene opens, is cast off by the king, stripped of the great seal, comes to self-awareness, bids farewell to his greatness, and makes his final exit to die, his mind turned to God. Here is presented a classic wheel of Fortune tragic fall; and it is created through the omission of a full year of events that occurred between Wolsey's dismissal in November 1529 and his death in November 1530—a year during which, according to Holinshed, Henry watched with fury as Wolsey rebuilt castles, staged grand processions, and attempted a new rise to power in the North as archbishop of York—as he, in Henry's words as reported in Holinshed, "remained presumptuous and proud," though supposedly "under foot." The play's powerful scene of Wolsey's disgrace and conversion, with its pathos, resignation, and immediate turning to God, was the dramatist's rewriting of history.

We find comparable compressions, rearrangements, and inventions in the falls of Buckingham and Katherine—changes that align their stories with the medieval tradition of wheel of Fortune falls. And even in the last act of *Henry VIII*, with its focus on the rise of Anne and Archbishop Cranmer, the wheel of Fortune pattern is operative. If we grant that Shakespeare's audience would have known much of the story of Henry and Anne and the result of their union in Elizabeth, we must also grant that they would have known the fates of those involved in that final, triumphant tableau: that Henry's destruction of wives had just begun; that Elizabeth, at the age of two, would be declared illegitimate by Cranmer himself; and that Cranmer would be burned at the stake. Anne, too, would very soon fall and die at the executioner's hand—primarily for having given Henry this daughter instead of a son. The joyful moment of the christening and the prophecy, then, can easily be seen as simply that: a moment at which Fortune's wheel is briefly still before it spins on again, carrying victim after victim in a series of tragic circles that spin out of the play and on into history.

The play is thus shaped around two emotionally contradictory patterns, behind which, I would argue, is yet a third. This one—not immediately obvious, but a constant in the play—is a pattern of jockeyings for position and favor, of bribery and subornation, of treachery and betrayals that we might call the "political ladder" design. The play's opening scene is illustrative. It begins with a lengthy description of Henry in France at the famous Field of the Cloth of Gold, a vision of peace and of golden splendor; and it ends with the duke of Buckingham's arrest, and his recognition that "My life is spanned already. / I am the shadow of poor Buckingham" (1.1.265–66). Behind these larger events, layers of political intrigue and horror are, in the course of the scene, opened to audience inspection. We learn, first, that the marvelous moment of peace and amity of the Field of the Cloth of Gold was purchased at crippling cost to the now-impoverished peers of England; we learn that the peace has already been broken, not through the action of Providence (though the tempest that followed the signing of the articles was generally seen as a sign from God that the peace was doomed) but rather through bribery and corruption in very high places: Emperor Charles V had bribed Cardinal Wolsey; Wolsey had in turn sold his and Henry's honor and had drawn up the articles of peace so that they could not hold but "like a glass / Did break i' th' rinsing" (196–97). As for Buckingham's arrest, we learn that Wolsey had found a man who hated Buckingham—a former servant named Knevet, dismissed for taking bribes. Wolsey has shown Knevet gold; Knevet has, in return, betrayed Buckingham by reporting treacherous statements he claims that the duke made. Buckingham falls, that is, not because of Fortune but because he has made an enemy of Wolsey, who is rich and powerful, and because a servant, for money and for spite, betrays him. The common feature linking the whole of this opening scene is, appropriately, gold—gold for splendor, gold for bribery, gold for subornation. The scene appears to be controlled by Providence and by Fortune, but its central action actually takes place on the political ladder, where Wolsey, on his way up, kicks Buckingham off.

The play is filled with stories of positions won and lost, with rumors, with intrigues, with factions forming and breaking, with attempts to secure that which can never be truly secured—that is, favor. Behind all of the play's reminders of Fortune and of the guiding hand of Providence, we are repeatedly faced with the realities of life in a world where gold buys subversion and false witness, and where treachery and self-serving are the rule. In this world, one survives through constant vigilance—with an eye on the person above on the ladder and an eye on the person below. Both are equally dangerous. A momentary failure of vigilance, a trust or affection unwisely given, a carelessly spoken or a maliciously misinterpreted word, an action or a decision that, even though commendable, creates an enemy, and one's position—and often one's life—lies forfeit.

Buckingham's final lament includes this moral from the political-ladder world: he and his father, he says, are "one in fortunes" in that both fell through the

treachery of servants, of "those men we loved most."
"Heaven has an end in all," he says:

> yet, you that hear me,
> This from a dying man receive as certain:
> Where you are liberal of your loves and counsels
> Be sure you be not loose; for those you make friends
> And give your hearts to, when they once perceive
> The least rub in your fortunes, fall away
> Like water from you, never found again
> But where they mean to sink you.

> (2.1.141–51)

Katherine, too—destroyed presumably by Fortune and
by Providence—describes accurately the corruption of
the court that secures her destruction. When asked to
trust the judges Henry has appointed, she says bitterly
that she'll put her trust in heaven: "there sits a judge /
That no king can corrupt" (3.1.113–14). As for the political world that determines her fate, she says, "Can
you think . . . / That any Englishman dare give me
counsel, / Or be a known friend, 'gainst his Highness'
pleasure, . . . / And live [his] subject?" (93–97).

Every incident in the play is touched by reminders of
this political-ladder world—by intrigue, by rumor and
half-lies and malice, by behind-the-scene glimpses of
how power is actually attained and, briefly, kept. The
design shows itself in countless tiny incidents. Wolsey,
for instance, at the side of the stage, congratulates the
king's new secretary: "Much joy and favor to you. / You
are the King's now"; the new secretary replies, "But to
be commanded / Forever by your Grace, whose hand
has raised me" (2.2.138–41). The secretary is Gardiner
(just beginning a rise that will take him eventually to
the chancellorship of England). Wolsey has placed

Gardiner in the king's household because Gardiner is a "good fellow": "If I command him [he] follows my [direction]." Gardiner's predecessor, says Wolsey, "was a fool, / For he would needs be virtuous" (157–59)—so Wolsey has destroyed him.

This world of self-seeking, of false service, of jockeying for position, of destruction through rumor and calumny, would have seemed familiar to the audience for which it was written—not so much from their reading (though Machiavelli describes it well) or from earlier literary forms as from direct observation. Though the play is set in Henry VIII's time, the political world it reveals is remarkably like the court of King James as it was described by contemporaries. By 1613, when *Henry VIII* was performed, the patronage system was in decay, having been corrupted into favoritism. Combat among lords was carried out not on battlefields but through political intrigue. Letters and records of the era reveal a world of treachery and corruption, especially in the period just before the play's first appearance. It was in 1612 that Robert Carr, James's then-current favorite, brought down the all-powerful Secretary of State and Lord High Treasurer, Robert Cecil. The rounding of the pack on Cecil, his miserable death, and the concerted attacks on his memory give us all the elements we need to put his story in the wheel of Fortune tradition, but his fall was politically, and maliciously, engineered. Again, it was in 1613 that Carr's own favorite, Thomas Overbury, was betrayed by Carr himself, and died, poisoned, in the Tower. This was the very real world so accurately reflected in the political-ladder scheme of *Henry VIII*.

What, then, can we say about the play's odd design? First, through its overlay of three dramatic patterns, the play gives us, almost simultaneously, three versions of a familiar story, each of which is presented as somehow "true." As one version has it, history, under the hand of God, sweeps on, bringing England providentially to the birth of Elizabeth. In the second version, under the power of capricious Fortune, individuals fall from power and are destroyed. In the third version, political intrigue and personal greed determine the countless small actions that eventuate in public, visible historic moments. The three designs, the three versions, intermingle in such fashion that the play's original title—*All Is True*—becomes an accurate description of history as the play shows it.

The scene in which Anne Bullen begins her rise to power illustrates the point nicely. Here Anne enters, lamenting the fall of Katherine, her mistress, and all such falls from greatness:

> Much better
> She ne'er had known pomp; though 't be temporal,
> Yet if that quarrel, Fortune, do divorce
> It from the bearer, 'tis a sufferance panging
> As soul and body's severing.
> . . . .
> Verily,
> I swear, 'tis better to be lowly born
> And range with humble livers in content
> Than to be perked up in a glist'ring grief
> And wear a golden sorrow.
>
> (2.3.14–18, 22–26)

Anne here interprets Katherine's fall in the wheel of Fortune tradition; and, in a few moments, Anne will herself begin to be lifted on Fortune's wheel. The closing lines of the scene suggest that Anne foresees her own fall: "It faints me / To think what follows" (124–25). Yet within the scene, the Lord Chamberlain sees in Anne's rise the hand of Providence:

Beauty and honor in her are so mingled
That they have caught the King. And who knows yet
But from this lady may proceed a gem
To lighten all this isle?

(93–96)

The bulk of the scene, however, takes place on the political ladder. Anne accepts a title and a gift of a thousand pounds a year from Henry, verifying the Old Lady's sardonic prediction that Anne yearns for eminence, wealth, and sovereignty just as every woman does, and that should such gifts be offered her, she would stretch her conscience and accept them. That the gifts are a payment in advance for Anne's sexual favors is again made clear by the Old Lady, who sarcastically calls the money a "compelled fortune" and asks rhetorically: "The Marchioness of Pembroke? / A thousand pounds a year for pure respect? / No other obligation?" (105, 114–16). And Anne's closing mention of Katherine—"The Queen is comfortless and we forgetful / In our long absence" (126–27)—reminds us that Anne is in the service of the queen. Anne's request to the Old Lady, "Pray do not deliver / What here you've heard to her," with the Old Lady's cynical "What do you think me?" (127–29), reminds us that Anne is one among many in this play who betray the one they serve for their own profit.

"All is true": Anne is a traveler on Fortune's wheel; Anne has been placed by Providence in Henry's eye to bring joy to the English nation; Anne is a woman who betrays her mistress for money and power. The three readings of her story—as of the stories of Wolsey, Katherine, and others—are built into the very structure of the play. We may, like some critics, respond to the composite vision of history that such a structure yields by seeing in its author a deep ambivalence; or we may say, with Northrop Frye, that this "tragic play" yields "an irony so corrosive that it has almost a comic dimension."[10] Or we may observe that we have in this play neither ambivalence nor corrosive irony. By 1613, dramatists could hardly be shocked by the discovery that history's means and ends are at odds, or that idyllic visions of any age are inevitably oversimplifications of life in this fallen world. The play simply says to the chroniclers of the Tudor myth: yes, that's true; to the wheel of Fortune poets: yes, that's true; and to the contemporary observers of James's court: "That's true, too."[11]

History, then, is given to us in a very complex form. The play allows us no single point of view, in that each of the three designs entails its own stance. The providential design is history viewed in hindsight, but expressed as prophecy. This is the storytelling, mythmaking stance, familiar to us from Shakespeare's eight English histories about the reigns of Richard II through Richard III: history, that is, viewed from a distance and interpreted as a clear pattern leading up to and explaining the story's ending; history interpreted for us by the news analyst who can now see how events conspired to bring us to a particular wonderful or terrible moment.

The wheel of Fortune design, in contrast, is history as filtered through the emotions of the person rising or falling on the wheel. We listen as Fortune's victims tell their stories. The tone is elegiac, theatrical, and often self-pitying (as in Wolsey's final words, doubtless the most famous words in the play: "Had I but served my God with half the zeal / I served my king, He would not in mine age / Have left me naked to mine enemies" [3.2.535–37]—very moving, but inappropriate for the Wolsey we have seen and judged). This is history as it *feels* to the person who has been powerful, who faces ruin and public exposure, and who seizes the chance to bid farewell to his greatness and to a curious public. In contrast, the political-ladder design gives us history close-up but nonengaged. The video recorder is on, but the observed are unaware and carelessly self-damning.

In watching the play, as in watching events in the world around us, we see the story now from one angle, now from another. Again, as in observing events in our world, we never know for certain who is telling "the truth." Did Henry, as he claims, put away Katherine because of a "scruple" in his conscience (2.4.190–91)? Or did his conscience simply "cre[ep] too near another lady" (2.2.20–21)? The play never tells us. Did Buckingham die a martyr to the machinations of Wolsey and the treachery of Knevet, or had he actually threatened the royal succession, as his peers decided at his trial? Again, both views are provided and we never know which is "true." Without private access to the characters' minds and hearts—with almost no revelatory soliloquies or pregnant asides to the audience—we can judge motive only indirectly. Rumor and public address determine much of the play's action, and even more of its dialogue, and the play refuses to sort out for us facts from near-facts, or near-facts from slanderous lies. It uses dramatic structure to eliminate dramatic structure, giving us instead the illusion of public life as we, as spectators, actually perceive it.

The result is a play that, while set definitively at a given long-ago moment, shows us, through its design, ourselves in our own world. It shows us, for example, our propensity to find patterns in the events around us and our propensity to identify emotionally with those falling from power—or, conversely, to characterize those falls as necessary parts of the progress of history or as the result of the characters' or others' machinations. Once one has experienced history as it is presented in *Henry VIII*, one can only with difficulty return to a more innocent view of events in one's own nation or in the world. The designs are there, the global explanations are there, but the play has taught us that events fall into multiple patterns, that there are conflicting explanations for every action, that the human impulses of greed and self-protection should never be underestimated. Thus the curious design of the play produces for the careful observer a new wisdom about the world—especially the political world—and how it works. The design of the play is a challenge, but a challenge of the same sort posed to us by our life among our contemporaries.

1. Wotton's letter to Sir Edmund Bacon, dated July 2, 1613, is printed in *Shakespearean Criticism: Excerpts from the Criticism of William Shakespeare's Plays and Poetry . . .* , ed. Laurie Lanzen Harris and Mark W. Scott, vol. 2 (Detroit: Gale Research, 1985), p. 14.

2. James Spedding, "Appendix: Shakspere's Share in *Henry VIII*," *New Shakspere Society's Transactions*, no. 1 (1874): 2–3, 11, 16 (originally printed as "Who Wrote Shakespere's Henry VIII?" *Gentleman's Magazine*, August 1850, pp. 115–23, and excerpted in *Shakespearean Criticism: Excerpts*, vol. 2, pp. 28–31).

3. Algernon C. Swinburne, *A Study of Shakespeare* (London: Chatto and Windus, 1880), p. 81.

4. Of the works listed in "Further Reading," p. 271 below, the following present versions of providential readings: R. A. Foakes, G. Wilson Knight, and Alexander Leggatt. See also, as one of the earliest of such interpretations, Edgar I. Fripp, "1612–13: *King Henry the Eighth*," in his *Shakespeare, Man and Artist* (London: Oxford University Press, 1938), vol. 1, pp. 770–80.

5. For versions of "wheel of Fortune" readings, see, e.g., in "Further Reading," works by Edward Berry, Lee Bliss, Frank Cespedes, and Paul Dean.

6. Raphael Holinshed, *Chronicles of England, Scotland, and Ireland* (London, 1587), vol. 3, pp. 850–939.

7. Holinshed, *Chronicles,* vol. 3, pp. 796–97.

8. Frank Kermode, "What Is Shakespeare's 'Henry VIII' About?" *Durham University Journal,* n.s. 9 (1947): 48–54.

9. England's most influential collection of *de casibus* stories was *The Mirror for Magistrates,* which first appeared in 1559, and which contained some one hundred poems narrating the lives of great men and women who fell from greatness. The book follows from Boccaccio's fourteenth-century collection of moral histories called *De casibus virorum illustrium,* which gave its name to the tradition.

10. Northrop Frye, "Romance as Masque," in *Shakespeare's Romances Reconsidered,* ed. Carol McGinnis Kay and Henry E. Jacobs (Lincoln: University of Nebraska Press, 1978), p. 33.

11. See *King Lear* 5.2.13.

Further Reading

Henry VIII

Abbreviations: *Cym.* = *Cymbeline; H5* = *Henry V;*
H8 = *Henry VIII; Per.* = *Pericles;*
RSC = Royal Shakespeare Company;
Temp. = *The Tempest; WT* = *The Winter's Tale*

Berry, Edward I. *"Henry VIII* and the Dynamics of Spectacle." *Shakespeare Studies* 12 (1979): 229–46.

Berry explores how Shakespeare combines the tragic pattern of political falls—namely, those of Buckingham, Wolsey, and Katherine—with the pageantry and spectacle of the masque tradition to create a self-reflexive history play "that redefines the truth, a *de casibus* play that moves beyond tragedy, and a masque that questions the value of spectacle." Henry's aversion of Cranmer's downfall allows history to achieve, at least momentarily, "the status of ideal," but the joy expressed in Cranmer's prophecy (5.4) is tempered by the reader's/spectator's awareness of the falls to come: Cranmer's, Anne's, and Cromwell's. The real flaw in *H8* is not lack of structural or thematic unity, the criticism most frequently leveled at the play, but the characterization of Henry, whose growth in wisdom (as he moves from being under Wolsey's control at the beginning of the play to protecting Cranmer at the end) is neither psychologically nor morally articulated. That flaw notwithstanding, *H8* is a rich blend of disparate modes, and thus "a fitting end to a career of remarkable assimilations."

Bliss, Lee. "The Wheel of Fortune and the Maiden Phoenix of Shakespeare's *King Henry VIII.*" *ELH* 42 (1975): 1–25.

Bliss cautions against both "interpreting [*H8*] backward" from the perspective of Cranmer's "romantic" prophecy and approaching it "as a culmination which *must* draw on and resolve the problems and interests of an entire career." The first scene is paradigmatic of the play's shifting perspectives that complicate the establishment of truth, for what at first appeared to be marvel at the Field of the Cloth of Gold turns out to have been nothing more than a political maneuver. Just as our understanding of events is continually subjected to reevaluation, so too are our perceptions of characters: e.g., the truth of Buckingham's guilt and Wolsey's responsibility for his fall are never made completely clear. Questions also surround the titular figure himself, whose private words and acts compromise the godlike image created by the pomp and majesty that attend him. The only "truth" the play "unequivocally teaches is that one cannot trust in the props of this world—not servants, friends, lovers, or monarchs." When viewed in light of the moral complexities and ambiguous motivations informing the first four acts, Cranmer's prophecy of a golden world functions more as a prayer than a statement. Hortatory in nature, it provides a glimpse of "what a transformed England, under an inspired monarch, might be," thereby ending the play with an "aesthetic rather than logical sense of resolution and finality."

Bosman, Anston. "Seeing Tears: Truth and Sense in *All Is True*." *Shakespeare Quarterly* 50 (1999): 459–76.

Bosman reads *H8* through the lens of its alternate title *All Is True* in order to demonstrate how sensory perception "is regulated, equivocated, and celebrated" in the play. The primary source of *H8*'s "skepticism toward truth is the indeterminacy of perception in general and of vision in particular." The most decisive testimony against Buckingham, for example, is neither auditory (a verbatim quotation) nor scriptorial (a written document) but visual: the surveyor's description of Buckingham's pose followed by the surveyor's embodiment or performance of what Buckingham did (1.2.235–41). The "truth" claims of the surveyor are those of the theater, where "seeing . . . a representation . . . is believing." Bosman uses the Prologue's distinction between "truth" and "show" (line 18) to establish the play's two visual modes: the gaze of "embodied reciprocity" (e.g., the tears of Cromwell as shed for and appreciated by Wolsey in 3.2.444–47 and 504–10) and the gaze of "rivalrous" or "spectatorial" show (e.g., the empty pageantry of the Field of the Cloth of Gold reported in 1.1). In *All Is True*, tears provide the "deepest form of visual authentication" because the "flowing eye is able to see beyond empirical [and seductive] 'show' into speculative 'truth.'" The peculiar theatricality of the play, then, is one of "'seeing tears,' a visual mode of which weeping is at once the subject and object."

Cespedes, Frank V. "'We are one in fortunes': The Sense of History in *Henry VIII*." *English Literary Renaissance* 10 (1980): 413–28.

Noting how critics frequently allege a disparity between the ending and the first four acts of *H8*, Cespedes argues for a unifying dynamic in the motif of Fortune's wheel, which suffuses the entire drama with historical irony. The play has a dual focus: the fortunate march of history toward the reign of Elizabeth and the unfortunate stories of individuals during Henry VIII's reign "who unwittingly helped to shape, and perished in the unfolding of, this historical process." Instead of suggesting the evolution of an ideal monarch (see Foakes below), Shakespeare used his sources to structure events so as to emphasize the king's political rather than religious motivations and to increase rather than mitigate his hypocrisy. In the final scene, the play's pervasive sense of the contingency of historical forces, symbolized by the amoral vicissitudes of Fortune's wheel, qualifies Cranmer's providential view of history. *H8* is "indisputably a history play" and not a political romance.

Clare, Janet. "Beneath Pomp and Circumstance in *Henry VIII*." *Shakespeare Studies* (Tokyo) 21 (1982–83; published 1985): 65–81.
    A consideration of *H8* as an answer to Samuel Rowley's *When You See Me, You Know Me* (1604; revived in 1613) shows Shakespeare's play to be history rather than romance. The alternate title *All Is True* and the assertions of the Prologue stress the drama's historical veracity in contrast to Rowley's version of Henry's life, which had little to do with the facts of his reign and treated the king more like a folk hero. Clare contends that *H8*'s pomp and splendor are intended not for the "wholesale glorification of sovereignty" as in the court masque but to reinforce the play's ironic political theme: "the precarious nature of earthly glory and the potency of its attraction." To classify *H8* as romance is to exaggerate the significance of the final scene, which, despite the joyous note struck by Cranmer's panegyric, contains nothing of the reconciliation and forgiveness nor the "lost and found" motif typical of those canonical plays generally classified as romances (*Per.*, *Cym.*, *WT*, and *Temp.*). Drawing on the same historical sources he had used for his two tetralogies and revealing the same integrity of purpose in his treatment of the historical record, Shakespeare wrote the history play he would have written earlier in his career had Elizabethan censorship allowed it.

Dean, Paul. "Dramatic Mode and Historical Vision in *Henry VIII*." *Shakespeare Quarterly* 37 (1986): 175–89.
    Dean tackles the genre issue to argue that the proper

question is not whether the play is "romance" or "history" but what kind of history play it is. Noting how the two terms are not mutually exclusive, he observes in *H8* a dialectical movement between a "romance" view of history with affinities to comedy and a "chronicle" view with affinities to tragedy. The first scene, with its contrasting perspectives on the events of the Field of the Cloth of Gold, illustrates the play's constant movement between the idealism of romance and the calculation of political reality; it is also a microcosm of the play's "insistence on the second-hand nature of our acquaintance with historical events." The play's "wavelike" structure, a "translation into dramatic terms of the undulations of the wheel of Fortune," allows Shakespeare to focus not on a single character but on "the larger movements of history to which all are subject." Throughout the play, but especially in Katherine's final verdict on Wolsey, her vision, and Cranmer's prophecy, Shakespeare uses the spatial and extratemporal elements of "romance" to rescue "chronicle history from collapsing into meaningless subjectivity." The image of the Phoenix (5.4.48–55), the mythic bird that "inhabits both time and eternity," provides Shakespeare's final word on a problem with which he had been wrestling from the beginning of his career: "the accommodation of the open, expansive movement of history within the close, concentrated, and intensified movement of drama."

Foakes, R. A. "Epilogue: A Note on *King Henry VIII*." In *Shakespeare, The Dark Comedies to the Last Plays: From Satire to Celebration*, pp. 173–83. Charlottesville: University Press of Virginia, 1971.

Foakes considers *H8* a natural sequel to *Temp.* in that both plays are set in modern, Christian times and display human activities within the framework and exigencies of human government or rule. In *H8*, the nature of "truth" and the business of "rule" are not only central to the action but structurally implicit in the play's emphasis on spectacle, i.e., "the public shows men make of themselves to each other. The action turns on what men observe, how they see one another, how they interpret and misinterpret, and often go wrong." As demonstrated in the shifting assessment of the events on the Field of the Cloth of Gold and in the treatment of Buckingham's fall, establishing the complete "truth" of an event or a person is a matter of multiple perspectives, the "truth" lying not in any one view but somewhere in the light of differing interpretations. What emerges from Katherine's and Griffith's opposing views of Wolsey's "true" character in 4.2 is the way of "religious truth," interpretation grounded in charity whereby one accepts the coexistence of both good and bad in the man (4.2.80–82). Foakes associates the emergence of Henry from a flawed ruler into the "panoply of kingship" with the "religious truth" that providentially "overrid[es] the contradictions, injustices and suffering" of the political realm, ultimately bringing all into the grace of heaven's blessing. The turning point for Henry's character occurs at the end of Katherine's trial when he voices praise for her and begins to distance himself from Wolsey's influence. Regarding the authorship question, Foakes argues that Shakespeare "planned the play, even if he did not write every word of it."

Frye, Northrop. "The Tragedies of Nature and Fortune." In *Stratford Papers on Shakespeare, 1961*, edited by B. W. Jackson, pp. 38–55. Toronto: W. J. Gage, 1962.

In an essay whose main focus is *Coriolanus* as a tragedy of human nature, Frye first discusses *H8* as a tragedy of Fortune. Using the idea of tragedy found in the *Mirror of Magistrates* and other collections from the Middle Ages, where the genre is symbolized by the wheel of Fortune, Frye discusses the three falls of Buckingham, Wolsey, and Katherine as exempla of the turning of Fortune's wheel. Although the "wheel" topos is essentially tragic in its conception, it is possible to achieve a "technically comic conclusion" by stopping its turn halfway, something that happens in only two of Shakespeare's histories, *H5* and *H8*. Despite what appears to be a happy ending, *H8* is tragic by implication since the triumphs of Anne Bullen, Cromwell, and Cranmer are temporary: "the wheel will go on turning" and their downfalls will eventually occur. The king, who comes into clearer focus as the play progresses, gradually achieves more control over his court, finally incarnating fortune himself by "turn[ing] the wheel" on which some rise and others fall. Countering the pervasive presence of fortune is a hidden providential force that is ready to dismantle the entire social and religious structure of the nation in order to achieve the birth of Queen Elizabeth. "These two polarized forces . . . make up the action of the play: a simple, almost naive action, yet one ideally suited to a processional and pageant-like history."

Harris, Laurie Lanzen, and Mark W. Scott, eds. *Shakespearean Criticism: Excerpts from the Criticism of William Shakespeare's Plays and Poetry from the First Published Appraisals to Current Evaluations*, vol. 2, pp. 11–86. Detroit: Gale Research, 1985.

This volume presents significant passages from published criticism on *H8*. The set of passages is introduced by a brief discussion of the "date," "text," and "sources," followed by a longer discussion of the "critical history" of the play. Each entry, beginning with Sir Henry Wotton's letter of 1613, is prefaced with a brief historical overview that places the excerpted document in the context of responses to the play. The passages are followed by an "Additional Bibliography." The

Shakespearean Criticism series is designed as "an introduction for the researcher newly acquainted with the works of Shakespeare."

Hodgdon, Barbara. "Uncommon Women and Others: *Henry VIII*'s 'Maiden Phoenix.'" In *The End Crowns All: Closure and Contradiction in Shakespeare's History*, pp. 212–34. Princeton: Princeton University Press, 1991.

In Hodgdon's reading, *H8* becomes an "early Stuart *Richard II*, a play which not only deposes a rightful Queen but crowns two others and, finally, through a sacramental procession, restores male rule." As the result of a gender economy that makes and unmakes wives, queens, and mothers, the play "eroticizes Anne's body and . . . beatifies Katherine['s]," thereby reproducing the familiar whore/virgin dichotomy. Through the structural juxtaposition of two scenes that "expose the central contradiction of Henry's sexual and political maneuvering"—Anne's coronation procession (4.1) and Katherine's vision (4.2)—the play "condenses the danger and pleasure of feminine power, and subjects both to Fortune, Time, and timing." The second half of this intertextual analysis of "closural form" deals with the play's various theatrical guises, which, through text and staging decisions, have affected the importance of Henry, Katherine, and Anne in the overall universe of the play. The major difference among productions lies in the choice of which queen's body to use as the concluding image. Hodgdon looks specifically at the productions of Herbert Beerbohm Tree (1910), Tyrone Guthrie (1949), Trevor Nunn (1969), and Howard Davies (1983) to show how some twentieth-century directors focused on Anne either in triumph (Tree) or as foreshadowing her ultimate fate (Guthrie), while others (Nunn and Davies) emphasized Elizabeth.

Kamps, Ivo. "Shakespeare, Fletcher, and the Question of History." In *Historiography and Ideology in Stuart Drama*, pp. 91–139. Cambridge: Cambridge University Press, 1996.

Kamps contends that much of the criticism of *H8* fails to appreciate the play on its own terms, i.e., as a Jacobean instead of an Elizabethan history play. In *H8*, Shakespeare and his collaborator, John Fletcher, were interested not in providing the "coherent and meaningful philosophy of history" that some critics look for but rather in tackling two problems essential to the development of Jacobean historiography: (1) the revising of the "Tudor conception of history *as* the history of great men," and (2) the shattering of the "Tudor propensity for unified (often providential) historiography." Kamps argues that how we respond to the play as a whole depends greatly on how we respond to Cranmer's concluding rendering of Tudor-Stuart history, an attempt to produce dramatic and historical closure that is undercut by other historical voices in the play. Instead of representing a failure of dramatic design, *H8*'s episodic structure is the consequence of the dramatists' deliberate rejection of a single view of history: Shakespeare and Fletcher give us not a "disunified play about history but a play about disunified history."

Knight, G. Wilson. "*Henry VIII* and the Poetry of Conversion." In *The Crown of Life: Essays in Interpretation of Shakespeare's Final Plays*, pp. 256–336. London: Methuen, 1947.

Knight cites meter, syntax, imagery, and stylistic mannerisms to argue that Shakespeare alone wrote *H8*, a play that marks Shakespeare's return to a national and contemporary theme. The author discusses the implications of the Prologue and deals at length with the play's three tragic figures: Wolsey, Buckingham, and

Katherine, who is "one of Shakespeare's most striking feminine creations." The tragic events involving these characters are countered by moments of gaiety and romantic warmth (e.g., 1.4) and robust humor (e.g., 2.3, 5.1.194–216, and 5.3). As for the titular figure, Henry is Shakespeare's only king in whom the man and office remain inseparable; he is "kingliness personified but . . . an eminently human kingliness." As the play moves toward its conclusion, Henry's speech becomes richer in sacred reference but he never loses his "bluff manner." The play's issues are human rather than ideological, and its pageantry holds "great architecture" and deep meaning. *H8* "bends and clasps [Shakespeare's] massive life-work into a single whole expanding the habitual design of Shakespearean tragedy: from normality and order, through violent conflict to a spiritualized music and thence to the concluding ritual. Such is the organic unity of Shakespeare's world."

Leggatt, Alexander. "*Henry VIII* and the Ideal England." *Shakespeare Survey* 38 (1985): 131–43.

Cranmer's prophecy in Act 5 may look like an exercise in nostalgia because of the way it idealizes the past (Elizabeth's reign); but by also idealizing the present of James's reign, it encourages us to "set the ideal vision against our sense of the world as it really is." Leggatt argues that this double perspective of the ideal and the actual enacts the historical vision of the play as it is reflected in the pervasive "rise and fall" pattern linking Buckingham, Wolsey, and Katherine, all of whom "at their highest moments . . . live in both worlds at once, half in heaven, and . . . constantly subject to the incongruities of that condition." Cranmer speaks of a golden age, but the play as a whole "shows the world of history to be complex, elusive and rather untidy." Nevertheless, the "shaping, idealizing vision that produces his prophecy is already at work, fitfully but unmistakably, in the main play." Like *WT* and *Temp.*, the plays immediately preceding it, *H8* illustrates Shakespeare's "abiding interest in the difficult but close relationship between what we dream of and what we are." To those who question whether *H8* is a Jacobean play or an "Elizabethan throwback," Leggatt answers that while the fusion of the two perspectives of the mortal world and the ideal vision may not be perfect, *H8* is Jacobean in its theatrical self-consciousness and evocation of "split judgments" about its major characters. Throughout, the author plays tricks on us, promising a somber play in the Prologue and ending with an Epilogue that is clearly designed to make us laugh. This sense of artifice nevertheless contributes to the play's unity.

Magnusson, Lynn. "The Rhetoric of Politeness and *Henry VIII*." *Shakespeare Quarterly* 43 (1992): 391–409. (Incorporated in her *Shakespeare and Social Dialogue: Dramatic Language and Elizabethan Letters* [Cambridge: Cambridge University Press, 1999], pp. 17–34.)

Magnusson uses ideas from discourse analysis and linguistic pragmatics, especially politeness theory, to explore the rhetoric of social maintenance in the play. Focusing on the discourse of Katherine and Wolsey, Magnusson examines "directives"—i.e., speech acts performed with the aim of getting others to do things—to show "how gender and class affect speech patterns" and how "an analysis of politeness forms . . . can help us toward a new understanding of the social construction in language of dramatic character." As understood in the "politeness" model developed by Penelope Brown and Stephen Levison, politeness consists of the "complex remedial strategies that serve to minimize the risks to 'face,' or self-esteem, of conversational participants." Positive politeness ("a rhetoric of identification") operates in low-risk social exchanges; negative politeness ("a rhetoric of dissociation") deals with high-risk exchanges that require deference behavior. An example of the latter occurs in 1.2 when Katherine asks Henry to remove unfair taxation imposed on the people by Wolsey; her gratitude to Henry for permitting her to "take place by us" and to assume "half our power" (1.2.10–12) works to "repair the risk of her suit by asserting a power difference between them." In *H8*, examples of negative politeness are dominant because so many of the speech situations involve addressing the king, whose power is greater than the speaker's. Katherine's "disjunctive speech behavior" with Wolsey and Campeius in 3.1 illustrates how politeness strategies can "pattern personality."

Micheli, Linda McJ. " 'Sit by Us': Visual Imagery and the Two Queens in *Henry VIII*." *Shakespeare Quarterly* 38 (1987): 452–66.

Micheli concentrates on the visual imagery—i.e., gesture, movement, stage grouping, and setting—associated with the two queens because our responses to Katherine and Anne, "polar characters identified with the old order and the new, respectively," are "central to our interpretation of the play as a whole." The contrasts between the queens are emphasized in a series of parallel scenes: 1.2 and 1.4, 2.3 and 3.1, and 4.1 and 4.2. Ceremonial gestures and movements that indicate hierarchical order in political, social, and domestic life (e.g., sitting, kneeling, taking by the hand, and kissing) establish the queens as "exemplars of opposing ideals of womanhood": Katherine, in her disruption of court proceedings, epitomizes the "primarily moral, spiritual, and strong-minded" type, while Anne, who at the banquet moves and speaks only when invited to do so, illustrates the "primarily sexual, [decorative], and compliant." Micheli claims that the visual images of *H8* also have a bearing on the genre of the play in that they emphasize romance as well as chronicle elements.

Noling, Kim H. "Grubbing Up the Stock: Dramatizing Queens in *Henry VIII*." *Shakespeare Quarterly* 39 (1988): 291–306.

Writing *H8* under the patronage of James I, Shakespeare "created a dramaturgy of queens that, although admitting some dissent" against the expedient usage of these royal women to beget male heirs, "ultimately endorses Henry's patriarchal will." The play's patriarchal ideology is bluntly and ruthlessly articulated by Bishop Gardiner, who wishes that "the stock" would be "grubbed up now" (5.1.29–30). Unlike Gardiner, who at least would preserve the fruit (Elizabeth), Henry gets rid of both fruit (Princess Mary) and stock when he has his marriage to Katherine declared to be "of none effect" (4.1.37). Shakespeare, however, treats Katherine more generously by giving her ample stage exposure, strong stage positions from which she upstages male characters, and a dream sequence to balance the ceremony of Anne's coronation. By interrupting ceremonies in order to turn them to her own advantage, Katherine distinguishes herself with an independence that temporarily challenges the play's patriarchal ideology. Nevertheless, such positive treatment should not be interpreted as "unalloyed feminism" on Shakespeare's part, for with both Anne and Elizabeth, the playwright "defines his queens by a dramaturgy that fully supports the institution of kingly power." Anne, for example, may be sympathetic but she is also forgettable, as her erasure from her daughter's christening makes clear. Regarding Elizabeth, not only does the image of the phoenix used to celebrate her in 5.4 "transcend . . . the threatening female body," but also the maker of the "flattering fiction," Cranmer, and not the phoenix, merits the king's gratitude: "O lord Archbishop, / Thou hast made me now a man" (5.4.72–74). Henry, in other words, becomes a new father not through a "redemptive daughter" but through the creative imagination of another man who "transforms that daughter into a male replacement." The presence of James, Elizabeth's "issue," in spirit, if not in body, at performances of *H8* by his own theatrical company, the King's Men, is "the play's final subversion of queens into no more than the means by which kings are produced."

Richmond, Hugh. *King Henry VIII*. Shakespeare in Performance Series. Manchester: Manchester University Press, 1994.

  H8's "diverse qualities of verbal realism and physical spectacle are so distinctive that they have had a sustained and decisive influence on the history of the English stage and even on the evolution of historical realism in the modern cinema." To support this thesis, Richmond examines revivals spanning the seventeenth century to 1991. Among those receiving special attention are the following: Davenant's Restoration "reinvention" (the first to exploit the play's "distinctive documentary texture"); J. P. Kemble's "pivotal" production in 1788 in which Sarah Siddons's "feminine naturalism" achieved "parity of interest" with the leading male roles of Henry and Wolsey; Herbert Beerbohm Tree's "florid historicism" in 1910 at His Majesty's Theatre, London (later replicated in the 1911 silent film); Tyrone Guthrie's "revisionism," which, at both the Shakespeare Memorial Theatre (Stratford-upon-Avon, 1949) and the Old Vic (London, 1950 and 1953), "restored vitality, viability and plausibility to a misunderstood script" and once again, as in the Restoration period, made Henry dominant over Wolsey (who had been played by the leading actor-managers of the late nineteenth century); Trevor Nunn's Brechtian approach for the RSC (1969), which underscored political and ecclesiastical issues; Kevin Billington's "very subdued" *H8* for the BBC/Time-Life Shakespeare Series (1978); and Howard Davies's postmodern staging for the RSC (1983). Richmond also discusses a production he produced at the University of California at Berkeley (1990), which crystallized for him and the student actors the text's "insistence on realistic communication of intimate behaviour" and the importance of the minor scenes. Richmond concludes that *H8* "is one of the few [plays] which almost necessarily have to be performed in historically accurate costume." A list of twentieth-century productions and cast lists for those discussed at length round out the volume.

Rudnytsky, Peter L. "*Henry VIII* and the Deconstruction of History." *Shakespeare Survey* 43 (1991): 43–57. Reprinted in *Shakespeare and Politics*, edited by Catherine Alexander, pp. 44–66. Cambridge: Cambridge University Press, 2004.

Rudnytsky argues that *H8* is, as the Folio classification indicates, Shakespeare's last history play; the presence of masque, spectacle, and the motif of succession through the female line—elements common to the late romances (*Per., Cym., WT,* and *Temp.*)—notwithstanding, *H8*'s spirit is "ultimately sceptical and not hierophantic." As ambiguous and unorthodox as any of its predecessors, the play carries to new heights the complexities of Shakespeare's earlier explorations of English history, especially the multiple perspectives found in the second tetralogy wherein the Tudor myth is both promoted and demystified. The Prologue offers a "litmus test" for reader/spectator responses to the play as a whole; in particular, its juxtaposition of weeping and wedding in the concluding couplet underscores *H8*'s pattern of contradiction. By allowing for laughter in a dramatic action that promises to be "full of state and woe" (Pro. 3), Shakespeare shows an interest in playing tricks on us, the most important of which lies in the enigmatic subtitle *All Is True* for a play dominated by deceptive appearances and the relativity of truth. In Pirandellian fashion, " 'all is true' means precisely that *any* interpretation of the past may be true if one thinks it so, and no point of view is allowed to contain or control all others." Central to Shakespeare's "deconstruction of history" is his treatment of Henry's contradictory motives for divorce and the portrayal of Henry himself, who, contrary to Foakes's view, does not evolve into ideal kingship as the minister of providence.

Smallwood, Robert, ed. *Players of Shakespeare 4: Further Essays in Shakespearian Performance by Players with the RSC*. Cambridge: Cambridge University Press, 1998.

This collection includes two essays by actors who played major roles in Gregory Doran's 1996–97 production of *H8* at the RSC's Swan Theatre in Stratford-upon-Avon: Paul Jesson's commentary on the titular figure (pp. 114–31) and Jane Lapotaire's on Queen Katherine (pp. 132–51). In his research for the role, Jesson was struck by both the extreme nature of the king, who "never did anything by halves," and his many contradictions: "energetic and lazy, generous and mean-spirited, brutal and tender." In Henry, Shakespeare creates a charitable portrait of a king who learns to rule, grows in wisdom and confidence, and finally comes to know himself; the affection of Katherine and Anne for him provides support for the reader's/spectator's sympathetic response to the character. In playing the role, Jesson found echoes of

Richard III, Falstaff, Petruchio, Othello, and, most important, Prospero, another "confident puppet-master . . . [whose] influence [is] felt even when . . . absent from the stage." Regarding the role of Katherine, Lapotaire shares her relief in learning that the director was determined to set the play in its actual "time zone": *H8* "is [so] essentially Tudor in its mores, its history, its hierarchy, in its treatment of women as male property and heir-bearing machines, that [to do otherwise] would be inappropriate and perverse." In order to underscore Katherine's status as an outsider, the production emphasized her Spanish heritage—e.g., the Spanish accent and the translation of the English madrigal in 3.1 into a song sung in Spanish. Katherine's quintessential character lies in her goodness, in her motto "Humble and Loyal," and in the four obligations (to her God, to her king, to her husband, and to her people) that "hold water" in each of the scenes where she appears. Like the other late plays in the canon, *H8* is about spiritual rebirth, "not just in the symbol of the baby who is to become Elizabeth I, but also through that most difficult of human experiences, the humbling of worldly state that leads to the spiritual state of forgiveness."

Shakespeare's Language

Abbott, E. A. *A Shakespearian Grammar*. New York: Haskell House, 1972.
This compact reference book, first published in 1870, helps with many difficulties in Shakespeare's language. It systematically accounts for a host of differences between Shakespeare's usage and sentence structure and our own.

Blake, Norman. *Shakespeare's Language: An Introduction.* New York: St. Martin's Press, 1983.

This general introduction to Elizabethan English discusses various aspects of the language of Shakespeare and his contemporaries, offering possible meanings for hundreds of ambiguous constructions.

Dobson, E. J. *English Pronunciation, 1500–1700.* 2 vols. Oxford: Clarendon Press, 1968.

This long and technical work includes chapters on spelling (and its reformation), phonetics, stressed vowels, and consonants in early modern English.

Houston, John. *Shakespearean Sentences: A Study in Style and Syntax.* Baton Rouge: Louisiana State University Press, 1988.

Houston studies Shakespeare's stylistic choices, considering matters such as sentence length and the relative positions of subject, verb, and direct object. Examining plays throughout the canon in a roughly chronological, developmental order, he analyzes how sentence structure is used in setting tone, in characterization, and for other dramatic purposes.

Onions, C. T. *A Shakespeare Glossary.* Oxford: Clarendon Press, 1986.

This revised edition updates Onions's standard, selective glossary of words and phrases in Shakespeare's plays that are now obsolete, archaic, or obscure.

Robinson, Randal. *Unlocking Shakespeare's Language: Help for the Teacher and Student.* Urbana, Ill.: National Council of Teachers of English and the ERIC Clearinghouse on Reading and Communication Skills, 1989.

Specifically designed for the high-school and undergraduate college teacher and student, Robinson's book addresses the problems that most often hinder present-day readers of Shakespeare. Through work with his own students, Robinson found that many readers today are particularly puzzled by such stylistic devices as subject-verb inversion, interrupted structures, and compression. He shows how our own colloquial language contains comparable structures, and thus helps students recognize such structures when they find them in Shakespeare's plays. This book supplies worksheets—with examples from major plays—to illuminate and remedy such problems as unusual sequences of words and the separation of related parts of sentences.

Williams, Gordon. *A Dictionary of Sexual Language and Imagery in Shakespearean and Stuart Literature.* 3 vols. London: Athlone Press, 1994.

Williams provides a comprehensive list of the words to which Shakespeare, his contemporaries, and later Stuart writers gave sexual meanings. He supports his identification of these meanings by extensive quotations.

Shakespeare's Life

Baldwin, T. W. *William Shakspere's Petty School.* Urbana: University of Illinois Press, 1943.

Baldwin here investigates the theory and practice of the petty school, the first level of education in Elizabethan England. He focuses on that educational system primarily as it is reflected in Shakespeare's art.

Baldwin, T. W. *William Shakspere's Small Latine and Lesse Greeke.* 2 vols. Urbana: University of Illinois Press, 1944.

Baldwin attacks the view that Shakespeare was an uneducated genius—a view that had been dominant among Shakespeareans since the eighteenth century. Instead, Baldwin shows, the educational system of Shakespeare's time would have given the playwright a strong background in the classics, and there is much in the plays that shows how Shakespeare benefited from such an education.

Beier, A. L., and Roger Finlay, eds. *London 1500–1700: The Making of the Metropolis.* New York: Longman, 1986.

Focusing on the economic and social history of early modern London, these collected essays probe aspects of metropolitan life, including "Population and Disease," "Commerce and Manufacture," and "Society and Change."

Bentley, G. E. *Shakespeare's Life: A Biographical Handbook.* New Haven: Yale University Press, 1961.

This "just-the-facts" account presents the surviving documents of Shakespeare's life against an Elizabethan background.

Chambers, E. K. *William Shakespeare: A Study of Facts and Problems.* 2 vols. Oxford: Clarendon Press, 1930.

Analyzing in great detail the scant historical data, Chambers's complex, scholarly study considers the nature of the texts in which Shakespeare's work is preserved.

Cressy, David. *Education in Tudor and Stuart England.* London: Edward Arnold, 1975.

This volume collects sixteenth-, seventeenth-, and early-eighteenth-century documents detailing aspects of formal education in England, such as the curriculum, the control and organization of education, and the education of women.

Dutton, Richard. *William Shakespeare: A Literary Life*. New York: St. Martin's Press, 1989.
Not a biography in the traditional sense, Dutton's very readable work nevertheless "follows the contours of Shakespeare's life" as he examines Shakespeare's career as playwright and poet, with consideration of his patrons, theatrical associations, and audience.

Honan, Park. *Shakespeare: A Life*. New York: Oxford University Press, 1998.
Honan's accessible biography focuses on the various contexts of Shakespeare's life—physical, social, political, and cultural—to place the dramatist within a lucidly described world. The biography includes detailed examinations of, for example, Stratford schooling, theatrical politics of 1590s London, and the careers of Shakespeare's associates. The author draws on a wealth of established knowledge and on interesting new research into local records and documents; he also engages in speculation about, for example, the possibilities that Shakespeare was a tutor in a Catholic household in the north of England in the 1580s and that he played particular roles in his own plays, areas that reflect new, but unproven and debatable, data—though Honan is usually careful to note where a particular narrative "has not been capable of proof or disproof."

Schoenbaum, S. *William Shakespeare: A Compact Documentary Life*. New York: Oxford University Press, 1977.
This standard biography economically presents the essential documents from Shakespeare's time in an accessible narrative account of the playwright's life.

Shakespeare's Theater

Bentley, G. E. *The Profession of Player in Shakespeare's Time, 1590–1642.* Princeton: Princeton University Press, 1984.

Bentley readably sets forth a wealth of evidence about performance in Shakespeare's time, with special attention to the relations between player and company, and the business of casting, managing, and touring.

Berry, Herbert. *Shakespeare's Playhouses.* New York: AMS Press, 1987.

Berry's six essays collected here discuss (with illustrations) varying aspects of the four playhouses in which Shakespeare had a financial stake: the Theatre in Shoreditch, the Blackfriars, and the first and second Globe.

Cook, Ann Jennalie. *The Privileged Playgoers of Shakespeare's London.* Princeton: Princeton University Press, 1981.

Cook's work argues, on the basis of sociological, economic, and documentary evidence, that Shakespeare's audience—and the audience for English Renaissance drama generally—consisted mainly of the "privileged."

Greg, W. W. *Dramatic Documents from the Elizabethan Playhouses.* 2 vols. Oxford: Clarendon Press, 1931.

Greg itemizes and briefly describes many of the play manuscripts that survive from the period 1590 to around 1660, including, among other things, players' parts. His second volume offers facsimiles of selected manuscripts.

Gurr, Andrew. *Playgoing in Shakespeare's London.* 2nd ed. Cambridge: Cambridge University Press, 1996.

Gurr charts how the theatrical enterprise developed from its modest beginnings in the late 1560s to become a thriving institution in the 1600s. He argues that there were important changes over the period 1567–1644 in the playhouses, the audience, and the plays.

Harbage, Alfred. *Shakespeare's Audience*. New York: Columbia University Press, 1941.
Harbage investigates the fragmentary surviving evidence to interpret the size, composition, and behavior of Shakespeare's audience.

Hattaway, Michael. *Elizabethan Popular Theatre: Plays in Performance*. London: Routledge and Kegan Paul, 1982.
Beginning with a study of the popular drama of the late Elizabethan age—a description of the stages, performance conditions, and acting of the period—this volume concludes with an analysis of five well-known plays of the 1590s, one of them (*Titus Andronicus*) by Shakespeare.

Shapiro, Michael. *Children of the Revels: The Boy Companies of Shakespeare's Time and Their Plays*. New York: Columbia University Press, 1977.
Shapiro chronicles the history of the amateur and quasi-professional child companies that flourished in London at the end of Elizabeth's reign and the beginning of James's.

The Publication of Shakespeare's Plays

Blayney, Peter W. M. *The First Folio of Shakespeare*. Hanover, Md.: Folger, 1991.
Blayney's accessible account of the printing and later life of the First Folio—an amply illustrated catalog to a 1991 Folger Shakespeare Library exhibition—analyzes the mechanical production of the First Folio, describ-

ing how the Folio was made, by whom and for whom, how much it cost, and its ups and downs (or, rather, downs and ups) since its printing in 1623.

Hinman, Charlton. *The Norton Facsimile: The First Folio of Shakespeare*. 2nd ed. New York: W. W. Norton, 1996.

This facsimile presents a photographic reproduction of an "ideal" copy of the First Folio of Shakespeare; Hinman attempts to represent each page in its most fully corrected state. The second edition includes an important new introduction by Peter W. M. Blayney.

Hinman, Charlton. *The Printing and Proof-Reading of the First Folio of Shakespeare*. 2 vols. Oxford: Clarendon Press, 1963.

In the most arduous study of a single book ever undertaken, Hinman attempts to reconstruct how the Shakespeare First Folio of 1623 was set into type and run off the press, sheet by sheet. He also provides almost all the known variations in readings from copy to copy.

Key to
Famous Lines and Phrases

No man's pie is freed
From his ambitious finger.

[*Buckingham*—1.1.61–62]

The mirror of all courtesy.

[*Second Gentleman*—2.1.68]

Go with me like good angels to my end,
And as the long divorce of steel falls on me,
Make of your prayers one sweet sacrifice,
And lift my soul to heaven.

[*Buckingham*—2.1.92–95]

This bold bad man.

[*Chamberlain*—2.2.49]

I swear, 'tis better to be lowly born
And range with humble livers in content
Than to be perked up in a glist'ring grief
And wear a golden sorrow.

[*Anne*—2.3.23–26]

Orpheus with his lute made trees . . .

[*Song*—3.1.3–14]

Heaven is above all yet; there sits a judge
That no king can corrupt.

[*Queen Katherine*—3.1.113–14]

Nay then, farewell!
I have touched the highest point of all my greatness,
And from that full meridian of my glory
I haste now to my setting. I shall fall
Like a bright exhalation in the evening
And no man see me more.

[*Wolsey*—3.2.274–79]

Farewell? A long farewell to all my greatness!
[*Wolsey*—3.2.420]

Cromwell, I charge thee, fling away ambition!
By that sin fell the angels. . . .

[*Wolsey*—3.2.520–21]

Had I but served my God with half the zeal
I served my king, He would not in mine age
Have left me naked to mine enemies.

[*Wolsey*—3.2.535–537]

He was a scholar, and a ripe and good one:
Exceeding wise, fair-spoken, and persuading. . . .

[*Griffith*—4.2.58–59]

She shall be—
But few now living can behold that goodness—
A pattern to all princes living with her. . . .
Truth shall nurse her;
Holy and heavenly thoughts still counsel her.
She shall be loved and feared. Her own shall bless her;
Her foes shake like a field of beaten corn
And hang their heads with sorrow.

[*Cranmer*—5.4.27–39]

THE FOLGER
SHAKESPEARE LIBRARY

The world's leading center for Shakespeare studies presents
acclaimed editions of Shakespeare's works.

For more information on Folger Shakespeare Library Editions, including
Shakespeare Set Free teaching guides, visit www.simonsays.com.

**WASHINGTON
SQUARE PRESS**
A Division of Simon & Schuster
A CBS COMPANY